Praise for *Coming Clean*

"Brune artfully exposes the shameless tactics employed at every level of the energy supply chain by those intent upon maintaining the status quo. Sharing proven methods to jump-start the necessary paradigm shift away from fossil-fuel dependency, Brune offers an enlightened yet impassioned manifesto on how to achieve clean energy."

— BOOKLIST

"A clearsighted indictment of our ugly marriage to fossil fuels. Brune … doesn't fail to name names and throw some light on both the plunderers and restorers of American energy."

— ORION

"Purging this country of its two-century addiction to fossil fuels is the great task of our time. Here is the resource we have long needed."

— BILL MCKIBBEN, AUTHOR OF *DEEP ECONOMY*

"A thoroughly engaging, reader-friendly analysis of our energy dilemma. Brune's empowering book tells us how to take back our future from the energy bullies leading us down a path to climate chaos."

— ROSS GELBSPAN, AUTHOR OF *THE HEAT IS ON* AND *BOILING POINT*

"This is a valuable odyssey through the coming world of clean, sustainable, resilient energy. As Brune puts it, 'Join us: it's fun over here.'"

— R. JAMES WOOLSEY, ENERGY-INDEPENDENCE EXPERT, FORMER CIA DIRECTOR

"An optimistic, realistic, pragmatic call to action. In this eloquent book, Mike Brune offers practical approaches, hope, and inspiration. A must-read for anyone who dreams of a sustainable, just, and peaceful future."

— JOHN PERKINS, AUTHOR OF *CONFESSIONS OF AN ECONOMIC HIT MAN*
AND *THE SECRET HISTORY OF THE AMERICAN EMPIRE*

"At last! A road map to a clean energy future. As Michael Brune says, embracing clean energy is not an obligation, it is an opportunity."

— VAN JONES, AUTHOR OF *THE GREEN-COLLAR ECONOMY*

"Straight from the front lines of the battle for a clean, cheap energy economy, Mike Brune tells the fascinating inside story. . . . His practical vision for how we can 'come clean' is tremendously important."

— WES BOYD, COFOUNDER OF MOVEON.ORG

"Strung out by high gas prices? Melting ice caps give you the sweats? *Coming Clean* is a road map to recovery, a smart, heartfelt guide to building a better world."

— JEFF GOODELL, AUTHOR OF *BIG COAL: THE DIRTY SECRET
BEHIND AMERICA'S ENERGY FUTURE*

COMING
CLEAN

COMING CLEAN

BREAKING AMERICA'S ADDICTION TO OIL AND COAL

Second Edition

MICHAEL BRUNE

Sierra Club Books
San Francisco

The Sierra Club, founded in 1892 by author and conservationist John Muir, is the oldest, largest, and most influential grassroots environmental organization in the United States. With more than a million members and supporters—and some sixty chapters across the country—we are working hard to protect our local communities, ensure an enduring legacy for America's wild places, and find smart energy solutions to stop global warming. To learn how you can participate in the Sierra Club's programs to explore, enjoy, and protect the planet, please address inquiries to Sierra Club, 85 Second Street, San Francisco, California 94105, or visit our Web site at www.sierraclub.org.

The Sierra Club's book publishing division, Sierra Club Books, has been a leading publisher of titles on the natural world and environmental issues for nearly half a century. We offer books to the general public as a nonprofit educational service in the hope that they may enlarge the public's understanding of the Sierra Club's concerns and priorities. The point of view expressed in each book, however, does not necessarily represent that of the Sierra Club. For more information on Sierra Club Books and a complete list of our titles and authors, please visit www.sierraclubbooks.org

Second Edition

Published by Sierra Club Books,
85 Second Street, San Francisco, CA 94105

Sierra Club Books are published in association
with Counterpoint (www.counterpointpress.com).

Sierra Club, Sierra Club Books, and the Sierra Club design logos
are registered trademarks of the Sierra Club.

Book and cover design by Blue Design (www.bluedes.com)

Library of Congress Cataloging-in-Publication Data

Brune, Michael
  Coming clean : breaking America's addiction to oil and coal / Michael Brune. — 2nd ed.
    p. cm.
  Includes bibliographical references and index.
  ISBN-13: 978-1-57805-190-8 (pbk. : alk. paper)
  ISBN-10: 1-57805-190-8 (pbk. : alk. paper)
1. Fossil fuels—Environmental aspects—United States. 2. Biomass energy—United States.
3. Renewable energy sources—United States. 4. Green movement—United States. I. Title.
  TD887.F69B78 2010
  333.790973—dc22   2010039211

Printed in the United States of America on acid-free paper that contains a minimum of 30 percent post-consumer recycled fiber

Distributed by Publishers Group West
14 13 12 11 10
10 9 8 7 6 5 4 3 2 1

To Mary, my love,

and to Olivia and Sebastian, for bringing
such joy and laughter

Contents

Acknowledgments

I grew up in a family of do-gooders, by which I mean to say that my parents often encouraged my two sisters, my brother, and me to try to make a positive difference in the world. My mother, Patricia Brune, is a public school teacher in New Jersey. My father, Robert, is a former mayor of Dover Township, New Jersey, and is passionate about energy and politics. Their commitment—to each other and to making the world a better place—inspired me to start writing this book.

I'm grateful to Jodie Evans, who first encouraged me to put this book together a few years ago. I had just become a father for the first time, was busy running Rainforest Action Network, and didn't take her suggestion too seriously at first. But without her persistence, and the support of RAN board chair Jim Gollin, I never would have started. Michael Marx and Safir Ahmed helped give the book its structure. I'm also indebted to my agent, Julie Castiglia, and to my tag-team editors at Sierra Club Books, Joan Hamilton and Diana Landau, who worked much harder than they should have. Sierra Club energy expert Fred Heutte and copyeditor Andrew Frisardi also made invaluable contributions.

Bill Twist, David Elliot, and the good folks at the Pachamama Alliance arranged for my trip to Ecuador. Matt Price and Larry Innes introduced me to First Nations leaders in Alberta. Mary Anne Hitt and Hillary Hosta put together a tour of West Virginia and taught me more about mountaintop-removal mining than I ever wanted to know. Thank you, all.

My colleagues and friends Jennifer Krill, John Sellers, Steve Kretzmann, and Ilyse Hogue are some of the most creative people I know of who are working for social change. Their fingerprints are all over this book. Chelsea Sexton, Dave Bernikoff-Raboy, Heather Bernikoff-Raboy, Marc Geller, Sarah Connolly, Jodie Van Horn, and Nile Malloy gave valuable insights into plug-in hybrids, electric cars, and the other topics in the chapters on transportation.

Equally helpful were Danny Kennedy, David Hochschild, Adam Browning, Elliot Hoffman, Dian Grueneich, Audrey Chang, John White, Art Rosenfeld, and Ralph Cavanagh, briefing me on the future of energy efficiency and renewable energy. Leila Salazar-Lopez, Shannon Coughlin, Heidi Quante, Andrea Samulon, Brihannala Morgan, and Alex Farrell helped me separate fact from fiction in the world of agrofuels.

Bill Barclay, Matt Leonard, Scott Parkin, Dana Clark, and Becky Tarbotton helped illuminate the specific role that corporate and public banks play in financing climate change. Thanks also to Brant Olson and Debra Erenberg for reviewing parts of the manuscript; to Branden Barber, Katie Steele, Joe Powers (at Tesla), Kevin Koenig, Eric Schaeffer, Paul West, and Chandra Kirana for their help; and to the staff and board of Rainforest Action Network for their patience and support.

I'm deeply grateful to Somer Huntley for her backbreaking research and documentation, always done with a smile.

For assistance in creating the second edition of this book, I'm grateful to my collaborator, Joan Hamilton; Sierra Club Books publisher Helen Sweetland and senior editor Diana Landau; Sierra Club staff members Rod MacKenzie, Dave Hamilton, John Coequyt, Ann Mesnikoff, Bruce Nilles, Mark Kresowik, Kate Colarulli, Lena Moffitt, Lyndsay Moseley, Ed Hopkins, Dave Willett, and Bob Sipchen; intern Edward Hill; and volunteers Fred Heutte, John Holtzclaw, and Ned Ford.

And most of all, I'm thankful for my family's love and encouragement.

Preface to the Second Edition

Since I checked the proofs of this book's first edition, early in the summer of 2008, our journey toward a future of clean energy has taken many twists and turns. We've celebrated a new president, then watched as hope for profound change faded into familiar partisan rancor. We've endured a recession that won't quit, two wars that won't end, and a hot summer in which approximately 200 million gallons of oil stained an entire coastline.

On a personal note, my wife and I welcomed a new baby boy into our family. And I have a new job: I'm now executive director of the Sierra Club, the country's oldest and largest grassroots environmental organization. Almost exactly two years after finishing the book, and just four months into my new job, I've taken a short break to refresh the page about what we need to do, together, to help our country kick its dirty-energy habit.

The changed landscape in the nation's capital is a good place to start. What's happened on the energy front since President Obama took office is a great example of why elections do matter. We've seen the Environmental Protection Agency revived from near death to institute new protections for public health and new rules to increase fuel economy and reduce oil consumption. We've seen automakers taken off life support and reenergized with new capital and higher standards for cleaner cars. Finance reform—which includes unprecedented disclosure for oil industry payments to foreign governments—is a done deal. And the 2009 stimulus funding gave a boost to everything from electric car batteries to high-speed rail to efficiency investments in major urban areas. All of this shows how things can change when we elect progressive leadership at the top and apply relentless pressure from the grassroots below.

At the same time, it's become painfully clear that the 2008 elections didn't guarantee the bold change we really need. Nearly unanimous opposition from Republicans and other conservative lawmakers weakened, watered down, and ultimately doomed climate and energy legislation in the Senate that would have cut pollution, created jobs, and made Americans more secure. As the EPA sought to hold polluters accountable, repeated attempts were made in Congress to strip the agency's authority and to weaken the Clean Air Act. Even President Obama, who came to office pledging to make climate change a top priority, missed repeated opportunities to hold Congress accountable and deliver a clear plan to move beyond oil and coal.

Despite such disappointments, it's critical to remember that we are not just passive spectators or victims of political posturing. Corporations and public officials are supposed to serve the public's interest. As taxpayers and consumers, investors, ratepayers, and shareholders, we *can* call the shots. We must build on the positive and respond to the painful in ways that help us and our neighbors heal wounds, address the common good, and move us forward under our own power. As radio commentator Scoop Nisker once said, "If you don't like the news, go out and make some of your own!"

In creating a revised edition of *Coming Clean,* we've had several aims. The chief impulse was to address the oil disaster in the Gulf of Mexico in a way that takes it outside the twenty-four-hour news cycle—to offer my personal perspective as an observer in the Gulf and inside the Beltway. I'll testify to what I witnessed and spotlight how our political leaders have—and haven't—responded. If you're one of those people who watched on your computer or TV screen day after day as oil spewed out uncontrollably, this book is for you. If you were offended by the comments of BP's former CEO Tony Hayward or were angered by investigative reports or congressional hearings on the disaster, and you want to do something about it—this book is for you in particular. Because we won't create a clean-energy future unless we work for it.

I've updated the story also to share some good news: a grassroots network of community organizations and national groups like the Sierra Club has made historic progress in stopping the planned construction of more than a hundred new coal plants. I'll explain why this is important and how they've succeeded. Meanwhile, the cost of clean energy has dropped significantly and installations of wind and solar have hit record highs. Not only can we stop new coal plants from being built, we can retire the oldest and dirtiest plants and begin replacing them with clean energy.

When I was on the Gulf this summer, I'd see small boats in the midst of a vast expanse, skimming tiny quantities of pollution from a sea filled with oil. I often thought to myself how futile the cleanup appeared and wondered whether it was worth the effort. I realize that many have the same reaction to our country's quest to break its addiction to oil and coal. "Why even bother?" they ask. "What can one person do?"

Providing direct answers to that question has always been this book's chief purpose. I've pulled lessons and stories from a couple of decades in the grassroots and have packed these pages with enough detailed information for almost any clean-energy project you might dream up. Above all, I want to remind you that it's never about what just one person can do, even the most powerful person on Earth. Whether it's parents, scientists, lawyers, and community members shutting down a coal plant, or college activists inspiring a giant corporation to reform its practices, when we work collectively, great things can happen. As candidate Obama once said, "If you love this country, you can change it." Let's prove him right.

It's Time to Refuel

There is one thing stronger than all the armies of the world, and that is an idea whose time has come.

— Victor Hugo

I did a double-take. On the magazine rack at my local grocery store was a photo of former Florida Marlins pitcher Dontrelle Willis. The photo had been altered so that the smiling baseball star was standing on the pitcher's mound, up to his thighs in water. You guessed it: *Sports Illustrated* had done its first cover story on climate change.

The cover announced, "As the Planet Changes, So Do the Games We Play." The article described how twice-a-day football practices were changing into once-a-night sessions due to the punishing Texas heat, and how the famous Hahnenkamm downhill ski race in Kitzbühel, Austria, had to be rescued by helicopters hauling in a hundred thousand cubic feet of snow. As sportswriter Alexander Wolff observed, "Global warming is not coming; it is here."

Since this book originally appeared, a lot has happened to sidetrack and confuse Americans' sense of how gravely we are threatened by climate change. Economic woes took center stage, gas prices rose and fell and inched up again, and a flap over scientists sharing climate data was inflated by climate deniers as proof of . . . who knows what? In any case, as *New York Times* columnist Thomas Friedman notes, "the climate-energy policy debate got disconnected from average people."

But as a new decade began, yet another deadly coal-mining disaster, the worst oil spill in our country's history, and the hottest six months on record brought home to people in a personal way the unacceptable costs of our addiction to dirty fossil fuels. For Americans living in the drought-parched

Southwest or in once-snowy mountain regions, the reality of climate change is ever harder to ignore. And by now, millions of Americans have in some way participated in creating a prosperous future based on clean energy—helping to retire a coal plant and replace it with power that doesn't pollute, protecting a shoreline from oil spills, or investing in clean-energy solutions for their home, school, or workplace.

Americans are also voting with their checkbooks. In 2007, sales of hybrid vehicles increased by 38 percent while total light-duty vehicle sales fell by 2.5 percent; though car sales overall fell in 2008 and 2009, hybrids fared much better than most. In May 2008, record-high oil prices led to cars outpacing pickup trucks as America's top-selling vehicles for the first time since 1992. A month later, General Motors announced that it would close four factories that make trucks and SUVs. Consumers can find smart replacements for almost any product, from energy-efficient refrigerators to superinsulated windows. Sales of compact fluorescent lightbulbs took off, as U.S. sales jumped from 57 million bulbs in 2001 to a projected 400 million shipped in 2010. During just one eighteen-month period, replacing incandescent bulbs with CFLs saved an estimated 16.9 billion pounds of coal and more than 72 billion pounds of carbon dioxide.

As Americans began to take steps against climate change, an NBC News/ Wall Street Journal poll in late 2009 showed that a solid majority of 74 percent remain convinced that the effects of global warming are caused chiefly by human actions such as burning fossil fuels.

Nearly three-quarters of all Americans support moving away from oil and coal in favor of clean-energy sources. You might think that such a groundswell would prompt corporate and political leaders to take action. Businesses even have a saying for it: "The customer is always right." But there is a game being played. Business and political leaders love to paint themselves as environmental champions, but too few of them take meaningful action.

General Electric's "Ecomagination," for example, promises to "imagine and build innovative solutions that benefit our customers and society at large." Thanks to its purchase of Enron Wind at a bankruptcy auction in 2002, GE is the largest manufacturer of wind turbines in the country. How ironic, then, that GE is also one of the largest financiers of dirty energy and a leading manufacturer of massive turbines for coal-fired power plants, which warm the planet more than any other source of electricity.

Ford Motor Company's ads tout the firm's "Bold Moves," and its chairman gives speeches about his lofty environmental goals. While Ford has taken a few steps in the right direction, what the company doesn't talk about is that its fuel economy has been below the industry norm for thirty-three consecutive years and that its overall fleet averages fewer miles per gallon than the Model T more than eighty years ago. Bold, indeed!

Corporate leaders aren't the only ones standing in the way of progress, however. In late May 2007, I attended an all-day hearing at the Environmental Protection Agency's (EPA) state headquarters in Sacramento, California. At issue was whether the agency would allow California to implement regulations it had finalized in 2004 to reduce greenhouse gas emissions from vehicles. The regulations required automakers to reduce greenhouse gas emissions by about 30 percent by 2016. More than fifteen states have adopted or have announced their intention to adopt the California standards, the most aggressive in the country.

Because the Bush administration opposed the state's law, it took the EPA a full eighteen months to even schedule a hearing on the issue, rousing the ire of political leaders on both sides of the aisle. Republican governors Arnold Schwarzenegger of California and Jodi Rell of Connecticut (which had followed California's lead on the legislation) placed an op-ed in the *Washington Post* the week before the hearing. "It's bad enough that the federal government has yet to take the threat of global warming seriously," they said. "But it borders on malfeasance for it to block the efforts of states such as California and Connecticut that are trying to protect the public's health and welfare."

This was truly an odd moment for California. The state had a law that united most of the business community. It would reduce vehicle exhaust, improve residents' health, save consumers' money, and cut greenhouse gas emissions. It was bipartisan and would reduce our dependence on oil and help the economy. Yet the only federal agency explicitly charged with protecting the environment was throwing up one roadblock after another.

More than fifty people—scientists, academics, business and political leaders—testified that day in favor of cleaner air. Two individuals (both representing the auto industry) testified in opposition. By the time it was my turn, it was clear that the panel had heard enough hard science and statistics for the day. I tried a direct approach.

I told the panel that, as the parent of a toddler, I was concerned about the world that today's children would inherit. By the time my daughter graduates from high school, up to 70 percent of coral reefs could be destroyed, unless we take strong action. By the time my daughter is in her midtwenties, up to a quarter billion people in Asia and Africa could face severe, life-threatening water shortages. When she reaches her midforties, more than 80 percent of all species in the Amazon would be threatened with extinction—all due to climate change. Closer to home, climate change is already responsible for dwindling snowpacks (and thus water supplies) in the mountain West; stresses on agriculture caused by rising temperatures, water shortages, and pests; risks to our coastlines from rising sea levels and storm surges; and threats to human health from smothering heat, choking air pollution, and waterborne diseases.

"How much more evidence do we need before taking action?" I asked. I urged the panel to stand up for what every person in the room knew was right.

As it turns out, the EPA leaders were unwilling to allow a state to limit its own pollution. In late December 2007, the Bush administration ruled in favor of the automakers, ignoring even the recommendations of EPA staff, one of whom told a reporter, "the most appropriate action is to approve the waiver." Which is, in fact, what happened in the early months of the Obama administration.

Our failure to secure energy independence is not a partisan issue. Under the last several administrations, with both Democrat- and Republican-controlled Congresses, our reliance on dirty energy has grown. America has fought wars for oil. Coal companies are blasting apart entire mountains in Appalachia for "cheap" energy. Congress allows oil companies to gouge Americans at the pump and to drill without any effective oversight but awards billions in annual subsidies to those same companies. And every year, the planet gets hotter.

The famed abolitionist and statesman Frederick Douglass once said, "Power concedes nothing without a demand. It never did, and it never will." It's time for a national intervention, because although many Americans are working individually to break our addiction to oil and coal, our business and political leaders are keeping us hooked.

Why We're Hooked

One reason it's hard to think about breaking our addiction to oil and coal is that we Americans owe our contemporary lifestyle to the ingenious ways both substances have been used. Let's face facts: without coal and oil, we wouldn't enjoy the conveniences that many of us take for granted. We mustn't overlook the determination and creativity of the engineers, entrepreneurs, and most of all, laborers who have helped raise the quality of life for millions of Americans.

Coal powered the Watt steam engine, which helped launch the Industrial Revolution. The discovery of oil in Titusville, Pennsylvania, in 1859 brought light and heat into homes and eventually allowed people to drive from one end of the continent to the other. Both fossil fuels were present in seemingly boundless quantities, could be transported cheaply, and, most important, could easily ignite. Today, nearly half of our electricity comes from coal, while oil is used for everything from pharmaceuticals and plastics to fertilizer, cosmetics, and about 71 percent of our transportation fuels.

Times have changed, however, and the costs of our fossil-fuel habit cast a huge and spreading shadow on the benefits. Coal is the world's biggest and fastest-growing source of greenhouse gas emissions. In the United States each year, pollution from coal-fired power plants kills an estimated twenty-four thousand Americans prematurely—more than homicides and AIDS combined—and causes thousands more heart attacks, asthma flare-ups, and respiratory disorders. Mountaintop-removal (MTR) mining in Appalachia has leveled more than five hundred mountains, killing streams, wasting landscapes, and wrecking homes and communities. More than a hundred thousand Americans died mining coal in the last century, and safety violations still abound at underground mines across the country; twenty-nine miners perished in the spring of 2010 at the Big Branch mine operated by Massey Energy, a company with a long rap sheet of safety and clean-water violations. Improper treatment and storage of toxic coal ash, produced by MTR mining, have polluted water supplies around the region.

Anyone with access to a newspaper, television, or Internet connection witnessed the devastation wrought by BP's Gulf oil disaster in the summer of 2010. In a new afterword to this edition, I describe my firsthand experiences in the Gulf region. As disturbing as the oil-soaked pelicans and tar-stained wetlands were, equally alarming was the absence of any effective regulatory oversight or even an intelligent backup plan (setting the sea on fire and plugging the well with golf balls do not count). It's useful to remember that this catastrophe was caused not by a fly-by-night rogue operator in a third-world country but by one of the world's most profitable corporations in the world's richest country. It shouldn't be this hard to force Big Oil to play by the rules.

America's desperate hunger for oil is one of the largest contributors to the U.S. budget and trade deficits. Oil companies pollute our air and water and gouge Americans at the gas pump. Oil exploitation destroys marine environments, rainforests, and other wild lands, infringes on human rights, subverts democracy, and poisons communities. For decades, our oil dependence has twisted foreign policy, causing the United States to underwrite corrupt and unjust regimes. Saudi Arabia, one of our chief sources of oil, doesn't allow women to drive, vote, or walk in the streets without an escort. Gays are imprisoned and tortured because of their sexual orientation. Its citizens lack real voting rights, its newspapers lack independence, and human rights reformists are often thrown in jail. Yet, under an agreement dating back to 1945, the United States provides military protection for the corrupt Saudi monarchy in exchange for guaranteed access to Saudi oil. What's going on here? Our energy policies should advance American values, not undermine them.

Breaking Our Addiction

Fortunately, change often happens in response to crisis. This is true in evolutionary biology, as species adapt to their environment; it's also true in human relationships. Personally or collectively, we can grow by facing and solving our problems, once we admit that we have them. We actually learn through conflict.

When you think about it, many of us first experience this in our families or close friendships. How many of us have had to personally intervene—sitting down with someone we deeply love and explaining how his or her destructive behavior has hurt him or her and others? Come to think of it, how many of us have *been* sat down by a spouse or partner who said the same thing to us? Be honest now.

It's hard to intervene, and it's even more difficult to be sat down yourself, but when we can take feedback, reflect on it, and change what we do, we become better people. This is true for individuals, for corporations, and for society. We can grow by confronting our problems and trying to solve them.

Rainforest Action Network (RAN), the organization I used to lead, has undertaken corporate-size interventions for years. In the late 1990s, RAN led a coalition of organizations that persuaded Home Depot to stop selling wood from endangered forests around the world. It took more than two years to convince Home Depot to change its ways, but to its credit the company made a commitment and has honored it. Today, Home Depot can track nearly every single two-by-four and sheet of plywood from stump to shelf and attest that it didn't come from an endangered forest.

RAN has also pushed other Fortune 500 companies to green their practices, including FedEx Kinko's, Goldman Sachs, Lowe's, Citi, Bank of America, and others. Sometimes it takes just one letter to convince a corporate executive to drive change. One note to Kinko's, for example, convinced the company to prohibit the use of paper made from old-growth forests in its stores.

Other companies require more persuasion. RAN coordinated nearly a thousand protests against Home Depot's old-growth wood sales, placed ads in the *New York Times* and *Atlanta Journal-Constitution*, and worked with shareholder activists and popular groups such as R.E.M. and the Dave Matthews Band to push the company forward. Some CEOs may have to be prodded, but many other executives realize that their customers, shareholders, and employees increasingly do not want to buy from, own, or work for a company that makes its profits from plundering the environment.

The Sierra Club uses a bottom-up and top-down approach. As the country's largest grassroots environmental organization, it has a chapter in every state, local volunteer groups in almost every major city and college campus, and 1.3 million members and supporters. Those supporters take action locally to fight coal plants and oil facilities while accelerating the development of clean-energy solutions. They're complemented by an elite team of lawyers and public-interest lobbyists who work on federal rules and legislation. What can all this achieve? The Sierra Club's Beyond Coal campaign, along with its grassroots partners, has stopped the construction of more than 130 new coal-fired power plants, as discussed in chapter 2. Our new Beyond Oil campaign will press for the most ambitious achievable plan to break America's addiction to oil over the next two decades.

Know Your Power

As Americans begin to work collectively to address the challenges posed by climate change, we have momentum on our side. Conditions are perfect for an energy revolution in this country. Melting glaciers, killing droughts, fouled coastlines, wars in the Middle East, volatile gas prices, and chronic air pollution should provide ample motivation. If they don't, there's the unhealthy trade deficit and the charges of corruption, cronyism, price gouging, obscene profiteering, and environmental malfeasance leveled against Big Oil and King Coal.

It's also a brave new world for political activism. Paul Hawken, visionary entrepreneur and author of *The Ecology of Commerce* and *Blessed Unrest,* believes that Americans concerned about the environment and social justice are part of the largest, most powerful, and most unified movement in the history of the world (thanks to the Internet). New technology makes it much more difficult for public leaders in the Beltway or the boardroom to escape public scrutiny.

Not long ago, campaigners would have needed to hire a videographer, a translator, and a local guide to document human rights abuses in Nigeria, Indonesia, or Ecuador. It would have taken months to edit the footage and write the report, and tens of thousands, if not hundreds of thousands, of dollars to bring this documentary film to a wide audience. Today, we can ship a video camera anywhere in the world, and with a steady hand and a couple hours of editing time, put a video on YouTube, where it can be watched, for free, by millions. Social networks such as Twitter and Facebook enable users to instantly share information, gather citizens at events, and connect with like-minded folks.

How far can we go with these new tools and this movement of unprecedented size and connectivity?

We can change the energy pathway for the entire country, that's how far. We can help Detroit and other automakers go emissions-free, or watch them go out of business, as GM and Chrysler very nearly did in 2009. We can replace dirty coal with solar, wind, and energy efficiency, using bulldozers not to construct new coal plants but to tear the most polluting ones down. Using technologies already available, we can generate power from clean energy that won't run out, build a twenty-first-century grid to distribute it, and create thousands of well-paying jobs in the process. We can take on the agribusiness industry and shine a spotlight on dangerous biofuels, because the world's poor shouldn't have to compete with automobiles for food.

In the late 1800s, the mining industry and railroad barons wrote laws that exploited workers, communities, and our air and water. More than a hundred years later, some of those laws are still on the books, but we can make new laws and set new standards now for sustainability and justice will that serve us for the next hundred years.

A Deeper Form of Patriotism

Imagine what this country can do if we fully dedicate ourselves to breaking our addiction to fossil fuels. If we become truly determined and fiercely committed, and insist that our leaders do likewise, we can create the clean and socially just economy that we deserve.

Americans' fundamental sense of fairness and justice led us to end slavery, ban child labor, and secure women's right to vote. American ingenuity and determination cured polio worldwide, mapped the human genome, and have put sixty thousand songs and videos in the palms of our hands. We invented jazz, rock and roll, baseball, and the Philly cheesesteak. Our self-reliance and individual sacrifice have, until recently, enabled each generation to do better than the one before it. And this country's historic respect for the messy processes of democracy and peaceful dissent has helped America enact civil rights legislation, promote human rights internationally, and end unjust wars.

How were these things accomplished? Often it was through the work of quiet heroes—ordinary Americans accomplishing extraordinary things. Citizen engagement has brought this country out of its darkest hours and helped us fulfill our promises of justice and equality to millions.

Remember, the Clean Air Act, the Clean Water Act, the Wild and Scenic Rivers Act, and the Environmental Policy Act were all signed by Richard Nixon. Nixon could hardly be accused of being a commie pinko tree-hugging hippie, and it's doubtful that he was a deep ecologist afraid to come out of the closet. He signed those bills because the public pushed him to do so.

It took organizers and committed Americans who believed in these basic ideas and who took action to make the world a better place. Those actions were often simple and mundane—talking to neighbors, making phone calls, handing out flyers—but the results changed the country and set an example for the world. Can we do it again?

Coming Clean

No doubt you've been told to update your lightbulbs, properly inflate your tires, turn down the thermostat, and vote every year or so. Those are all useful ways to help create a clean-energy future. But they're not nearly enough. Let me be blunt: if we only take individual action and do nothing else, we'll continue to cook the climate, degrade our coastlines and landscapes, poison our air and water, and lose vital clean-energy jobs to other countries. We need to aim higher by changing corporate America and challenging our political leaders.

Rather than hope that 200 million drivers will each buy the most fuel-efficient car possible, we can work together to convince Detroit and the world's automakers to make *all* cars clean, not just a token few. Rather than harangue each of 300 million Americans to buy the best dishwasher, refrigerator, or dryer, we can join forces to set national standards for efficiency so that all appliances, buildings, and factories are as efficient as possible, reducing costs and emissions at the same time.

Coming Clean sets its sights on identifying ways that Americans can work together to achieve big wins that will break our addiction to oil and coal. Plenty of books focus on describing the human and ecological costs of fossil fuels or climate change. This is not one of them. There are other excellent books that survey and evaluate the range of technological solutions to our energy crisis. Not this one.

This is a book about action. At its core, *Coming Clean* is inspired by two hopeful notions: that as a society we possess practical and attractive solutions that can replace oil and coal, and that as individuals we possess the ability to work together to improve each other's lives. I'll share enough information in the first two chapters to reveal the true social and environmental costs of dirty energy, without getting bogged down in policy minutiae. The rest of the book is devoted not only to which remedies we can employ most effectively but to how we'll ensure that those solutions are implemented. Each chapter ends with a list of ways to get involved—at home, in the workplace, or as part of a church, community group, or student or other organization.

One of the first things an addict loses is perspective: our leaders have been so fixated for so long on getting access to more oil and coal that they've lost sight of the true costs of our dependency. So the first two chapters of this book reveal those sometimes hidden burdens. "Getting Our Fix" examines how we're invading the last intact forests, deep oceans, and wilderness areas to extract oil at ever greater economic, ecological, and human cost—often to Indigenous peoples. "Smokescreen" explores the misleading claim that coal, our leading source of electricity, can be made clean, and looks at the industry's impacts on Americans from the mountains of West Virginia to the streets of Chicago.

The rest of *Coming Clean* highlights what we need to do to break the hold that oil and coal have on America and the rest of the world. We'll start at the top, showing why we must change the rules in government and on Wall Street. Chapter 3, "Separate Oil and State," shows how the country can declare political independence from Big Oil and King Coal. Chapter 4, "Follow the Money," exposes the cash behind climate change, supplied by corporate banks and the World Bank—and how to redirect it toward a clean-energy future, with success stories of how banks have been pressured to develop smart environmental policies.

Chapters 5, 6, and 7 explore how to retool our national transportation system, which now swallows nearly three-quarters of the oil we use. "Redesigning Mobility" begins on a Japanese bullet train and envisions how a diverse set of transit options will make traveling more fun, efficient, and far better for the climate. "Jump-Start Detroit" shows how individual persistence, technological innovation, and collective action can truly revolutionize the auto industry and promote America's energy independence. "Growing Gas" separates fact from fantasy in the biofuels industry, identifying policies that will allow biofuels to help relieve oil dependence while minimizing their potential for harm.

Moving from fuel to electricity generation, chapters 8 and 9 bring good news about how to accelerate a clean-energy transition. "Greening the Grid" focuses on how solar and wind—the renewables with the most potential to scale up quickly—can start putting coal-fired plants out of business and create new green-collar jobs along the way. "Less Is More" details some of the easiest steps we can take to beat our addiction and save money, by promoting smart policies on energy efficiency.

The last chapter, "Power Shift," begins with a sobering reminder of just how hard the fossil-fuel industries will fight to hold their position, with ad campaigns, lobbying strategies, scare tactics, distortions, and dirty tricks. But the shift is on, and if we act effectively, it cannot be stopped. To fuel your inspiration, I'll offer a glimpse of how thoroughly a clean-energy economy can permeate our lives by the year 2030.

Breaking our addiction to oil and coal is both patriotic and principled. Yet many are losing confidence that we can meet this challenge. The essential purpose of *Coming Clean* is to present evidence that we can and to provide a hopeful, helpful, do-it-yourself guide to making it happen. Big Oil and King Coal may have armies of lobbyists, lawyers, foreign diplomats, and even military advisors, but Americans know that we can do better for ourselves, our country, and our fellow humans. As the writer Arundhati Roy says, "Another world is not only possible, she is on her way. On a quiet day, I can hear her breathing."

CHAPTER 1

Getting Our Fix

The True Cost of America's Oil Habit

*The fact that oil is beginning to get more expensive
more quickly will contribute to the realization of how
dysfunctional our current pattern is. Take the tar sands
of western Canada. For every barrel of oil they extract
there, they have to use enough natural gas to heat a
family's home for four days. And they have to tear up
four tons of landscape, all for one barrel of oil. It is
truly nuts. But you know, junkies find veins in their toes.
It seems reasonable, to them, because they've lost
sight of the rest of their lives.*

—AL GORE

W e were a couple hundred feet or so above the canopy in the Ecuadorian Amazon jungle, and I felt the urge to shout—whether with joy or alarm, I wasn't sure. Squeezed into a tiny, four-seat plane, up front with the pilot, I was enthralled by the divine view of a lush green carpet of magnificent forest that extended in every direction as far as the eye could see. Below, the muddy waters of the Rio Bobonaza meandered through the dense rainforest. Soon I'd be digging my feet into the wet soil, smelling the musty rain, and maybe spotting some toucans, macaws, perhaps a king vulture or two.

We had taken off from the town of Shell (this was oil country, after all), and by now not a hint of industrial society could be seen. There was no smog, gridlock, fast-food restaurants, or strip malls, only the deep and seemingly impenetrable rainforest. We were flying over the traditional territory of the

Shuar, Achuar, and Kichwa peoples and could occasionally spot signs of their huts and villages from the air. This part of Amazonia is one of the most wondrous and biologically diverse forests on the planet, with thousands of plant and animal species unique to the region, including howler monkeys, pink river dolphins, jaguars, three-toed sloths, parrots, guacamayos, and more.

I looked forward to meeting both the human and wild inhabitants of this captivating landscape, but I found it difficult to fully enjoy the flight—for we weren't here on holiday, but to challenge one of the world's wealthiest and most powerful oil companies. With me in one plane were Bill Twist and Dave Elliot of the Pachamama Alliance, which works to protect Ecuador's rainforests. A second plane carried Hermann Edelmann from Pro-Regenwald, a German environmental group, and Randy Hayes, the founder of Rainforest Action Network. We were visiting the Kichwa community at Sarayaku, located deep in the rainforests of southwest Ecuador, near the Peruvian border.

Just after liftoff, as we left the frontier town behind, we passed dozens of bulldozers, tractors, and piles of garbage. Magnificent rainforests were being disfigured by new roads penetrating deeper and deeper into the rainforest—with logging, oil drilling, and other industrial operations soon to follow. Without strong pressure and decisive leadership, these forests and their residents would be sacrificed like so many other parts of the Amazon—all for just a little more wood or oil.

Soon we banked left and followed the path of the river, descending quickly. Within seconds we were under the treetops, then just fifteen feet over the water. I began to shift uncomfortably in my seat: did the pilot forget that we weren't in a floatplane? Just as I was about to say something, a turn in the river revealed a dirt runway ahead, beginning right at the river's edge. After an impressively smooth landing, the plane rolled to a stop, and what appeared to be the entire village of several hundred men, women, and children gathered around the plane. They had all come to welcome us.

Sarayaku is ground zero in the Kichwa people's battle to stop a massive oil-drilling project within their native territory, led by Burlington Oil Resources, since acquired by Houston-based ConocoPhillips. More than half of the oil Ecuador produces is shipped to the United States, where it meets about 1 percent of U.S. demand. To put this another way, America consumes its daily oil imports from Ecuador in less than twenty minutes. Any oil found in Kichwa territory would be a fraction of that amount.

Our visit, in March 2004, came just weeks after Ecuador's government had threatened to use military force to repress any resistance by the Kichwa, who have always opposed this project. The Kichwa have seen how similar oil projects nearby have introduced deadly new diseases, poisoned water supplies, decimated forests, and divided communities.

Shortly after landing, we all gathered under a thatched canopy, little children smiling shyly behind their parents' legs. One by one, for several hours, elders and other community leaders described how the oil company's plans would threaten their way of life. "You must make this case known," said one of them, Ricardo. "We are a Kichwa people. The jungle is our market. We live and eat off the jungle. We fish here. Our children play in these rivers. In the plane, you saw the river and the beautiful state of our forests. This is our home."

As people who had lived in the region for centuries, the Kichwa were incredulous that their refusal to allow oil drilling was not taken seriously. "We don't want oil, okay?" another leader declared. "We've been saying this for twenty years, but nobody listens. We live in the twenty-first century now, and somebody must know that we have rights that must be respected."

After the meeting, we were led on a tour of the village, past a solar-powered infirmary, two schools, and at the end of the tour, surprisingly, a volleyball court. One hour and buckets of sweat later, our largely California-based crew walked off the court in humbling defeat, much to the delight of our mostly fourteen-year-old opponents.

As I lay under a mosquito tent that night, I thought about how to describe what I'd seen and heard that day to my wife back home in California. We were expecting our first child later that summer, and all day long I had found myself imagining what I'd do if I was a father in the Kichwa community. I'd want to protect my family, that much was clear. No matter where they live, almost all parents share the instinct to do whatever it takes to keep their kids safe. But not all parents face the same challenges. It's one thing to hold your child's hand as you cross the street, or to install safety latches on your kitchen cabinets. It's another thing altogether to stare down an oil company and risk a military invasion.

Americans love an underdog. I think that most of us, if we had the option, would support a peaceful community against a corporate bully or corrupt government every time. But when it comes to energy policy in the United States, we're not given much choice. Americans aren't asked whether it's right to plunder the Amazon—or finance terrorism—to keep our country awash in oil. Instead, politicians mostly cater to the demands of multinational oil corporations and do very little to hold them accountable for damages to the environment or to human dignity. It's clear that our leaders don't usually calculate the true cost of our oil addiction—which is even more expensive than you might think.

The High Price of Peak Oil

Around the globe, conflicts like the one at Sarayaku are becoming more frequent. The reason is simple: the world's appetite for oil continues to grow at the same time as our reserves of easily obtained oil are steadily decreasing. As a result, oil companies are digging deeper and reaching farther into previously untouched areas to find every remaining pocket of oil. And they are digging deeper in areas already exploited, such as our own Gulf Coast. Increasing oil consumption by China and India heightens this tension even further.

Unless we change course, the trends are not in our favor. Global oil consumption is projected to increase from 85.5 million barrels of oil per day in 2007 to about 104 million barrels of oil per day in 2030. As we seek to burn more and more oil, many geologists and other experts believe that, very soon, less and less of it will be produced each year. If this occurs without planning for how to equitably distribute a dwindling resource—and without a crash program to implement oil-free solutions—we'll be in a world of hurt. This is the threat of "peak oil"—and it is growing every year.

Peak-oil theorists are like global-warming scientists: ridiculed at first, then politely dismissed, they now see their viewpoints gaining traction. The intellectual ancestor of today's peak-oil scientists is M. King Hubbert, a geologist and petroleum engineer who shocked the industry with his prediction in 1956 of a pending decline in U.S. oil production. Hubbert worked for Royal Dutch Shell for thirty years, later teaching at Stanford University and the

University of California, Berkeley, and putting in time at the U.S. Geological Survey (USGS). Hubbert developed an analysis that showed how the growth and decline of oil production in a nation would be like that of an individual oil well. He surmised that the discovery of new oil would rise, peak, and fall in a roughly bell-shaped curve, and that a nation's actual production of oil would follow a similar pattern approximately forty years later.

At the time of Hubbert's prediction in 1956, the United States was the largest oil producer in the world. Observing that American oil discoveries reached their zenith in 1930, Hubbert estimated that U.S. oil production would peak around 1970, then gradually fall. And that's exactly what happened. U.S. oil production topped out at 9.6 million barrels per day in 1970 and has since declined to barely more than 5 million barrels per day, despite advanced engineering and state-of-the-art recovery techniques.

Noting how global oil discoveries peaked in the mid-1960s, and citing a bevy of other statistics, many experts foresee a similar growth-peak-decline curve for oil production globally. They include Kenneth Deffeyes, a Shell oil man and professor emeritus from Princeton University; Colin Campbell, a geologist who has worked for Amoco, Fina, BP, Chevron-Texaco, Shell, and Exxon, and who founded the Oil Depletion Analysis Centre in London; and Matthew Simmons, a Texas businessman and energy expert.

These experts believe, with little variation, that global peak-oil production either has just occurred or will occur within the next several years. Deffeyes takes a whimsical but reflective view, writing, "I nominate Thanksgiving Day, November 24, 2005 as World Oil Peak Day. . . . We can pause and give thanks for the years from 1901 to 2005 when abundant oil and natural gas fueled enormous changes in our society. At the same time, we have to face up to reality: World oil production is going to decline, slowly at first, and then more rapidly."

Peak-oil theorists use several arguments. They begin with hard evidence, showing that for the past twenty to twenty-five years the world has been consuming oil far faster than it has been discovering it, thus depleting reserves more quickly than they can be replaced. Oil production has either leveled off or begun to decline in fifty-four of the world's largest sixty-five oil-producing countries. Many of the remaining countries, such as Saudi Arabia, Libya, and Iran, closely guard their data about remaining oil supplies. The lack of independent verification and transparency means that we simply don't know how much oil remains under their control.

Others are skeptical that the world will reach peak-oil production any time soon. They profess faith that the industry will always discover new technologies, efficiencies, and ways to drill profitably, particularly if oil prices remain high. "This is not the first time that the world has 'run out of oil.' It's more like the fifth," scoffs Daniel Yergin, author of the Pulitzer Prize–winning book *The Prize: The Epic Quest for Oil, Money, and Power* and chairman of Cambridge Energy Research Associates. This is a fair comment. The decline of oil production has indeed been prophesied since soon after the first commercial oil well was established in Titusville, Pennsylvania, in 1859, and plenty of times since then.

However, in a telling sign of the scarcity of conventional oil sources, the oil industry itself has cut its investment in exploring new oil sources. In the last decade alone, the share of major oil companies' exploration and production budget that has gone to exploration has declined from 30 to only 12 percent— most likely because oil executives know that most of the large reserves that can be profitably exploited have already been discovered. "Despite the fact that we're in the highest oil-price era, the level of exploration is not increasing," notes Michael Rodgers, senior director at PFC Energy. "The reason . . . is that, in so many regions of the world, the fields have gotten so small that even though you might be able to drill a well and get a positive rate of return, the incremental value doesn't mean a lot." But there are plenty of places, like Sarayaku, already explored and targeted, and clearly worth the effort to the companies seeking oil there. And as product gets scarcer and prices rise still more, the cost-value equation could shift again.

The chief economist at the respected International Energy Agency (IEA) believes that the crunch will come sooner than most believed only a few years ago. Fatih Birol warned in August 2009 that global production is likely to peak by 2019, at least a decade earlier than most public estimates by governments. A detailed assessment of more than eight hundred oil fields in the world (three-quarters of global reserves) determined that most of the biggest fields have already peaked and that the rate of decline in production was more pronounced—nearly twice that calculated two years earlier. Birol warned that the market power of the very few countries that hold substantial reserves of oil—mostly in the Middle East—would skyrocket as the oil crisis really sets in after 2010. "One day we will run out of oil. . . . [W]e have to leave oil before oil leaves us, and we have to prepare ourselves for that day," said Birol.

Deffeyes points out, too, that though U.S. refineries have been running at close to capacity for years, no new refineries have been built since 1976. "Oil tanker ships are fully booked," he adds, "but outdated tankers are being retired faster than new ones are being built." Sadad al-Husseini, the former head of exploration and production for Saudi Aramco, the national oil company of Saudi Arabia, says that global oil production likely reached its peak in 2006, and in fact, it has not increased since then.

Pass It On

For every barrel of oil discovered, we now consume three. Production has leveled off or declined in fifty-four of the largest sixty-five oil-producing countries, yet oil demand is expected to soar by nearly 40 percent in coming decades. Welcome to peak oil.

While it's debatable whether we've reached peak production, there's no question about the problems that will ensue when oil supplies do start to decline. Gasoline prices will rise, affecting working families and truckers in particular, as well as airlines and other sectors across the economy. Tens of billions more will be spent each year on military operations to safeguard access to oil in the Middle East, Latin America, and across Asia. Wars for oil will become more frequent and may drag on for years. Human rights, human health, protection of wilderness areas, and other environmental concerns will be subordinated to meet America's energy demand, as we've seen in the renewed push for offshore drilling. Wait—you think this is already happening? Imagine what will take place when less and less oil is available each year. And then consider a future in which China's and India's levels of oil consumption approach our own.

Whether peak oil is imminent or a few decades away shouldn't make much difference in how we respond to the threat. Oil is a finite resource. For every barrel of oil we discover, we now consume three, and global demand is expected to increase nearly 40 percent in the next few decades. You don't need to be a math expert to calculate that trouble lies ahead. Given this reality, it's not surprising that some policymakers are seeking to exploit parks and wilderness areas or to cut deals with unsavory governments to get access to every puddle of oil available. But like a junkie searching for veins in his toes, this irrational and desperate scramble for oil is corrupting the idea of what it means to be an American. Trying to drill our way out of our oil addiction could end up costing us not just our economic future but our souls.

Drilling at Home: From the Arctic to the Gulf

Consider first the long-running debate over the Arctic National Wildlife Refuge (ANWR), the Alaskan wilderness area that is sacred to the native Gwich'in people and is a wildlife haven for caribou, grizzly bears, arctic wolves, and other species. Teams of corporate lawyers and oil-friendly officials have struggled mightily to drill in the region, while opposing lawyers and other passionate citizens are equally determined to keep the refuge pristine. As in the Amazon, the social and environmental costs of oil extraction in the Arctic are enormous compared to the actual benefit to society.

Ninety-five percent of all known oil reserves in Alaska have already been made available for exploration and production. Geological surveys indicate that oil in the Arctic Refuge, rather than being concentrated in one major field, may be scattered in thirty or more small deposits. And since the potential oil fields are more than thirty miles from the nearest pipeline and more than fifty miles from the nearest road, exporting oil from the refuge would require significant investments in new infrastructure across the melting landscape.

If exploration did proceed, thirty-two-ton "thumper trucks" would traverse the sensitive wild lands, sending jolts of seismic waves underground. In their wake, bulldozers and large rigs would roam over the delicate tundra, drilling exploratory and production wells throughout the refuge. Several dozen oil fields would need to be constructed, plus numerous airstrips, gravel mines, water reservoir excavations, water withdrawal sites, seawater treatment plants, utility lines, loading docks, dormitories, and garbage dumps across the landscape.

In addition, several hundred miles of seismic exploration trails and ice roads would have to be built, as well as countless more miles of pipelines and other access roads. Eventually the oil would be shipped to Prudhoe Bay and travel through the eight-hundred-mile Trans-Alaska Pipeline System to Valdez, to be loaded onto oil tankers that must navigate the rocky shoals of once-pristine Prince William Sound (where the *Exxon Valdez* ran aground in 1989) to ports in the Lower 48. Analysts estimate it would take at least ten years for the first drops of oil to reach our gas tanks. All this for much less oil than the United States consumes in a year.

With plans to drill in the refuge repeatedly blocked in Congress due to public pressure, oil companies have looked elsewhere in Alaska for oil. Shell has ambitious plans to drill offshore in the Chukchi and Beaufort Seas off northern Alaska, and the Minerals Management Service (since broken up into three federal agencies) approved its Chukchi Sea drill plan in December 2009. The company had intended to drill up to three exploration wells in the Chukchi and two in the Beaufort the following summer and fall.

President Obama suspended all offshore Arctic drilling permits in the aftermath of the BP Deepwater Horizon disaster, and in the summer of 2010 a federal judge blocked, at least temporarily, the Chukchi Sea project. But the Obama administration has sent mixed signals, at best, about offshore drilling, arguing at first that it can be done safely, then installing a short-term moratorium in response to the Gulf oil disaster.

It might be a good time to remind ourselves that offshore drilling was banned on all our coastlines for more than two decades, and for very good reasons. In 1969, a Union Oil Company platform six miles off the coast of Santa Barbara, California, suffered a blowout, causing two hundred thousand gallons of crude oil to spread into an eight-hundred-square-mile slick. Incoming tides spread thick tar over thirty-five miles of coastline, washing ashore dead seals, dolphins, and some four thousand birds. In a statement reminiscent of Tony "I Want My Life Back" Hayward, the former CEO of BP, Fred Hartley, president of Union Oil, said at the time, "I am amazed at the publicity for the loss of a few birds."

Congress renewed the moratorium each year since then. The first President Bush strengthened it in 1990, deferring new leasing until 2002. President

Clinton extended that deferral until 2012, but the moratorium was lifted under the second Bush administration, leaving waters from Alaska to the Gulf and on both coasts at risk of future drilling.

It's true: there's still a lot of oil under the Gulf of Mexico and in Arctic waters. And as global oil supplies continue to shrink, oil companies will want it more and more. But it's getting more expensive to reach and more dangerous to extract, whereas other onshore oil sources are even dirtier.

Tar Sands: America's Next Tank of Gas?

If drilling efforts in the Amazon and the Arctic illustrate the high social and environmental risks that are incurred to produce small amounts of oil, the development of oily tar sands in the Canadian province of Alberta presents entirely different challenges. Everything about Canada's tar sands industry, from the size of its reserves to its impacts on human health and the environment, is extreme. Those reserves are large enough to potentially meet a portion of U.S. oil demand for years to come, which is a frightening prospect if you care about clean air and water and a stable climate.

"I've lived in Fort Chipewyan most of my life," recalls Allan Adam, chief of the Athabasca Chipewyan First Nation (ACFN), a native community of Alberta's boreal forests. "When we were kids, we were living out in the bush. My father taught us how to hunt, and my mother taught us how to dry meat and fish. We used to drink right from the Athabasca River."

But this was before the oil industry arrived to convert Canada's vast tar sands into a source of fuel. "We can't drink freshwater any longer. We have to bring it from the treatment plant. They say it's good for us, but we know better. Too many people here [in the communities at Fort Chipewyan and Fort McMurray] are getting sick—and it's because our water is being poisoned," Adam explains.

Residents of Fort Chipewyan, a town of about twelve hundred people, have been afflicted with unusually high rates of debilitating illnesses, including rare cancers, lupus, leukemia, lymphomas, and autoimmune diseases. The region's former medical examiner, Dr. John O'Connor, has called for epidemiological studies to be completed before more permits to develop tar sands are approved, urging that such studies be started as quickly as possible. "For years the community has believed that there's lots of cancer," says Donna Cyprien, a local health director. "When they drank from the water, there was an oily scum around the cup. We now know there is something wrong." "The river used to be blue. Now it's brown. Nobody can fish or drink from it. The air is bad. This has all happened so fast," says Elsie Fabian, an elder in the native community.

Underlying the northeastern part of Alberta, Canada's tar sands cover an area larger than the state of Florida. They're quite different from a conventional oil site such as in Texas or Saudi Arabia, where the liquid oil flows easily when drilled. Here the "oil" is a thick, heavy substance called bitumen, mixed with dirt, rock, and minerals beneath the surface. The processes of mining and refining bitumen, which is then converted into oil for fuel, create waste and pollution on a scale that boggles the mind.

Pass It On

To get oil from Canada's tar sands, more landscape must be excavated than was moved for the Great Wall of China, the Suez Canal, the Great Pyramid of Cheops, and the ten largest dams in the world—combined.

For every barrel of oil refined from Alberta's tar sands, four tons of dirt, rock, and bitumen must be dug up, producing enough waste to fill Yankee Stadium every two days.

The mining, refining, and transport of tar sands oil is also extremely energy intensive and thus a huge climate risk, producing almost three times as much greenhouse gases as conventional oil sources. In recent years, development of the tar sands is the largest contributor to the growth of climate-change pollution in Canada.

Approximately 20 percent of the bitumen can be excavated using strip mines, one of which, operated by Syncrude, is already the largest strip mine in the world. Another will soon be six miles in diameter. Dozens more strip mines are planned for the region.

The other 80 percent of the bitumen lies too deep for strip mining. At these sites, massive quantities of natural gas are piped in to produce steam, which is injected into the ground to heat up the bitumen and liquefy it so that it can be drilled. The process is highly inefficient: for every three barrels of oil produced, the energy equivalent of one is consumed in the process. Within the next few years, tar sands oil production will consume enough gas each year to heat every home in Canada. As Eric Reguly commented in the Canadian newspaper *Globe and Mail*, "Burning a clean fuel to make a dirty fuel is a kind of reverse alchemy, like turning gold into lead. It also leaves less gas for more sensible uses, like making electricity or heating your home."

Many who question the wisdom of mining tar sands look for justice to the United States, Canada's largest oil customer. Fed by ever-increasing U.S. oil demand, the production of oil from Alberta's tar sands has skyrocketed. At the end of 2007, about 1.3 million barrels of oil were produced each day. Expansion plans would bring production to about 2.2 million barrels daily by 2015 and about 3.5 million in 2025.

All that natural gas needed to produce oil from tar sands has to come from somewhere. To increase the flow of gas, Exxon, Shell, and others have proposed building the Mackenzie Gas Project, a 758-mile pipeline from the Arctic to eastern Alberta—much of it along the wild and scenic Mackenzie River. The Mackenzie Valley is part of the Canadian boreal forest, one of the largest intact forest ecosystems in the world, hosting healthy populations of grizzly bears, caribou, and millions of migratory birds.

The pipeline also would bisect the territory of the Dehcho First Nation, an Indigenous community that has fought the proposal for decades. "People think of a pipeline like a garden hose in your yard," says Dehcho grand chief Herb Norwegian. "But a pipeline of this magnitude is like building a China Wall right down the valley, and the effects will be there forever and ever."

Furthermore, oil production in the tar sands is extremely water intensive, using from two to five barrels of water for each barrel of oil produced. Every year, up to 349 million feet of cubic water is allowed to be diverted from the Athabasca River in Alberta—more than twice the amount of water used each year by the residents of Calgary, Canada's third-largest city. Mining tar sands depletes local freshwater aquifers, drains wetlands and muskegs, and produces massive amounts of waste associated with water treatment. Although oil companies are required to attempt to restore these natural systems, none has done so in nearly forty years of development. Much of the waste is sent to poisonous tailings ponds, many of them so large that they can be seen from outer space.

In September 2006, Chief Norwegian helped form the Keepers of the Water Coalition, an alliance of two dozen First Nations and other concerned citizens whose water is being poisoned and territories destroyed. The Keepers' declaration stated, "Water is a sacred gift, an essential element that sustains and connects all life. It is not a commodity to be bought or sold. All people share an obligation to cooperate to ensure that water in all of its forms is protected and conserved with regard to the needs of all living things today and for future generations tomorrow."

They are resisting powerful forces, though. The province of Alberta and the federal government hope to increase production to 5 to 6 million barrels of oil per day by 2030, and several energy analysts predict that output could reach as high as 11 million barrels per day by 2047. To bring in still more natural gas and to export the oil that expanded tar sands would produce, another pipeline has been proposed, this one cutting through temperate rainforests in British Columbia's Great Bear Rainforest. Fifty-two angry First Nations communities along the coast have already sued to stop the plan.

Allan Adam views all this with a historical perspective. "We have all this oil in our backyard, yet there's no benefits coming to our community and our people are still being neglected. Not only that, but cancer rates have skyrocketed. It's not going to get better. It's just going to keep getting worse. People around here say that the oil industry is just the twenty-first-century version of General Custer. They're here to finish the job of what's been done to Indigenous people all over the continent."

Nor do the ill effects of mining and transporting tar sands oil stop at the border. The United States is the main consumer of tar sands oil. In fact, we import more oil from Canada's tar sands than we do from any other country. Within our borders, oil and pipeline companies plan to build an extensive, two-thousand-mile tar sands pipeline and refinery infrastructure that will lock us in to receive this high-carbon fossil fuel for many decades to come. The proposed Keystone XL pipeline would pass through freshwater aquifers used to irrigate farms throughout middle America, bringing a serious danger of oil spills to America's agricultural heartland.

In addition to risks associated with the pipeline, pollution from refineries threatens midwestern communities and the Great Lakes region. Refining tar sands oil that contains sulfur, nitrogen, mercury, lead, and arsenic can produce pollutants that cause acid rain and a wide range of debilitating health problems.

Americans whose lives are likely to be seriously affected by tar sands pipeline development are clear on why they don't want it. South Dakotan landowner Kent Moeckly says, "The big oil companies stand to make millions of dollars with the sludge that they're going to put through the pipe, and yet they won't even set up a fund for cleaning up spills. South Dakotans historically are reasonable, methodical people, not easily swayed and misled by the smoke and mirrors of snake oil salesmen and the like." And Ben Gotschall, whose family has ranched for four generations in Nebraska's Sand Hills, worries that any leaked oil from the pipeline—which would run right by his property—would affect the adjacent wetlands and their important bird migrations. "In my mind," he says, "oil and water don't mix no matter where it is."

The Bucket Stops Here

The problems associated with oil use—from extraction to combustion—aren't limited to other countries. America's dependence on oil is poisoning its own citizens. Federal officials estimate that approximately 90 million Americans live within thirty miles of one of the nation's 153 oil refineries. These refineries release millions of pounds of benzene, butadiene, formaldehyde, and other cancer-causing chemicals, as well as particulate matter, nickel, lead, sulfur dioxide, nitrogen oxides, and other pollutants linked to heart disease, severe asthma, and other respiratory ailments.

Although these refineries are subject to the Clean Air Act, enforcement has been, shall we say, lax. An investigative report by the Ecological Integrity Project and the Houston Galveston Association for Smog Prevention found that the U.S. EPA and state governments routinely underreport toxic air emissions, and that the presence of certain

Pass It On

In the United States, more than 90 million Americans live near oil refineries that release millions of pounds of cancer-causing chemicals, particulate matter, and other pollutants into the air each year.

cancer-causing chemicals in the air may be four to five times higher than what the EPA reports to the public.

More than half of the nation's refineries are located in Texas and Louisiana, including nine of the top ten carcinogen emitters. There and elsewhere around the country, refineries are often located in low-income communities and communities of color. In Port Arthur, Texas, dangerously high levels of ozone and benzene have been reported. Yet public officials often side with industry. Here's one uplifting statement: "This city is not going to change. It is a refinery town—tomorrow, next year, a hundred years from now. It will always be a petrochemical area," says Oscar Ortiz, the town's former mayor. Asked about the health impacts from the refineries' pollution, Ortiz replied, "We've all got to die of something."

Increasingly, communities are fighting back with an unlikely weapon: the humble, everyday, five-gallon bucket. Most people use these buckets as toolboxes, planters, even as makeshift drums on street corners. But more recently they've been put to a new and higher use: holding refinery owners accountable to local communities.

Here's how it works. Before the mid-1990s, residents concerned about releases of dangerous pollutants in their neighborhoods had to rely on costly air-sampling equipment brought in by government agencies to determine what they were breathing. In 1994, ailing citizens living near a Unocal refinery in Rodeo, California, filed a lawsuit to address excessive pollution from the site. Their lead lawyer was Edward Masry, who, along with his colleague Erin Brockovich, would soon be immortalized in an Oscar-winning movie. Masry realized that his clients in Rodeo had no economical way to monitor their air quality, so he hired an environmental engineering firm to design an inexpensive air-sampling device.

The engineers' solution was the five-gallon bucket. For about $75 citizens could draw a "grab sample" of air into a gas-sampling bag, seal it in the bucket, and send it to analysts for testing. Rodeo residents immediately put the buckets to use and used the data on air quality in negotiations with the company. Two years later, Unocal settled the lawsuit, paying $80 million to the plaintiffs.

Denny Larson was a community organizer at the time. Today he is executive director of Global Community Monitor, an environmental justice organization, and has helped create "bucket brigades" in dozens of U.S. cities and at least nineteen countries around the world. Larson sees the bucket brigades as a key tool for community empowerment. No longer do citizens have to trust refinery operators to volunteer air-pollution data. Nor must they rely on government regulators and local politicians like Mayor Ortiz. Citizens can "use simple but effective and credible testing methods to document their toxic exposure. Armed with that information, they can fight to reduce their exposure to unnecessary pollution from large industrial sources," Larson says.

Dorothy Jenkins of New Sarpy, Louisiana, used the data from a local air sample to confront a manager of Orion Refining. "That was one of the greatest moments of my life," recalls Anne Rolfes, founder and director of the Louisiana Bucket Brigade and a colleague of Jenkins. "He was so smug and rude, insisting that there wasn't a problem, and she just slammed her air sample results down on the table and said, 'Then why did you violate the state benzene standard?'"

"People get so excited when they build the bucket, get the test results, and find out what they're breathing for the first time," Larson says. "Man, when they go after companies and regulators, you'd better not be in their way."

Freedom from Oil

As oil refining further degrades the environmental quality of poor communities, both inside and outside the United States, oil development often makes poor countries even poorer—an effect that Stanford University professor and author Terry Lynn Karl calls the "paradox of plenty." Many poor countries with large oil reserves become dependent on oil to fund their governments and increase public spending rather than develop stable and diversified economies. Increased oil prices create the illusion of prosperity in these countries; actually, they mask deeper troubles and destabilize governments that become too dependent on oil as a primary source of revenue. As a result, developing countries that have significant oil reserves are in worse economic shape than neighboring countries that don't have much oil. A report by Christian Aid states that poor countries dependent on oil revenues have a higher likelihood of "four great and interconnected ills. Oil, in these instances, becomes the key ingredient in a lethal cocktail of: greater poverty for the mass majority of the population, increased corruption, a greater likelihood of war or civil strife, [and] dictatorial or unrepresentative government."

From Alberta to the Amazon to the Arctic to Alabama, the list goes on. Dependence on oil is causing human rights and environmental integrity to be trampled in Nigeria, Colombia, Burma, and many other countries. It's giving power to tyrants, as multinational oil corporations cozy up to corrupt, oil-rich governments in Sudan, Libya, Uzbekistan, and elsewhere. As the world's largest consumer of oil, the United States bears the greatest responsibility. And as oil grows scarcer, the human, economic, and ecological consequences of our addiction—whether it's a ballooning trade deficit, a destabilized climate, polluted air and water, or human rights violations—will only become more severe.

On the morning I left Sarayaku, as the sun was coming up and the howler monkeys were quieting down, I sat in the village and spoke with several of the Kichwa leaders. One gave me a handmade necklace: a gift, she said, for my pregnant wife. As we walked down to the riverbed where her own children were playing, she told me, "Our people will never be free as long as your country drinks oil like it is water. Until you stop, we will never truly be free."

Based on the most rosy industry forecasts, the oil under Sarayaku would meet U.S. demand for slightly more than a month. To get this oil, the Ecuadorian military would have to invade a peaceful community. Oil companies would threaten the water supply and wildlife upon which the Kichwa have depended for generations, and risk introducing deadly new diseases. If somehow that oil could be drilled profitably in such a hostile environment, oil companies would have to cut a pipeline through miles of pristine rainforest to load the oil onto a tanker for sale in the United States before it is refined into gasoline, belching more pollution into the air. Pumped into American gas tanks, each fifteen gallons would add three hundred pounds of carbon dioxide to the atmosphere.

Here's a better idea: leave the oil there and prevent another community from suffering because of our energy cravings. It wouldn't be that hard to do. We can easily save more oil than Sarayaku could produce if Congress or the president or any of the major automakers showed some courage and foresight.

Just one solution—equipping all new vehicles with hybrid engines and other minor modifications—would save much more oil than we currently import from the entire Persian Gulf.

And we can go much further: by challenging every politician and corporate executive to get serious about climate change and clean energy. Personal responsibility is important—the choices we make about where we live, how we commute and heat our homes, and which vehicles we drive (or don't) can have an impact on how much oil our nation consumes. But the game is rigged, because we aren't given the best choices. Automakers have historically refused to utilize the best technologies to clean up emissions. Airlines are slow to transition to more fuel-efficient models, and our mass transit systems have been underinvested and neglected for decades.

I believe that most Americans are fair-minded and compassionate. If more of us witnessed or understood the harm to families and natural systems that comes from wresting oil from the earth and bringing it to our country, we would demand more and better alternatives from our politicians and CEOs. Our choice is to act now to convert to a clean-energy economy, or to fight over every last barrel of oil that can be found—and suffer the consequences of burning it.

Take Action

Take it personally

1. Do your homework. To learn more about our oil addiction and the real price of oil, check out the books, movies, and Web sites recommended in the Resources section at the end of this book:

2. Know your adversary. Oil companies are the richest corporations in the world, with plenty of spare change to hire the cleverest PR professionals. Visit Chevron's site, www.willyoujoinus.com, where a leading source of greenhouse gas emissions and human rights controversies is attempting to reposition itself as a company that cares. BP for a time adopted the brand "Beyond Petroleum"; check out its site at www.bp.com to see how one of the world's largest polluters congratulates itself on its response to the Deepwater Horizon blowout, while on a deeper page it defines "sustainability" as the capacity not to ensure that future generations live in a clean and healthy environment but simply to sustain itself as a business.

Express yourself

Raise your voice in support of ethical policies that support human and environmental rights:

1. Contact the premier of Alberta, Ed Stelmach (or his successor), and urge him to adopt an immediate moratorium on expansion of Alberta's tar sands.

2. Write or call James Mulva, the current chairman and CEO of ConocoPhillips, urging him to withdraw all plans to drill for oil within Kichwa territory in Ecuador.

3. Write to the CEOs of BP, Chevron, ConocoPhillips, Exxon, Shell, Total, and Occidental—some of the world's largest oil companies—to demand that they stop drilling for oil in endangered ecosystems and accept local communities' right of refusal to reject projects that will harm their health or livelihoods.

4. If you live near an oil refinery (or a coal plant or any other source of industrial pollution), take action to improve health and air quality in your community. You can contact your local Sierra Club chapter, work with Global Community Monitor, Communities for a Better Environment, and other organizations to hold polluters accountable; see the Resources section for more information.

Stay engaged

As you learn more about the costs of our oil dependency, don't stop with one call or letter to a CEO. Stay involved! Suggest this book or others named above to your reading club. Host a movie night to screen *Syriana* or one of the powerful documentaries about oil exploitation, such as *Oil on Ice* (oil in Alaska) and *Crude Impact* (peak oil and the urgent need for action). Urge your family and friends, your employer, church group, or school to take action as well.

To reform the world's richest and most powerful industry, we'll also need to weaken its control over our government (chapter 3), enlist the support of fossil-fuel financiers (chapter 4), and change the industry's biggest markets (starting with the auto industry, chapter 6).

Challenging Big Oil will also require working collectively. Get to know the organizations that work on the issues mentioned in this chapter and support those whose aims and approach best match your interests. In the Resources section you'll find an extensive list, along with brief descriptions and Web sites. A good place to start is the Sierra Club Web site, www.sierraclub.org/oilspill, and the satellite site letsmovebeyondoil.org. There you'll learn how to get involved in helping move the United States beyond oil in the next twenty years.

CHAPTER 2

Smokescreen

The Dirty Side of "Clean Coal"

You can fool all the people some of the time, and some of the people all the time, but you cannot fool all the people all the time.

— ABRAHAM LINCOLN

Most Americans have never heard of Larry Gibson or Maria Gunnoe, but both have become heroes of mine. It takes determination to stand up for what's right, but it really takes guts to do so while being violently threatened and harassed.

Gibson is a stout firecracker of a man whose voice shakes with passion when he talks about the coal mining that has been leveling the mountains around his home in West Virginia and throughout much of Appalachia. "I never thought I was poor until I went to the big city, in Cleveland," Gibson says. "Living here we had everything we needed—apple orchards, walnut trees—there were bears in the valleys, berries on the trees, even ginseng on the mountaintops. Now it's all gone."

One hot summer day, I visited Gibson to see what he was talking about. West Virginia boasts some of the country's most picturesque landscapes, from the whitewater rapids in the southeast to the Allegheny Mountains, the Monongahela National Forest, and the Ohio River Valley. Appalachia's forests are famously rich in the range of plant and animal life they support; like parts of central China, they still contain remnants of pre–ice age habitats. Driving the state's back roads, you remember why John Denver began one of his most famous songs, "Almost heaven, West Virginia . . ."

We took a short walk from Gibson's home in the town of Kayford toward the blast zone of a mountaintop-removal mining site. When we got to the edge, I had difficulty accepting what was in plain sight in front of me. I've had the sad experience of seeing plenty of ecological devastation—barren clear-cut forests, bleached and dying coral reefs, toxic waste incinerators, massive oil spills. Yet this scene was so jarring it took my breath away: an entire mountain being methodically blown apart.

Work had been halted for the day. Across the mine's entire thousand-acre expanse, not a single sound could be heard. Where we were standing, the forested ridge that once soared several hundred feet above was now an industrial waste zone that dropped five hundred feet below. All the trees were gone. "Most people think of coal mining as a process of removing coal from underneath a mountain," says Mary Anne Hitt, director of the Sierra Club's Beyond Coal campaign. "Mountaintop removal entails removing the mountain from the coal."

In the distance, several dozen large piles of dynamite were organized in rows, ready for detonation. Following an explosion, giant bulldozers push what the coal industry calls overburden—trees, soil, rock, everything that isn't coal—over the edge into the valley below, burying the stream that once ran through the valley. Coal mining accounted for 65 percent of all explosives use in the United States in 2006. Throughout Appalachia, explosives can be set off within three hundred feet of a home, and blasting occurs all day, often seven days a week. The stories of what local residents have to endure will break your heart.

As reported in the *Washington Post*, on the evening of August 19, 2004, Dennis Davidson came home from work as an inventory clerk and played catch in his family's front yard in Inman Hollow, Virginia, with his two sons, three-year-old Jeremy and six-year-old Zachery. His wife, Cindy, made dinner inside. After dinner, young Jeremy was so worn out that he crawled into his mother's lap, fell asleep, and was soon tucked into bed. At about 2:30 in the morning, a mining crew was working just 650 feet uphill from the Davidsons' home, leveling a road from the nearby strip mine to a coal-processing plant. A bulldozer operator dislodged a thousand-pound boulder and sent it careening down the hillside, directly into the house. The boulder tore through a bedroom wall, crashed through a closet, and came to rest at the foot of Zachery's bed. Zachery was scared but unhurt. His younger brother Jeremy was crushed instantly.

The scale and impact of mountaintop mining are terrible, yet many Americans don't even know about it. Opponents have described mountaintop-removal coal mining as "strip mining on steroids." The mines are located throughout West Virginia, eastern Kentucky and Tennessee, parts of western Virginia, and, more recently, Maryland. In excess of five hundred mountains have been leveled throughout Appalachia in just the past two decades. In that same period, more than twelve hundred miles of rivers and streams have been completely buried. "The individual and cumulative impacts to both aquatic and terrestrial ecosystems are unprecedented," the U.S. Fish and Wildlife Service's West Virginia field office concluded in its September 2001 report.

Pass It On

Mountaintop-removal coal mining has permanently destroyed more than five hundred mountains throughout Appalachia, burying more than twelve hundred miles of streams.

Dynamite blasts routinely rattle the windows in Gibson's home. Unwilling to sell his land to coal companies, he's also been the victim of persistent harassment and intimidation. Gibson has been threatened, shot at, and had his car run off the road. His small home is now guarded by security cameras on the roof and on trees in his yard. One of his dogs was shot, and another escaped an attempted hanging. But Gibson grew up there, and he isn't leaving.

"What do you hold so dear in your own life that you won't put a price on it?" Gibson asks. "And when somebody comes to take it, what will you do? For me, it's this mountain and the memories I had here as a kid. I'm fighting for my life here, and I will never give up."

Gibson's not alone. An hour away in Bob White, West Virginia, I sat on the front porch of Maria Gunnoe's home as she described the horrors of mountaintop-removal mining operations directly to the east, south, and west of her home. The entire region is facing an onslaught of air and water contamination, landscape scars, mudslides, and floods from coal mining and processing. Since mountaintop mining began near her home several years ago, seven floods have ripped through her farm, destroying her barn and the bridge that connects to her property. Waste from the mining operation washes through the creeks in front of and behind her home, poisoning the water and soil.

"My family first settled this area over three hundred years ago. My grandparents lived right here. I was raised in this house," Gunnoe says. "We used to have the most beautiful garden over there, with the richest soil—up to your elbows! It's poisoned now. The well water is ruined, too. Ten coal trains pass by this house every day, and the blasting up in the mountains goes from daylight till dark."

Gunnoe has been fighting back, organizing with the Ohio Valley Environmental Coalition to stop the mountaintop mining around her home and throughout the region. This work has earned her the prestigious Goldman Environmental Prize as well as the enmity of some of her neighbors. "In doing this, I've had a little bit of everything done to me," she says. "I've been accused of all kinds of stuff. I've had sand put in my gas tank—it cost $1,200 to keep my truck on the road. Teachers make comments to my kids. It's not their place to tell my children that their water isn't poisoned by coal, when my children know they can't drink their water. I've had my tires cut, my dog shot. People spit on my truck all the time—big, gross tobacco juice spit. One of my dogs was shot and left in the parking lot where my kids catch the school bus.

"One thing about West Virginia people is, we're not the kind to give up and walk away. If we was the kind to give up and walk away, we would never have settled this area years and years ago. Because this was a very rough terrain—a very rough life here. But people loved it—people like my great-grandmother, people like my grandfather before me. They loved this land and tended this land. It's land that wasn't meant to be developed. It's a special land. God put it way up high so they'd leave it alone. I've had people tell me that God put the coal there for us to mine. I have to disagree with that. He buried it because it's so doggone nasty!"

I asked Gunnoe what she thought of "clean coal." Her jaw clenched. "Clean coal is the biggest lie that coal companies and the United States government have ever created. There's no such thing as clean coal. The two words together quite honestly anger me." She paused. "Wow—how can you steal a life from a family and clean it up? How can you rob people of who they are and where they are, and make that look like it's clean in any sense?"

The Seductive Myth of Clean Coal

The term *clean coal* has been used to describe a variety of industrial processes, everything from installing scrubbers mandated by law to making minor improvements in coal processing or burning techniques. Most commonly, "clean coal" describes a series of methods—most of which are in the small-scale, experimental stage—that attempt to reduce greenhouse gas emissions.

Here's the industry's theory: As coal is burned, carbon dioxide gas would be removed, either mechanically or through chemical processes. The gas would then be compressed and pressurized until it became a liquid with a consistency similar to oil. Then it would be sent through pipelines to carefully selected geologic sites and injected into the ground. If these potent greenhouse gases were held underground permanently, they wouldn't wreak havoc on the earth's climate.

But when you hear coal advocates describe "clean coal" as a way to fight climate change, put your BS detector on alert. The dirty secret of "clean coal" is that, after more than twenty years of government and industry research and billions in subsidies, not a single coal plant in the world can be called clean. Not a single power plant has ever captured all of its carbon dioxide emissions, much less compressed the carbon and stuffed it underground.

Moreover, the "clean coal" techniques that industry is talking about do not address most other forms of air and water pollution. They do not give the millions of Americans living near coal-fired power plants their basic human right to clean air and safe water. They do not stop mountaintop removal and other unsafe and destructive forms of coal mining, nor do they prevent the creation of millions of tons of toxic waste. And "clean coal" certainly does not address the steady decline of well-paying

Pass It On

After years of research and billions in subsidies, not a single coal plant has ever effectively captured and stored all of its greenhouse gases.

union jobs or the coal-mining industry's atrocious health and safety record. From 1985 to 2008, coal-mine production increased by 32 percent, while the number of coal-mining jobs decreased by 48 percent in that same period.

In the coalfields I visited in West Virginia, many of the mountaintop-removal mining jobs were nonunion, paying significantly less than comparable union jobs. Meanwhile, more than a hundred thousand miners died in coal mines in the twentieth century, including twelve thousand from black lung disease as late as the years from 1992 to 2002.

Coal is also the dirtiest and most carbon-intensive fossil fuel, containing 70 percent more carbon per unit of energy than natural gas. Three tons of carbon dioxide are produced for every ton of coal that is burned. It is the largest and one of the fastest-growing sources of greenhouse gas emissions in the country. As climate change exacerbates droughts across the country, burning coal produces another problem: coal plants use far more water than all other forms of electricity besides nuclear power. If that's not bad enough, consider that the American Lung Association estimates that air pollution from coal-fired power plants kills an estimated twenty-four thousand people prematurely each year.

Despite all of this, industry executives and their political allies are propagating the "clean coal" myth in order to justify the largest proposed expansion of coal-fired power plants in more than half a century. In 2008 there were about six hundred U.S. coal plants in operation, and the industry planned to build many more. An unprecedented citizens' effort stopped most of them (see the last part of this chapter), but the industry won't stop trying, especially if it can convince us that coal power can be made clean. There's much at stake. More than a billion tons of coal is mined in the United States each year, producing nearly half our country's electricity. On average, every man, woman, and child in the United States uses about twenty pounds of coal each day. Our heavy reliance on coal to produce power gives the industry plenty of ammunition with which to bring American public opinion into line.

Of course the notion of "clean coal" is tempting. I'd vote for it myself if coal could be made genuinely clean and safe, from the mine to the processing plant to the generating station. But if you clear away the hype, it just doesn't add up. "Clean coal" is an oxymoron, like clean dirt or healthy Twinkies. If

America bets its energy future on the promise of "clean coal," the worst predictions of climate change are likely to come true. We will also increase the poisons in our water and air, imperil human health and safety, and do further irreparable harm to our natural heritage. Most important, we'll squander the best opportunity this country has ever had to create an energy-efficient economy that uses truly clean power.

Why, then, does "clean coal" have so many powerful and vocal advocates? It boils down to profits, politics, and relentless PR. The U.S. coal lobby is strong and has powerful friends in coal states on both sides of the aisle. This influence allows coal companies to flout safety regulations without fear of large penalties, to circumvent or roll back environmental regulations, and to secure billions of dollars of federal government subsidies. Big Coal has big friends on Wall Street, and in Democratic and Republican Party circles. And if these friends can't help change the dirty realities of the coal industry, they can certainly help polish its image.

In defense of Big Coal, an industry group called Americans for Balanced Energy Choices launched a new marketing campaign in 2004. On the group's Web site, an irrepressible twelve-year-old skateboarder in baggy pants extolled the wonders of the coal industry. ABEC also commissioned a series of ads for its site, featuring a collection of cute kids as the coal industry's mouthpiece. In one ad, a young student in a lab said, "Kids are just better at technology than their parents. Like, by the time I graduate college, we'll be building clean coal power plants that are pollution-free."

I like a can-do, optimistic story and smart, perky kids as much as the next person. It would be great if somehow coal could be mined cleanly without threatening drinking water for millions. It would be wonderful if conditions were safe, unions restored, and workers paid salaries and benefits commensurate with the risk they take every day. It would be a comfort if coal's neurotoxins were eliminated, and it sure would help if burning coal somehow

Pass It On

Coal is the country's largest source of greenhouse gas emissions and mercury poisoning, and produces about three times more solid waste than all the municipal trash in the country. The American Lung Association estimates that coal-fired power plants kill more than twenty-four thousand people prematurely each year.

could not destabilize the planet's climate. While we're at it, it would also be great if babies didn't cry at night and eating ice cream gave us six-pack abs, but wishing things were true doesn't make them so.

In 2008 Americans for Balanced Energy Choices merged with Center for Energy and Economic Development to form a new coal industry front group, American Coalition for Clean Coal Electricity. A project of this group, America's Power Army, exhorts visitors to its Web site to do the patriotic thing and "keep America's energy supply based on American resources."

If cute kids and powerful lobbyists can't sell clean coal, then maybe sex can. General Electric, a leading coal financier and manufacturer of turbines and other equipment for coal-fired power plants, gave pickaxes, miner's helmets, and not too much clothing to some sexy supermodels in a 2005 coal ad. The women in tank tops pose provocatively with jackhammers and drills, as bare-chested men preen under spotlights—while the soundtrack appropriates Merle Travis's classic anticorporate ballad "Sixteen Tons." The voiceover concludes, "Thanks to emissions-reducing technologies from GE Energy, harnessing the power of coal is looking more beautiful every day."

Too Much Hot Air

The central idea behind "clean coal" is that coal could be separated from its carbon dioxide, which could then be stored—forever—safely and effectively underground, where it wouldn't reach the atmosphere and contribute to global warming. The technique is called carbon capture and storage (CCS), carbon sequestration, and other names. My preferred term is "boondoggle." But whatever your preference, "clean coal" is a huge risk, a gamble that we can't afford to make.

Let's start with the promise of capturing carbon. Theoretically, this can be done in one of two ways. In one method, high-tech scrubbers would remove the CO_2 before it is released through a power plant's smokestack. Engineers are experimenting with capturing a portion of a plant's emissions, but to date haven't been able to capture all of even one plant's emissions. Another way to capture carbon is to build a new type of coal plant, called integrated gasification combined cycle (IGCC), in which the coal is refined, then heated and turned into a gas. In an IGCC plant, the CO_2 is removed during the "gasification" process, before the gas is burned and electricity is produced.

Both methods are costly in terms of fuel and funds. Using scrubbers on pulverized-coal plants to capture carbon emissions would increase the cost of electricity generation by 40 to 70 percent, according to the Intergovernmental Panel on Climate Change. (The wide range in cost estimates is attributable to a series of variables associated with the coal plant itself, including its size, overall efficiency, and so on, and also with the carbon-capture process.) According to the same report, an IGCC plant that captured its carbon would increase the cost of power production by 20 to 55 percent, primarily because IGCC plants produce fewer emissions and also require less energy to capture them. IGCC plants are more costly to construct, however.

Much of the increased cost to capture and compress carbon for either the IGCC or traditional coal plants method is due to the additional energy needed to separate and compress the carbon. IGCC plants that capture carbon require 14 to 25 percent more energy. Pulverized coal plants seeking to capture carbon need 24 to 40 percent more power. It's a coal company's dream: we would have to mine, refine, transport, and burn more coal just to create the energy to reduce the greenhouse gas emissions from burning coal in the first place. For every three to six coal plants currently in operation, an entirely new plant would have to be built to supply the extra power needed to capture the plants' carbon.

Just for a moment, let's set those issues aside and suppose that somewhere down the road these problems are solved and carbon can be captured inexpensively. Then the carbon needs to be stored somewhere. Compressed carbon can be shipped by pipeline and injected into saltwater aquifers, into old oil and gas pits, or under the seabed. One project in Norway injects approximately 1 million tons of carbon annually into a depleted oil field under the North Sea. A project in Saskatchewan has stored a total of 5 million tons of carbon in the past decade. In comparison, a single medium-sized coal plant typically emits about 3 million tons of carbon dioxide into the atmosphere each year.

Burning coal in the United States caused the release of more than 2 billion tons in 2006. If you think "clean coal" has a future in this country, then it would be wise to reflect upon the scale of carbon sequestration that would be required. In *The Future of Coal,* a 2007 analysis from MIT, the authors write, "If 60 percent of the CO_2 produced from U.S. coal-based power generation were to be captured and compressed to a liquid for geologic sequestration, its volume would about equal the total U.S. oil consumption of 20 million barrels per day."

You read that correctly. To store less than two-thirds of the carbon dioxide produced by U.S. coal plants, we'd need to construct a new set of pipelines and tanker ships and then inject as much carbon into the ground as the amount of oil that is extracted around the world and then burned in America each year.

Pass It On

Nationwide, if 60 percent of greenhouse gas emissions were captured from U.S. coal plants, compressed into liquid form, and injected underground, that liquid carbon would equal the total quantity of oil the United States consumes on an annual basis.

Again, let's set aside concerns about mountaintop removal and the expense and energy requirements of capturing and compressing carbon from coal plants. Let's also suppose that a new system of pipelines can be constructed around the country to allow the carbon to be transported and injected underground. Then safety issues loom: condensed carbon is buoyant underground and becomes lethal at concentrations of 15 percent or more. At concentrations of 25 percent or more, people can experience convulsions and lose consciousness after just a few breaths. In Cameroon in 1986, a natural release of poisonous CO_2 at Lake Nyos caused the deaths of more than seventeen hundred people.

One wonders who will want to live above these pockets of gas, and who will accept liability once leakages occur. "Clean coal" advocates frequently cite Texas as a location with abundant subterranean real estate, thanks to a century of pumping petroleum. But who would want to live over a carbon sequestration site? And can we trust coal companies or utilities to safely construct and monitor these sites, essentially forever? One coal company alone, Massey Energy, violated the Clean Water Act more than forty-five hundred times between 2000 and 2007. And during just one year beginning in April 2008, Massey violated its effluent limits at various operations at least 971 times, the plaintiffs in a 2010 civil suit alleged. Utilities have resisted regulations that would protect human health and the environment for decades. We'd be smart to question their commitment to safety.

Let's review. The coal industry touts "clean coal" as the way of the future, but most of the talk about "clean coal" ignores the damage caused by destructive coal mining and processing. Furthermore, not a single coal plant to date is capturing and sequestering all of its annual greenhouse gas emissions. The process of capturing carbon hasn't been perfected, but if it is, costs are expected to increase by 20 to 70 percent, while energy use at coal plants also would increase, by an estimated 14 to 40 percent. Meeting the increased energy requirements will in turn cause more air and water pollution and increase demand for coal. The carbon can be compressed and piped to specific sites, but this will add still more costs and require construction of thousands of miles of new pipelines or shipping passages. The carbon can be sequestered underground, but to fully mitigate coal's climate impacts, we'd need to inject into the ground more carbon than the amount of oil that is drilled and extracted for American consumption each year. And if any of the carbon escapes from underground, a person breathing the air could be dead within two minutes.

But if this all works, will coal then be clean? Not even close.

Air America

"Run in place for three minutes," instructs Kidshealth.org. "Then place a straw in your mouth, close your lips around it, and try to breathe in and out—but only through the straw. . . . Now, narrow the straw by pinching it in the middle. That's what it feels like when someone tries to breathe during an asthma flare-up. During a flare-up, the airways narrow and become obstructed, making it difficult for air to move through them. Asthma can be very scary—and when not controlled, it can be life-threatening."

Approximately 20 million Americans suffer from asthma each year, including 6 million children. Asthma leads to 2 million emergency room visits and five thousand deaths each year in the United States. Asthma attacks can be triggered by many things: secondhand smoke, anxiety or excitement, allergic reaction to cats or dogs, mold, and other factors, such as air pollution. The

American Lung Association estimates that more than 550,000 asthma attacks, 38,000 heart attacks, and 12,000 hospital admissions due to air pollution from coal-fired power plants help cause 24,000 people to die prematurely in America each year. Those premature deaths are twice as many people as die from traffic accidents each year, and more than half as many as are murdered.

Maureen Damitz works for the Respiratory Health Association of Metropolitan Chicago and is the proud mother of two boys, Jeff and Kyle. Both suffer from asthma. When Jeff, the older, was diagnosed soon after birth, the Damitzes did what many parents of children with asthma do. They educated themselves about how to respond in the event of an attack and took every precaution to prevent such attacks from occurring, by removing curtains and stuffed animals and pulling up the rugs in their Chicago home. "We followed all the rules and did everything we could," Maureen Damitz says. "But we can only do so much. We cleaned up our house, but someone needs to clean the air."

We're not talking just about asthma here. Each year, burning coal to make electricity creates more than 120 million tons of solid waste—about three times the amount of municipal waste produced in the entire country. Coal plants dump more than five dozen different types of hazardous air pollutants, as defined by the EPA, including poisons such as arsenic (100,000 pounds a year), lead (176,000 pounds), and chromium (161,000 pounds). Power plants also emit two-thirds of all sulfur dioxide and 22 percent of nitrogen oxides, which both cause acid rain and a range of respiratory disorders. Coal is also the country's largest source of poisoning from mercury—a potent neurotoxin that can cause severe birth defects, learning disabilities, lowered IQ, convulsions, and even death.

Particulate matter is another danger altogether. Airborne particles invisible to the naked eye burrow into the lungs, where they cause breathing difficulties, lung disease, and even cancer. Smaller particles can do even more damage by entering the bloodstream and contributing to cardiovascular disease. The American Heart Association published a study showing that air pollution can significantly increase the risk of ischemic strokes, which block the flow of blood to the brain and are a leading cause of death in the United States each year.

The burden of this pollution falls disproportionately on poor and minority communities. According to a 2002 report by a coalition of environmental organizations called Clear the Air, 68 percent of African Americans live within thirty miles of a coal-fired power plant—the distance within which the worst effects of the pollution from a coal plant are expected to occur. The same report shows that 71 percent of African Americans live in counties that violate federal health standards for ozone and particulate pollution.

Chicago, where the Damitzes live, has some of the worst air pollution in the country. The city is ringed by aging coal-fired power plants. A Harvard University study released in 2001 estimated that the nine coal plants in northern Illinois caused three hundred premature deaths and more than fourteen thousand asthma attacks each year. Two of those plants, the Crawford and Fisk Generating Stations, are located within Chicago city limits in lower-income communities with large African American and Latino populations. They were both built in the late 1950s and do not have the scrubbers or other pollution-control equipment mandated by law since the Clean Air Act was passed in 1970. In 2006, the two plants released more than fourteen thousand tons of sulfur dioxide and nearly four tons of nitrogen oxide. Not to mention that the Crawford plant produces more than 3.18 million tons and the Fisk plant more than 1.78 million tons of CO_2 annually.

A coalition of organizations has pushed to have the Crawford, Fisk, and other area coal plants equipped with modern equipment that would reduce their pollution. As a result, Fisk, Crawford, and other plants are due to be modified, but not until as late as 2017. Sam Villasenor, who campaigns for the Little Village Environmental Justice Organization, wants the plants shut down as soon as possible. "These plants should have been updated with scrubbers three decades ago, but they avoided regulation," he says. "Now they want us to be happy because they promise to fix them in ten years? These plants should be shut down now."

I stood outside the Fisk power plant one sweltering day in July 2010 with several dozen local residents determined to improve air quality in their community. In August 2008 the EPA and the attorney general of Illinois filed suit against Midwest Generation, which owns the plants, and momentum was building. At our press conference that morning, we were joined by members of the Chicago city council to advance a clean power ordinance that would force the utility either to install pollution controls to cut down on air emissions or to retire the plants outright. Many of the activists with me that day were veterans of fights to oppose new coal plants throughout the Midwest and were keen to use their skills in their own backyard. Their enthusiasm was contagious: I asked them to invite me to the victory party when the plants were retired and replaced with clean-energy sources.

Beyond Coal

Remember those closed-door meetings of Vice President Cheney's Energy Task Force? Well, here's what they were up to. Coal consumption had tripled in the United States between 1970 and 2000, and it was being burned for electricity in an outdated fleet of aging coal-fired power plants. Federal policymakers called for an aggressive expansion of coal mining and combustion years into the future, including a burst in constructing new coal plants around the country. The 150 new coal-fired power plants proposed by industry and supported by the Bush-Cheney administration would have emitted more carbon dioxide collectively than 178 of the world's 186 countries: an estimated 585 million tons every year for perhaps the next half century. The coordinated campaign to defeat those coal plants is one of the most important environmental and public health victories of the past several decades, and it can serve as a model for the important fights ahead. Here's how it worked.

In 2002 the Sierra Club began a campaign to fight one of the first proposed coal plants. The Elwood Indeck Energy plant, sited fifty miles south of the Chicago Loop, would have dumped an annual 3.6 million tons of carbon dioxide into the atmosphere and released significant amounts of mercury, arsenic, lead, and other toxic compounds into the air over the greater Chicago region, home to more than 9 million people. Led by Bruce Nilles, Verena Owen, and a small team of committed activists, the Sierra Club and local organizations such as Citizens Against Ruining the Environment and the American Lung Association of Metropolitan Chicago fought hard against the developer and then governor Rod Blagojevich to stop that plant from being built. They testified at numerous public hearings. They filed three lawsuits arguing that the air permit was too weak and that regulators had failed to assess air impacts on residents and the nearby Midewin National Tallgrass Prairie, the nation's first nationally protected prairie ecosystem. They enlisted help from the city of Chicago and Lieutenant Governor Pat Quinn and reached out to local reporters to educate the public about the health and environmental threats associated with this massive new plant. Despite Governor Blagojevich's efforts to fast-track the project, the campaigners repeatedly delayed it. And they won.

Emboldened, the Sierra Club's campaign then took aim at a cluster of other plants proposed throughout the upper Midwest, including a proposed Peabody Thoroughbred coal plant in Kentucky, the LS Power coal plant in Iowa, an Associated Electric Cooperative coal plant in Missouri, and the Alliant Energy project in Wisconsin, among two dozen others. Again working with a broad and growing coalition of determined community groups, the campaigners documented how the plants would pollute the atmosphere and local air and water while costing ratepayers more money. They defeated more than 90 percent of the proposed plants.

One that got through was Peabody Energy's Prairie State coal plant, a massive 1,600-megawatt dinosaur in southwestern Illinois. In the summer of 2010, the plant had only begun construction but had already suffered cost overruns of $2 billion—costs to be borne by local ratepayers. As the headline in the *Chicago Tribune* read, "Clean Coal Dream a Costly Nightmare."

Fortunately, the Peabody plant is one of the few plants to have broken ground in the last few years. Together with Earthjustice, Physicians for Social Responsibility, and literally hundreds of grassroots groups, the Sierra Club's nationwide Beyond Coal campaign stopped more than 130 coal plants from being built across the country as of the summer of 2010. But the coal and utility industries are not giving up—new plants are still being proposed. As of August 2010, approximately fifty coal plants totaling 25,000 megawatts of output are still on the drawing board. They are concentrated in a dozen states, including Texas, Illinois, Kentucky, and Georgia.

Perhaps it's time to consider Will Rogers's "first rule of holes": if you find yourself in one, stop digging. The Earth's climate has warmed slightly more than one degree Fahrenheit in the past hundred years, and we may see an increase of two to ten more degrees over the next century. Already we are seeing the melting of glaciers and polar ice caps, the warming of the deepest oceans, and species migrating to higher altitudes and latitudes. Severe droughts, severe storms, and severe floods are all increasing. The fourteen warmest years in recorded history have all occurred since 1990. We simply cannot afford an additional 3 million tons of annual greenhouse gas emissions every time a new coal plant goes online. And considering the toxic effects of air and water pollution, as well as the impact that coal mining and processing has on families across the country, isn't it time for at least a moratorium on new coal plants?

James Hansen thinks so. Hansen is director of NASA's Goddard Institute for Space Studies, an adjunct professor at Columbia University, and perhaps the country's most eminent climatologist. Hansen first drew national attention in a series of briefings and testimonies given to Congress in the late 1980s warning policymakers that the costs of responding to climate change would only increase as time passed. Although Hansen is a government scientist, he was highly critical of the Bush administration's ideology on climate and has found wanting the Obama administration's limited action thus far.

As the climate crisis has deepened, Hansen has become increasingly vocal. In 2006, he warned that humanity had about ten years to address climate change effectively, before feedback loops in natural systems (such as melting ice and thawing permafrost) caused runaway climate change that can't be stopped. In late February 2007, Hansen made a dramatic proposal calling for a complete moratorium on the construction of new coal-fired power plants, at least until carbon sequestration problems could be solved. Hansen further declared that any existing coal plant would need "to be bulldozed" within the next decade or two, if it could not capture and store its carbon in a safe and cost-effective way. In the summer of 2009, Hansen participated in civil disobedience to stop mountaintop removal in West Virginia, literally going to jail to protest coal industry activities there.

It's time to unleash our country's ingenuity and put coal in our rearview mirror. Proposed new coal plants have already been rejected in red states and blue states, with support from Democratic and Republican governors. We've defeated coal plants on economic grounds, because of concerns about contamination of air and water, because Wall Street has pulled its investments, and because of climate change. This is a great start. We should sink our teeth into every coal plant proposal in the country and defeat each one.

We shouldn't stop there. As I describe in chapter 8, we have a historic opportunity to build a new economy powered by clean energy. More than two-thirds of the country's existing coal plants were built before 1980—some in the 1920s and 1930s—and many utilize outdated, inefficient technologies not capable of limiting mercury and other harmful emissions, not to mention greenhouse gas pollution. We can retire the country's most polluting coal plants one by one, replace them with clean power and efficiency investments, and rejuvenate our economy in the process.

Consider the Four Corners Power Plant on the Arizona-Nevada border. In 2006 this was ranked top among coal plants in emission of nitrogen oxides, which destroy lung tissue and cause a long list of dangerous cardiovascular effects. The Four Corners Plant is also ranked eighteenth in greenhouse gas emissions among the country's power plants and was thirty-eighth in mercury poisoning. It's located in a region bathed in solar energy. Wouldn't a concentrating solar farm paired with an aggressive regionwide program of efficiency rooftop solar systems be a better idea? Let's shut this dinosaur down.

How about shuttering the largest greenhouse gas emitter in the country? That's the Robert W. Scherer Power Plant in Georgia, jointly operated by Southern Company and Georgia Power. Retiring this plant and replacing it with renewable energy and aggressive efficiency measures would save 25 million tons of CO_2 annually, using 2006 figures. Southern Company also jointly operates (with Alabama Power) the second-ranked greenhouse gas emitter for 2006, the James H. Miller Jr. Electric Generating Plant in Alabama.

Here are some other coal plants asking to be mothballed:

- Bowen Power Plant: operated by Georgia Power, this was the top-ranked coal plant in sulfur dioxide emissions in 2006. It's also ranked number three in carbon dioxide emissions and number fourteen for nitrogen oxides.

- Martin Lake Steam Electric Station: operated by Texas Utilities (commonly known as TXU), this plant released more mercury poisoning than any other coal plant in 2006. It was ranked number thirty-two in sulfur dioxide emissions and number five in carbon dioxide pollution. TXU operates three coal plants that are among the nation's six worst for mercury emissions.

- Sherburne County Generating Plant: operated by Northern States Power Company in northern Minnesota, land of steady winds and community-based energy development. This plant is ranked number thirteen in total carbon dioxide emissions but is ranked number two by emission rate (pounds of CO_2 per megawatt-hour). The plant is also ranked number twenty-two in nitrogen oxide emissions.

There are plenty more. The mayor of Los Angeles has made commitments to use electricity more efficiently, to scale up clean energy, and to end coal use by 2020. But the city council is balking because Los Angeles owns the Intermountain Power Plant—which provides much of its power to Southern California but which is located in Utah's Sevier Desert and leaves its pollution in that state. Intermountain has ranked among the top twenty polluting power plants in the country for carbon dioxide (number twenty in 2006) and nitrogen oxide (number twelve).

In every region of the United States, there are coal plants whose time is up: the Boardman coal plant outside Portland, Oregon; the Centralia plant in Washington State; the Fisk and Crawford plants on the South Side of Chicago; the Valley plant in downtown Milwaukee; and the two filthy plants in downtown Kansas City.

It won't be easy. The coal industry has fought bitter battles against its own workers for more than a century, busting unions and routinely violating safety regulations. For decades, coal executives have defied scientists and citizens demanding clean air and water. The industry's close relationships in the White House, Congress, and statehouses across the country have been used to convince many policymakers that increased coal burning is a responsible energy choice. The myth of "clean coal" is a powerful one, and millions are being spent to sell it to American citizens.

But this emperor is wearing no clothes. We can recognize the myth as a distraction and a tease, and reject it. Even better, we can transition to clean-energy sources that don't pollute our air and water—and our politics—and that provide sustainable jobs for working families across the country. We'll stop the expansion of the coal industry and start to downsize it. Big Coal has had a long reign, but it has no further place in a society that values well-paying, sustainable jobs, clean air and water, and a stable climate.

Take Action

Take it personally

1. Do your homework. Check out the books and films listed in the Resources section to learn more about the myth of "clean coal."

2. Know your adversary. Big Coal is ruthlessly effective and has hired some of the most talented PR firms in the business. Observe some of the masters of corporate doublespeak at www.americaspower.org. Learn how they deflect criticism, omit key information, and clothe a dirty and deadly industry in a shiny suit of feel-good patriotic optimism.

3. Know your power. Use the EPA's Power Profiler (at www.epa.gov/cleanenergy/energy-and-you/how-clean.html) to determine the energy mix for the power grid in your area. Type in your zip code to find out what percentage of your power comes from coal versus renewables and other power sources.

4. Visit www.ilovemountains.org to watch a Google Earth presentation of mountains that have been leveled throughout Appalachia. Type in your zip code and find out whether the power supplying your home or business was generated by a company that engages in mountaintop removal. You can also find out if your bank is financing destructive mining.

Express yourself

If you read an article or hear a radio broadcast in which someone offers the industry line that coal is being made clean, call or write to set the record straight. If politicians or corporate spokespersons cite the wonders of "clean coal," challenge them. Here are five questions you can ask elected officials:

1. Why do you support proposals for additional coal plants, knowing they will continue to poison our air, water, and families? (You might cite these facts: 6 million U.S. children have asthma; mercury poisoning threatens human health everywhere; coal is the largest source of air pollution and mercury.)

2. Since we know that coal accounts for approximately 40 percent of global greenhouse gas emissions and is also one of the fastest-growing sources of these emissions, is coal really the best investment in our future?

3. The nation's top climate scientist, James Hansen, has urged a moratorium on new coal development. Will you?

4. As the coal industry becomes more mechanized, well-paying jobs are disappearing, while energy efficiency and renewable energy can create more jobs per kilowatt of electricity. Isn't this a better investment for our economy and our country?

5. If you are a politician or an elected official, how much money have you taken from the coal industry since you entered politics?

Stay engaged

There are plenty of ways you can help make the transition from the dirtiest form of energy to clean, renewable power. Chapters 8 and 9 outline specific actions to advance clean energy and energy efficiency. We also need to support the rights of people whose health and way of life are endangered by mining and burning coal. See the resources section for information about organizations such as Coal River Mountain Watch, Ohio Valley Environmental Coalition, and others that focus on these issues.

CHAPTER 3

Separate Oil and State
Getting Fossilized Power Out of Politics

Sunshine is said to be the best of disinfectants.

— SUPREME COURT JUSTICE LOUIS D. BRANDEIS

I f you're like me, when you learn more about offshore oil drilling, the illusion of "clean coal," or our government's anemic response to climate change, you shake your head and wonder what has happened to our country's leadership. America's energy policies bankroll our enemies, pollute our air and water, and imperil our economy. This is no secret. It's been talked about, debated, dissected, and then largely ignored by the leaders of both parties since the first oil shock in 1973. Every administration and every Congress since then has had the opportunity to break our addiction to dirty energy, but more often than not they end up making it worse.

Take climate change. A major report from the U.K. government concludes that not taking strong action on global warming "could create risks of major disruption of economic and social activity . . . on a scale similar to those associated with the great wars and economic depression of the early 20th century." The world's most respected scientists insist with increasing alarm that by 2050 the world needs to reduce its greenhouse gas emissions by at least 80 percent from 1990 levels to stave off wrenching changes to our planet and our way of life. The U.S. government has responded for the most part with policies that encourage more drilling, more mining, more burning, and more pollution. We're running in the wrong direction: total U.S. greenhouse gas emissions actually increased by about 14 percent from 1990 to 2008.

If all it took to make progress were clever speeches, dense policy proposals, press conferences, and pilot projects, we would have licked our addiction to dirty energy years ago. Both Republican and Democratic politicians routinely make happy talk about energy independence and intone gravely on the risks of global climate change, yet very few propose and fight for solutions that match the problem in scale.

If Republicans were serious about these issues, they'd advocate making our economy more efficient, rather than building more coal-fired power plants. And if Democrats were truly committed to breaking our dependence on oil, they wouldn't still be coddling an automobile industry in which the former top-selling vehicle, the Ford F-Series truck, gets lower gas mileage than the Model T nearly a hundred years ago. Even the rise in automobile fuel efficiency standards that the Obama administration pushed through Congress will improve gas mileage in America's cars, trucks, and SUVs only to a modest 35.5 miles per gallon by 2016. At that time, we'll reach the fuel efficiency that China's drivers enjoy today. Are you inspired yet?

There's no mystery about what needs to happen to end our fossil-fuel habit, as you'll learn in the chapters that follow. We would save more oil than is rumored to be under the Arctic National Wildlife Refuge by using highly fuel-efficient replacement tires in every new American car, truck, and SUV. We'd save all the oil that America imports from the Persian Gulf by putting hybrid engines and other fuel-saving technologies in all our vehicles.

These steps are just a start. When America gets truly serious about creating a new energy economy, our country will restore its reputation for world leadership, clean up its air and water, rejuvenate its manufacturing base, create clean, well-paying jobs, and show that we can do more than just talk about a stable climate and energy independence.

But none of this will happen without political courage. To break free of oil and coal will require that politicians stand up to some of the richest corporations in the world. Large donations and the sophisticated campaign machinery behind the coal and oil lobby make that hard to do, so most politicians attempt to have it both ways—by talking a good game on clean energy, yet voting for only the mildest proposals. Don't let them fool you. Most of our top political leaders are not yet taking energy independence and climate change seriously. If they were, we wouldn't be in the mess we're in today.

Each of the chapters to come suggests specific ways to break our addiction to dirty energy. In the first part of this chapter, we'll explore the relationship between lawmakers and the corporations that earn enormous profits by cooking the planet. In the second half, you'll meet some people who are challenging those cozy ties. If we are serious about coming clean, holding our politicians accountable is a good place to start. Because to get clean energy, we'll need a clean government.

Friends with Money

Do you know why coal companies like Massey Energy can violate the Clean Air Act, Clean Water Act, and other state and federal regulations *thousands of times* and still be allowed to stay in business? Because they've bought friends in Congress—on both sides of the aisle. How do oil companies like BP, Exxon, and Chevron pollute our air, water, and climate, yet still get preferential treatment and subsidies? Because they've made large investments in the lucrative field of lawmaking, and they're cashing in.

You would think that an industry as prosperous as Big Oil wouldn't even ask for handouts from the federal government. You also might think that those in government who profess to be fiscally conservative, environmentally responsible, or dedicated to free markets would refuse to fund corporate welfare for dirty energy.

You might even believe that a functioning democracy would call utility owners to task. Utilities and coal companies spend millions on teams of lawyers to delay or avoid compliance with laws and safety standards. Have they forfeited any rights to gifts from American taxpayers? Not exactly.

Executives in the oil and coal sectors are keen, if cynical, observers of the political process; they know the benefits of having good buddies in high places. In 2009 alone, oil and gas companies spent a total of more than $175 million in lobbying expenses. Exxon invested $27.4 million. Chevron spent $20.8 million and BP almost $16 million. All told, oil companies spent $888.5 million from 1998 through the first half of 2010 on politicians, political parties, and lobbyists, according to the nonprofit organization Center for Responsive Politics.

The late Kenneth Lay, former CEO of now-defunct Enron, might have been the poster child for political cronyism. "Kenny boy," as President George W. Bush was fond of calling him, and his wife gave $882,580 to federal candidates from 1989 to 2001, all but $86,470 of which went to Republicans. Lay personally donated $139,500 to Bush's campaigns for governor and the presidency, gave an additional $100,000 to Bush's inauguration in 2001, and raised at least an additional $100,000 from others for Bush's 2000 presidential campaign, making him a Bush "Pioneer" and one of the president's most valued fundraisers. Other Enron employees also supported Bush, donating $602,000 to Bush's campaigns for governor and the presidency, making the company Bush's top political patron.

Pass It On

From 1998 through the first half of 2010, oil companies spent $888.5 million on politicians, political parties, and lobbyists, according to the Center for Responsive Politics.

These were wise investments. Lay was appointed to the transition team for the Bush administration's Energy Department, helping to appoint two out of five members of the Federal Energy Regulatory Commission. Lay also met four times with Vice President Cheney's Energy Task Force, at one meeting delivering a memo with a series of policy recommendations. A subsequent investigation by Representative Henry Waxman found that "all or significant portions of Enron's recommendations" were adopted in seven of eight policy areas.

On April 17, 2001, Vice President Cheney met with Lay during the California energy crisis. In a memo, Lay advised, "The administration should reject any attempt to re-regulate wholesale power markets by adopting price caps." The next day, Cheney announced that the Bush administration would not support price caps on California's energy prices, a decision that ultimately made billions for Enron at the expense of the state's citizens.

There are plenty of examples of dirty-energy money driving politics. In the 2002, 2004, and 2006 election cycles, the oil industry doled out more than $70 million to politicians, more than 80 percent of which went to Republicans. In mid-2006, the U.S. House and Senate each voted on separate pieces of legislation to weaken the country's long-standing moratorium on oil drilling off America's coastlines. Of the top twenty recipients of oil industry cash in the 2006 election cycle (all of them Republicans), every one of them sided with the oil industry on those votes.

Cronyism and corruption between Big Coal and federal regulators is legendary. It ought to be criminal. Since 2001, mining companies have given more than $180,000 to Kentucky's Republican senator Mitch McConnell, a big friend of the coal industry. Soon after taking office, President Bush appointed McConnell's wife, Elaine Chao, to the post of secretary of labor, the department that oversees the Mine Safety and Health Administration (MSHA). Chao was a Bush Pioneer who raised more than $100,000 for his presidential campaign. Chao's deputy labor secretary, Stephen Law, also helped raise funds for the Republican Party. In the wake of the Big Branch mine collapse in the spring of 2010, a *Huffington Post* article called on McConnell to return campaign contributions from mine owner Massey Energy: some $13,550 from "people and PACs associated with Massey Energy," according to the Center for Responsive Politics. Matt Sledge wrote in his article, "This is not a company America's leaders—the ones tasked with writing our mining and climate change laws—should be doing business with."

Another of McConnell's donors is mining executive Bob Murray, CEO of Murray Energy. Murray, who has characterized concerns about climate change as "hysterical global goofiness," in 2010 gave $25,000 to the campaign of Carly Fiorina, who was opposing California senator Barbara Boxer. Boxer, who supports tighter controls on greenhouse gas emissions, had drawn Murray's wrath—notably at a 2007 Senate hearing in which he accused Democrats in Congress of trying to export "the draconian so-called 'global warming' measures already enacted in California . . . to the rest of America."

Murray's company operates the Crandall Canyon mine in Utah, which gained notoriety in 2007 when six miners were killed in a shaft collapse. Another three workers tragically died in a subsequent rescue attempt. Federal inspectors had issued 324 violations at the mine since 2004, including 107 that were "significant and substantial." Meanwhile, Murray's Galatia mine in southern Illinois was cited more than twenty-seven hundred times in just two years, and another Murray company—Ken American Resources—and four top managers have been convicted in a federal court of conspiring to violate federal mine safety rules.

Years earlier, in 2002, MSHA officials had brought Murray to the district office in Charleston, West Virginia, to discuss safety concerns. Murray shouted at the table full of MSHA officials, warning that he'd get the inspectors fired. "Mitch McConnell calls me one of the five finest men in America," Murray told the inspectors. "And the last time I checked, he was sleeping with your boss." Murray pointed at two inspectors: "They are gone."

Sure enough, one of the men, Tim Thompson, was soon transferred to a district with no jurisdiction over Murray's mines. He unsuccessfully appealed his transfer for three years before eventually accepting retirement. "The ironic part is, I'm a Republican," Thompson told the *Kentucky Herald-Leader*. "But I don't think you should bring up politics at a meeting like that, involving safety."

Human Resources

One of the most effective ways that fossil-fuel companies influence government is not with cash but by getting their own people into powerful government positions. People like Phil Cooney.

For about a decade, Cooney worked for the American Petroleum Institute (API), an oil industry trade association. He served as the "climate team leader" at API, which has fought tenaciously for more than fifteen years to resist any regulation of greenhouse gas emissions. A primary strategy was to sow seeds of doubt about whether climate change was real and whether U.S. action was justified.

The strategy worked—in part because of the media's "equal time" mandate. The *Seattle Times* reported on a study conducted by science historian Naomi Oreskes, prompted by a conversation with her hairdresser, who had said she wasn't worried about climate change because even the scientists didn't know what was happening. Oreskes set out to examine whether there was, in fact, much disagreement in the scientific community. In a random sampling, she selected a thousand research papers on global warming from 1993 to 2003. Not one study rejected the idea that the planet was warming and that humans were to blame. However, in a separate analysis of 636 articles covering climate change from 1988 to 2002 in the *New York Times, Washington Post, Los Angeles Times,* and *Wall Street Journal,* researchers found that 52.7 percent gave "roughly equal coverage" to the competing notions that climate change either is caused by humans or is simply a result of natural fluctuations.

Cooney was very good at his job, and in 2001, he followed the Bush administration into the White House, serving as chief of staff for the President's Council on Environmental Quality. In March 2001, EPA chief Christine Todd Whitman traveled to Italy for climate talks with European leaders, assuring them that the Bush administration would honor its campaign pledge to regulate greenhouse gas emissions. Concerned that Whitman might be successful in pressing the administration to keep its climate commitments, Cooney took the unusual step of organizing public criticism of a fellow Bush administration official. He asked for assistance from Myron Ebell, policy director for global warming at the Competitive Enterprise Institute (CEI), another organization fighting responsible action on climate change. For years, CEI has counted Exxon as a top funder. In a memo later obtained by Greenpeace, Ebell replied, "Dear Phil, Thanks for calling and asking for our help," proceeded to strategize about how CEI would call for Whitman's firing, and asked for support from the administration for a "strident and noisy" campaign. Whitman kept her job, but was effectively muzzled and ultimately resigned in 2003.

Two years later, in June 2005, internal White House documents were leaked to the *New York Times* showing that Cooney—not a scientist—had made a series of small but significant edits to U.S. scientific climate change reports in 2002 and 2003. At least 181 of those edits sought to downplay the significance of the scientific consensus on climate change. Another 113 attempted to sow doubts about the extent to which this change was caused by humans, or even to proclaim the benefits of global warming.

Cooney resigned almost immediately after this story broke. Two days later, he was hired by Exxon. In March 2007, Cooney resurfaced at a congressional hearing, expressing no regrets about how his policies distorted scientific findings and misled the public. "My sole loyalty was to the President and advancing the policies of his administration," he said.

Cooney's story was broadcast throughout the mainstream media, including National Public Radio and *Meet the Press*. The connections between corporate polluters and the White House were in plain view, at a time when U.S. citizens were facing gas prices near historic highs and the oil industry was enjoying record profits. Yet the billion-dollar federal subsidies to Big Oil—the richest industry in the world—went on.

Those subsidies are tended carefully by crack teams of industry lobbyists, many of whom got their training in energy matters on congressional or administration staffs. As a 2010 *Washington Post* story observes, those staffs can be a kind of human resources pool for the extraction industries. The paper's analysis showed that three of every four lobbyists who represent oil and gas companies previously worked in federal government, "a proportion that far exceeds the usual revolving-door standards on Capitol Hill." In all, more than 430 out of some 600 industry lobbyists once held jobs in the legislative or executive branches.

The *Post* story went on to demonstrate how this influence "has been on full display in the wake of the BP oil disaster," noting that efforts to impose new restrictions or curb oil use were blocked by stiff resistance from both Republicans and Democrats in oil-producing states. And just two weeks after the Deepwater Horizon blowout, New York representative Edolphus Towns lost a staff member who took a lobbying job with BP. Perhaps Jack Gerard, president of the American Petroleum Institute, put it best: "If you want somebody to work on energy issues, you don't hire health-care workers."

Return on Investment

Consider the irony. Not only do oil and coal companies pollute our air and water and destabilize our communities and our climate, but we taxpayers pay them to do so. It's not enough that oil companies inflate gasoline prices while earning more profits than any industry in the history of the world—they're also world-class operators at squeezing billions in subsidies out of the government and at securing other tax breaks, regulatory loopholes, relaxed regulations, and reduced royalty payments. You almost have to admire the chutzpah.

Robert F. Kennedy, Jr., president of the Waterkeeper Alliance, says, "You show me a polluter, and I'll show you a subsidy. I'll show you a fat cat using political clout to escape the discipline of the free market and load his production costs onto the backs of the public." These are indeed fat cats. The top five oil companies brought in more than $800 billion in revenue in 2006, earning nearly $83 billion in profits. In 2006, Exxon became the most profitable corporation in history, earning $39.5 billion in profits in a single year.

Coal and oil executives aren't hurting personally, either. John Drosdick, top oil man at Sunoco, brought in a tidy $46.2 million in total compensation in 2006. Don Blankenship earned $34 million from Massey Energy the year prior, while Ray Irani, the chief executive of Occidental Petroleum, has averaged nearly $40 million for the past five years. The grand-

Pass It On

Money in, money out: according to one analysis, oil companies received a total of $39 billion in U.S. federal subsidies in 2006, a year in which some of those same companies earned more in profits than any corporation in modern history. Coal companies received $8 billion in subsidies that same year.

daddy of gilded executives, however, is the former chief executive of Exxon, Lee Raymond. On Capitol Hill in 2005, when Raymond was asked to account for record gas prices, he proclaimed his sympathy, telling lawmakers, "We're all in this together." The next year, Raymond retired with a parting gift from Exxon of nearly $400 million, including access to Exxon's jet, a car and driver, and a $1 million a year gig as a part-time consultant to the company.

More troubling is the cash these corporations get at the public trough. According to a 2007 analysis of federal policies by the environmental group Friends of the Earth, oil companies will receive more than $31.6 billion in handouts from Congress alone over a five-year period from 2007 to 2011. These include more than $16 billion in tax breaks, nearly $10 billion in reduced royalty payments, research and development subsidies totaling nearly $2 billion, plus an additional $4 billion or so in other accounting tricks. Friends of the Earth estimates that these figures could "dramatically increase over the next 25 years if current tax breaks are extended and if an estimated loss of up to $60 billion in royalty revenue from offshore oil drilling occurs."

Other analysts have a broader perspective. Doug Koplow is the founder of Earth Track, a Cambridge-based consulting firm that analyzes subsidies to natural resource industries. "While subsidies are most commonly thought of as cash payments to a particular person or corporation, this definition misses most of the ways in which governments transfer value to private entities," he wrote in a paper for the Organization for Economic Cooperation and Development. "A range of policies . . . offer politicians less visible ways to provide benefits to constituent groups."

Koplow estimated that total U.S. subsidies for the oil industry topped $39 billion in 2006 alone. This figure includes the cost of guarding the Alaska pipeline, providing accelerated depreciation benefits to lower taxes, and keeping oil shipping lanes open in the Persian Gulf. (The larger costs of the Iraq War are not included in his estimate.) According to Koplow, total U.S. federal energy subsidies in 2006 were $74 billion, of which fossil fuels received 66 percent, or $49 billion. Total investments in conservation: $2 billion. State and local subsidies to the fossil-fuel industries are not included in the calculations, nor are the billions in subsidies that the World Bank and other international financial institutions give each year. (I discuss those in the next chapter.)

In 2010, the Web site of Americans for Energy Leadership drew attention to a comprehensive new report by the Environmental Law Institute on the cost of fossil-fuel subsidies during fiscal years 2002–2008—"a smorgasbord of tax and royalty relief measures"—and contrasted it with government support for renewable energy during the same period. "Subsidies to fossil fuels—a mature, developed industry that has enjoyed government support for many years—totaled approximately $72 billion over the study period, representing a direct cost to taxpayers," the report found. "Subsidies for renewable fuels, a relatively young and developing industry, totaled $29 billion over the same period." The report also noted that most of the largest fossil-fuel subsidies were written into the U.S. Tax Code as permanent provisions, whereas subsidies for renewables are often linked to energy bills, with time limits that make them less useful to the renewables industry.

To broaden the idea of subsidies even further: sometimes the biggest gift the government can give to an oil or coal company is to simply look the other way. It's a story Jack Spadaro knows well.

Mine Your Own Business

On a rainy Sunday morning in West Virginia in February 1972, a toxic waste impoundment from a nearby coal-mining and processing facility collapsed, releasing an estimated 132 million gallons of black sludge in a twenty-foot wave into the raging waters of Buffalo Creek. Within minutes, 125 people were killed and four thousand homes were destroyed.

A young research engineer from the West Virginia School of Mines was sent to investigate. "Memories of those conversations are still with me," Jack Spadaro said in an interview. "Buffalo Creek wasn't necessary. The neglect, the disregard . . . of the mine operators caused it."

Spadaro subsequently helped write safety regulations aimed at preventing a repeat occurrence. Twenty-eight years later, disaster struck once again. In October 2000 in Martin County, Kentucky, another waste impoundment burst, releasing more than 300 million gallons of toxic sludge—almost thirty times the size of the *Exxon Valdez* spill in Alaska's Prince William Sound. Amazingly, no one was killed, although a seventy-five-mile plume of waste extended from the creek where the spill originated to the Ohio River. Water supplies for 27,623 people were contaminated. The EPA ruled it

Pass It On

Three out of every four lobbyists who represent oil and gas companies previously worked in the federal government, the *Washington Post* reported in 2010.

the worst environmental disaster in the history of the southeastern United States. Spadaro was asked to help lead an investigation of the spill for the Mine Safety and Health Administration (MSHA).

Less than a month after the Martin County spill, President George W. Bush was elected, in part because of his upset victory in West Virginia. Coal executives shelled out $3.65 million in the 2000 federal election, giving 88 percent to the Republican Party and its candidates. One executive, Bush Pioneer James H. "Buck" Harless, raised $275,000 for Bush's run, donated to his Florida recount campaign, and contributed $100,000 to his inauguration party. In turn, Bush nicknamed Harless "Big Buck" and invited him to join Ken Lay in the administration's transition team on energy. "We were looking for friends, and we found one in George W. Bush," Harless told the *Wall Street Journal*.

Two days before the inauguration, as Spadaro and his nine-person team were quickly building evidence of negligence on the part of Martin County Coal Company, a subsidiary of Massey Energy, the investigating team was suddenly given a new supervising officer, Tim Thompson. Thompson (who two years later would arouse the ire of Bob Murray) demanded that the investigation be closed within a week. Later that year, Harless was given a seat on the board of Massey Energy, the company ultimately responsible for the spill.

Can you guess how this story ends? Spadaro's team had to cut short its investigation. It recommended eight substantive violations on the part of Massey's subsidiary, which could have resulted in multimillion-dollar fines, demands for significant remediation measures, and potential criminal proceedings. Only two of those recommendations were approved by MSHA bosses, however. Spadaro and his team continued to press the case, charging that the MSHA had covered up negligence on the part of Massey. Spadaro was forced off the team, reassigned, demoted, and fired. He appealed his termination under whistleblower's protection, but eventually quit in disgust. The total fine issued by the Labor Department to Massey, for the worst environmental disaster in the history of the southeastern United States? Just $55,000.

It falls outside the scope of this book to explore the many other cases where energy policy has been corrupted by corporate cash (but see the resources section at the end of this book if you want to find more). Although the media and watchdog groups have exposed many such corporate giveaways, the net effect actually may have been to lower the expectations many Americans have for our government. It's easy to be cynical when a government that is ostensibly of, by, and for the people looks more like a government of, by, and for big business.

Empowering Democracy

It's time to get dirty-energy money out of politics and to end corporate welfare to the richest industries in history. Politicians need to show some backbone to help our country create a clean-energy future. Elected officials can step up and disavow campaign contributions, travel junkets, or other financial perks from the coal and oil industries. It's really quite simple: if we want our government to be independent of the fossil-fuel industry, then politicians have to prove they can't be bought. And if we want to move decisively to safe and sustainable forms of energy, then we should stop using taxpayer dollars to subsidize some of the oldest and dirtiest forms of energy.

Imagine what we could do with the fossil-fuel industry's billions in annual subsidies. We could provide Head Start schooling for all eligible children in the United States (about $2 billion) and medical care for uninsured U.S. kids ($6 billion). Rather than dole out taxpayer dollars to Exxon and other oil companies, we could subsidize the rapid development of plug-in hybrid vehicles (more on this in chapter 5) or residential and industrial-scale solar arrays (see chapter 8). We can declare independence from oil and coal and clean up government in the process.

An array of energetic public-interest groups is turning up the heat. Veteran energy strategist Steve Kretzmann has sparred with the oil industry in the halls of the World Bank and United Nations and around the world in Ecuador, Colombia, Nigeria, Kazakhstan, and beyond. *Rolling Stone* calls him a "whip-crack petroleum economics analyst." I first met Steve in 1995 when he was campaigning to save the life of Nigerian poet Ken Saro-Wiwa, who was imprisoned for criticizing the vicious Nigerian military dictatorship and the oil operations of Royal Dutch Shell. Tragically, Shell refused to intervene in Saro-Wiwa's case, and he and eight others were hanged in November of that year.

More recently, Kretzmann founded and now directs a new organization, Oil Change International (full disclosure: I'm on the board). Oil Change is focused on identifying and overcoming the political barriers to a transition to clean energy. Kretzmann describes how his approach has evolved over time. He says that while it is crucial to hold the oil industry accountable for human rights abuses, accelerating climate change, fomenting war, deepening poverty, and greedy pricing, "we must also confront the system that allows these injustices to occur. To create a clean energy future, we have to separate oil and state."

Oil Change wants to make it as easy as possible for people to persuade their elected officials to come clean. The organization's Web site helps you find out if your representatives are on the take from Big Oil. Next, the site guides you to immediately send a letter to congratulate the representatives who have refused contributions from Big Oil and encourage those who haven't to declare their independence. Oil Change staff members coordinate with people on the ground, too, helping them arrange face-to-face meetings with their representatives, or at least key staff members, in their home districts.

Joining Oil Change in this campaign is a broad alliance of organizations, including the Sierra Club, Energy Action Coalition, Global Exchange, Public Citizen, Greenpeace, Rainforest Action Network, the Ruckus Society, and many others. In the summer of 2006, these organizations were joined by thousands of MoveOn.org members, holding rallies at more than three hundred gas stations across the country that called for an "oil-free Congress" and a responsible energy policy.

Along with the rising awareness and indignation of informed citizens around the country, this campaign is having an impact. In the 2006 congressional midterm elections, every single candidate who refused to accept money from the oil industry won election. Four out of the top five largest recipients of oil money contributions in Congress were voted out of office in 2006.

And in more recent news, Congress acted in 2010 to require that extraction companies publicly disclose how much they pay to the U.S. government and to other countries for access to oil, gas, and minerals. This "publish what you pay" provision, included in the Dodd-Frank Wall Street Reform and Consumer Protection Act, will help citizens here and around the world track the money that flows from dirty-energy companies to their governments.

"We can do this. We know how to power a society in a way that does not fuel global warming and war," Kretzmann insists. "At the end of the day, it's about politics. Once our political system isn't bought and paid for by the big energy giants, a whole world of possibilities will emerge."

Turning a Bright Light on Government

Cleaning up our government won't happen overnight. And there's bound to be some backlash from the oil and coal giants. To take them on, we'll need to be prepared with the most accurate, specific, and up-to-date information about how big money dominates the political process. A handful of organizations do this well, but no one illuminates the connections between money and politics better than a new group, MAPLight.org.

MAPLight.org was started by Dan Newman, who studied biomedical ethics and psychology before cofounding Say I Can, a speech-recognition firm. As a campaign volunteer and an observer of politics on the side, Newman grew frustrated by the influence of big money on the lawmaking process. "It's obvious to me how much corporate money is preventing change from happening, and how hard it is for citizens to band together and get anything done when they're competing against big campaign donations from special interests," he says. "So I started this Web site to give people specific examples of how the money and political system works."

MAPLight.org uses public information to make the political process more transparent by combining several distinct sets of data. The site shows who gave money to lawmakers in the U.S. Congress and the California state legislature (other states are to be added soon). Then it shows how those lawmakers voted on dozens of bills in the past several years. Finally, it reveals the positions taken on those bills by the donors themselves. Pick a bill, a legislator, or an issue, and you'll see a clear and consistent pattern of how big money and the political process intertwine.

Pass It On

In the 2006 congressional election, four of the top five recipients of oil industry contributions were defeated, whereas all the candidates who refused all oil money won their elections.

Newman gave me a guided test drive to show how the Web site can be used. We picked a bill introduced by former congressman Richard Pombo (R-CA) to allow drilling in the Arctic Refuge. The bill actually passed in the U.S. House of Representatives in 2006 but stalled in the Senate. From the MAPLight.org home page, we clicked on "U.S. Congress," then "Bills," then entered into the search engine "American-Made Energy and Good Jobs Act," Pombo's creatively named bill to exploit the pristine wildlife refuge. We picked "major (multinational) oil and gas producers" and "oilfield service and equipment providers" to measure the influence they had over the eventual vote. Sure enough, the industry gave $10,863 to each legislator who voted for the bill.

We went a step deeper, and the story became even more interesting. Clicking the tab "Timeline of Contributions" revealed a surge in donations right before the vote took place in late May 2006. Two and a half weeks before the vote, Occidental Petroleum made a series of donations to Representatives Duncan, Weller, Bono, Neugebauer, and McCaul. All voted to drill in the refuge.

A few days later, Chevron kicked in contributions to Representatives Mica, Pickering, Ros-Lehtinen, Wilson, and Barton. They all voted for the bill, too. In the month before the vote, Pombo himself received donations from Shell (five separate ones), Exxon, Marathon, BP, and Chevron.

Is this a coincidence? Just because an oil company gave money to politicians does not necessarily mean that their votes were bought. But, as Newman says, "sometimes the money influences the vote, which means the money is making the difference rather than the strength of the policy or what constituents want. Other times, money goes to people who already support industry." Either way, democracy is weakened. If industry money can't buy votes, it can ensure that polluter-friendly candidates get more cash for their election campaigns. Even if no individual person changes his or her vote in direct response to a corporate donation, Congress as a whole can be bought.

The scope of the challenge of restoring accountability in government can be daunting. Newman has a healthy perspective, however, reminding us that Americans have the power. "The desire for change among Americans is so broad," he says. "People know the political system is corrupt, and by giving people something visibly good they can do, we're showing that this corruption is a solvable problem. It's a political system that 'we the people' have created, and that 'we the people' can change."

Indeed we can. Year by year, support is growing for an end to corporate welfare for dirty energy. Following the defeats of four of the top five beneficiaries of oil industry donations in the 2006 election, Democratic leaders in Congress, having gained the majority, took action within the first hundred hours of the new session. Led by Speaker Nancy Pelosi, the House passed a bill to cut subsidies, restore oil royalty fees, and redirect as much as $15 billion toward renewable energy programs. Although the Senate narrowly defeated a similar provision in December 2007, it's clear that oil-industry subsidies are becoming a threatened species. It's only logical: if even former president Bush admits that "America is addicted to oil," then it's time to stop paying the pusher.

Take Action

Take it personally

1. Find out how much money your federal, state, and local representatives are taking from Big Oil by visiting Oil Change International's www.priceofoil.org.

2. See how much your representatives in Congress receive from the coal industry and other special interests. Visit the Center for Responsive Politics Web site at www.opensecrets.org.

3. Observe the connections between money and politics at www.maplight.org.

4. Want more examples of the corrupting influence of corporate cash? Check out Robert F. Kennedy, Jr., *Crimes against Nature: How George W. Bush and His Corporate Pals Are Plundering the Country and Hijacking Democracy.*

Express yourself

It's time for our political leaders to come clean. Contact your elected officials and urge them to:

- *Declare independence from dirty energy* by refusing to accept political contributions, gifts, or travel junkets from oil and coal companies.

- *Stop the giveaways!* Demand that they oppose all tax breaks, royalty reductions, subsidies, and gifts of taxpayer funds to oil and coal companies. No dirty money should be accepted by government officials, and no taxpayer money should be given to fossil-fuel companies in return.

- *Reinvest in America.* Every subsidy taken from oil and coal should be redirected toward energy efficiency and renewable power. Recommitting these funds will accelerate the transition to clean energy.

Stay engaged

Join the effort to separate oil and state by getting involved with one of the organizations mentioned above or in the resources section. Internationally, support the Publish What You Pay campaign (www.publishwhatyoupay.org)—an initiative that seeks to "help citizens of resource-rich developing countries hold their governments accountable for the management of revenues from the oil, gas, and mining industries." This coalition of more than three hundred organizations worldwide seeks to eliminate corruption by forcing corporations to disclose what they pay governments for their extraction rights.

CHAPTER 4

Follow the Money

How Your Bank Is Funding Climate Change, and What You Can Do about It

*Permit me to issue and control the money of a nation,
and I care not who makes its laws.*

— MAYER ANSELM ROTHSCHILD, BANKER

You might not know it, but there's a good chance that you're funding climate change. Do you have a credit card or checking account with Citi, JPMorgan Chase, or Bank of America? How about an investment fund, student loan, or even a home mortgage? These giant institutions aren't just the country's three largest consumer banks. They're also the largest financiers of the dirtiest and most carbon-intensive industries in America today. And they're bankrolling those industries with your money.

Banks are one of the best recyclers in America—of money that is. Every bank in the country takes consumer dollars in the form of ATM fees, credit card interest payments, savings and checking deposits, mortgage payments, and so forth, and then reinvests that money to earn a higher rate of return. Many of these investments or loans are helpful; the economy needs credit and liquidity in order to function properly.

But banks also direct hundreds of billions of dollars each year to oil and coal operations that blast mountains apart, drill in sensitive ecosystems, and destabilize our climate. Although fossil-fuel industries attract criticism for these practices, banks often enjoy almost complete anonymity—even though they're paying for and profiting from the entire operation.

It has become almost a cliché: follow the money. It was the famous advice that "Deep Throat," FBI insider Mark Felt, gave to *Washington Post* reporters Bob Woodward and Carl Bernstein during their Watergate investigation. In the film *JFK,* Donald Sutherland's mysterious character "X" advises Kevin Costner's Jim Garrison to "follow the money" to understand the motivations behind JFK's assassination. After the 9/11 attacks, one of the first things the Bush administration did was to freeze the financial assets of terrorist suspects and conduct financial investigations to determine who was behind the attacks. Whether you're a grassroots environmental group or a giant multinational oil company, financing keeps you afloat.

The role of banks in providing loans, advice, liquidity, and a range of financial services to dirty-energy companies must not be underestimated. Cleaning up our government won't be enough. To create a future in which we enjoy safe, secure, and sustainable energy, we also need Wall Street and the global financial system to stop the flow of easy money for the world's biggest polluters.

Banking on Addiction

The banks' press materials say all the right things. On Bank of America's Web site, Anne Finucane, the chair of the company's Environmental Council, states, "We . . . recognize that climate change and atmospheric pollution represent a risk to the ultimate stability and sustainability of our way of life."

In 2007, Bank of America announced a $20 billion commitment over ten years to address climate change. "Today, we have a tremendous opportunity to support our customers' efforts to build an environmentally sustainable economy," said then-CEO Ken Lewis in a press release. The company pledged to introduce a new credit card to help customers offset greenhouse gas emissions, a mortgage program with incentives for energy efficiency, and expanded advisory services to help clients take advantage of "carbon-offset" markets.

Two months after Bank of America's announcement, Citi raised the ante with a pledge to invest $50 billion over ten years in clean energy and reductions in the firm's own greenhouse gas emissions. "We believe very strongly that addressing climate change is one of the most important issues being faced by chief executives, investors and governments today," declared Michael Klein,

Citi's co-president of markets and banking. Citi, Chase, and Bank of America each invest in some clean-energy technologies and have each pledged to reduce the energy use and resulting greenhouse gas emissions from their own offices and bank branches. (Citi says that it will cut its emissions 10 percent worldwide by 2011.)

With big numbers and promises such as these, what's the worry? Only that these policies are an easy distraction from a much bigger problem: the exponentially larger loans and investments that are profoundly damaging to our climate and our way of life. It's difficult to take a bank too seriously regarding climate change when it continues to finance the world's largest climate polluters. For example, while Bank of America was announcing its new climate change commitment, the company also extended credit to AES Corporation, which at one time sought to build new coal-fired power plants in four states. Bank of America funds Massey Energy, Arch Coal, and Alpha Natural Resources, three of the largest coal companies engaging in mountaintop-removal coal mining throughout Appalachia; Dynegy, which planned to build up to eight or more new coal-fired power plants across the United States; the world's largest coal company, Peabody Energy, which has poisoned the groundwater for Hopi and Navajo in Arizona and sought to build three more coal plants; and many other companies and utilities seeking to expand markets for coal-fired power.

Similarly, Citi has provided financial assistance to American Electric Power, which proposed new coal plants in West Virginia, Virginia, Ohio, Arkansas, and Oklahoma; Florida Power and Light, which proposed adding four coal plants; Southern Company, which operates two plants that are the largest emitters of greenhouse gases in the country; TXU Energy, whose coal plants include several that are among the nation's top emitters of greenhouse gases and mercury pollution; and plenty of other coal companies and operators of dirty-power plants.

Pass It On

A single coal plant with financing from Citi, Chase, or Bank of America will produce more greenhouse gases in three weeks of operation than Citi's entire annual commitment to reduce emissions from its offices in a hundred countries around the world.

There's some good news to report on those coal company plans: thanks to the efforts of thousands of citizens working nationally and locally, nearly all of the proposed plants mentioned above went down to defeat before they could be permitted, as reported in chapter 2. And Bank of America (along with Credit Suisse, Wells Fargo, Citi, Morgan Stanley, and JPMorgan Chase) has adopted policies that begin to limit financing for companies engaged in mountaintop-removal coal mining. In the case of Credit Suisse such financing was ended completely. This work is far from over, as most banks do not have an outright ban on financing MTR, much less firm prohibitions on the construction of new coal-fired power plants. Nevertheless, we're making progress, and groups like Rainforest Action Network, Waterkeeper Alliance, and the Sierra Club's Beyond Coal campaign, along with key investors, deserve lots of credit.

Financing oil development is another story. Kenneth Derr, the former chairman of Chevron, sits on Citi's board of directors, and you can bet that Citi is knee-deep in controversial oil deals in the Amazon and beyond. As recently as 2007, Citi's largest shareholder was the Gulf Arab emirate of Abu Dhabi, the world's sixth-largest oil exporter. Another large shareholder is Prince Walid bin Talal of Saudi Arabia.

"Too many investors and companies are vested in not addressing climate change," declares Leslie Lowe, a former program director at the Interfaith Center on Corporate Responsibility. "They have assets that will be devalued, personal holdings that will be devalued, and so they're fighting a rear-guard action to preserve those assets, or what we'd call 'business-as-usual.'"

The approach these banks take to addressing climate change would be amusing if it weren't so serious. It's a nice gesture for banks to use less energy at their branch offices. But compared to the extensive financing that companies like Citi offer to coal companies and utilities, this is like rearranging deck chairs on the *Titanic*. Consider this: A single medium-sized coal plant with financing from Citi will produce more carbon dioxide in just three weeks of operation than the reductions Citi plans to make annually in all of its offices around the world. And there are hundreds of coal plants in the United States alone. In a year, one large coal plant releases as much carbon as six hundred thousand cars and trucks.

Let's look more closely at Citi's 2007 $50 billion climate-change commitment. Citi will spend $31 billion over ten years for investment and financing in energy efficiency, renewables, and upgrading existing infrastructure, an average of $3.1 billion per year. Compare that to the $63 billion in Citi's corporate credit portfolio dedicated to the utilities and petroleum sectors in 2006 alone. That figure doesn't even include the income earned for underwriting stocks and bonds, advisory, and other services related to financing for these two sectors. Bank of America will spend an average of $1.8 billion per year to help corporate clients reduce greenhouse gas emissions. Meanwhile, the company extended $35.6 billion in credit to oil and utilities in 2006.

Pass It On

Reform is slow but starting: thanks to citizen action, six of the largest banks have adopted policies that begin to limit financing for companies engaged in mountaintop-removal coal mining.

It might seem daunting to attempt to change the policies of institutions as large as Citi, Bank of America, or JPMorgan Chase. They're the three most powerful financial institutions in the world. Citigroup alone had almost $25 billion in profits in 2006, maintains offices in more than a hundred countries, and employs more than 320,000 people. Bank of America, one of the world's most recognized brands, has nearly six thousand branches within the United States and net assets of more than $1 trillion.

But it's been done before. Earlier this decade, a small collection of nonprofit organizations organized tens of thousands of volunteers to persuade Citi, Bank of America, JPMorgan Chase, and others to help protect threatened ecosystems and address indigenous rights. If we can get banks to protect biodiversity and human rights, then we can also compel them to join the fight to stabilize our threatened climate in more meaningful ways. Here's how we did it.

Inside a Campaign

When I worked for Rainforest Action Network (RAN), I was often asked how the organization determines which issues to prioritize. Deciding between different campaigns and potential corporate targets is a complex process. The first step involves detailed research: identifying the top causes of climate change, deforestation, or human rights abuses; specifying which industries or particular companies are most implicated in contributing to the problem; deciding whether there are reasonable steps those companies can take to address that problem, or effective national or international laws that can be applied or strengthened.

Other questions are more strategic: Is the company vulnerable to public pressure? If so, how? What is the psychological profile of its CEO and senior management team? What allies can be cultivated? Which constituencies can be mobilized? Can people get involved in ways that are both fun and meaningful? And then questions of funding and organizational capacity must always be answered, too.

No matter what the proposal, mounting a new campaign almost always provokes a friendly but fierce debate within the organization. In late 1999 and early 2000, as RAN was considering taking on the company then known as Citigroup, the discussion was particularly passionate. RAN had recently persuaded Home Depot to stop selling wood from endangered forests, a big victory that provided much-needed momentum to protect British Columbia's Great Bear Rainforest. *Time* magazine named it the top environmental story of 1999, and we were plotting our next move.

A major issue was whether we thought Citi could be pushed forward. And if so, how far would the company go? At that time RAN had a staff of just a few dozen people. Citi was about to become the world's largest bank and soon the world's most profitable corporation. Pick your problem area—logging, mining, oil and gas, large hydroelectric dams—and Citi was a top financier. Pick your favorite threatened ecosystem—California redwoods, the Amazon basin, tropical forests in central Africa and Southeast Asia—and Citi was also implicated in its destruction.

The breadth of its operations was both a danger and an opportunity—a huge David-versus-Goliath scenario. How could we possibly take on a company so large? On the other hand, Citi was a symbol of corporate-led globalization. If we could change the policies of the world's largest bank, the impact would be profound.

Ultimately, it was Citi's size and global reach that convinced RAN to give the campaign a go. Perhaps just as important, it was the size of Citi's brand.

For years Citi had spent hundreds of millions of dollars on a whimsical "Live Richly" advertising campaign designed to position the company as a friendly, full-service bank that protected not just your assets but your true interests in life. "Hugs are on a 52-week high," announced a typical Citi billboard. "The best blue chips to buy are the ones you dip in salsa," offered another. We loved the prospect of juxtaposing these feel-good corporate slogans with images of Citi-financed environmental decay and exploitation. James Gollin, a former investment banker with Nomura Securities and Morgan Stanley International and the current chair of RAN's board of directors, calls it "corporate jujitsu"—using the power of a company's brand against itself.

The more popular the brand, the easier it is to subvert. *Adbusters* magazine took on cigarette advertising to kids with its brilliant "Joe Chemo" campaign, which placed the mascot formerly used to sell Camel cigarettes in a hospital bed hooked up to life support. On the poster, a spoof of the surgeon general's warning reads, "The Surgeon General warns that smoking is a frequent cause of wasted potential and fatal regret." Another ad challenges the sexiness of alcohol advertising: "Absolute [*sic*] on Ice" features a toe tag on a dead body at the morgue with the text, "Nearly 50 percent of automobile fatalities are linked to alcohol. . . . A teenager sees 100,000 alcohol ads before reaching the legal drinking age."

Before we would start a new initiative at RAN, we sent a short note to the corporate executive whose policies (and mind) we wanted to change. Our letter in early 2000 to Citi CEO Sandy Weill was respectful but direct: we informed Mr. Weill that his company was damaging human rights and the environment and asked that he join us to solve the problem collaboratively. Each time RAN sends such a letter, the hope is that it will inspire the CEO to simply do the right thing—to show that his or her company can do well by doing good, by taking responsibility for its environmental and social impacts.

Sometimes one letter is all it takes. Lowe's, the country's second-largest home-improvement retailer, agreed to phase out all wood products from endangered forests after a letter and meeting with RAN. Similarly, Kinko's responded to a letter by adopting the country's strongest policies to increase the recycled content of paper and eliminate purchases of wood from endangered forests.

Our note to Citi didn't quite have that effect, but it did lead to a meeting with Citi executives at its headquarters in New York. The goal was a comprehensive policy that would include strong environmental and social standards affecting forests, human rights, climate protection, labor standards, and more. "We wanted Citi to model what a responsible and equitable twenty-first-century bank could be," recalls Ilyse Hogue, former director of RAN's global finance campaign. "But we were light-years apart at that time." Years later, a Citi executive joked that it seemed RAN wanted an "intergalactic, universal policy that would abolish everything that we do."

We had been warned that this would be difficult. Michelle Chan, a campaigner with Friends of the Earth who pioneered financial advocacy with corporate banks in the mid- to late 1990s, had had some frustrating early encounters. "When we first started, banks didn't factor in most environmental issues, and certainly didn't have comprehensive policies," she said. "If we brought a controversial project to a bank, they would routinely try to pass any criticisms off either to the company involved or to the government. Our first challenge was simply getting banks to accept responsibility for their loans and investments."

It became clear that Citi wouldn't move voluntarily. It was time to make some noise.

Not with Our Money!

Challenging Citi to stop bankrolling bulldozers in the Amazon and elsewhere was an effort in which RAN was joined by hundreds of small groups around the country and thousands of concerned individuals around the world. Many were students—who were particularly important in this case because Citi needed them and their money. High school and college students are red meat for banks. Once a bank starts doing business with a young person, it won't let go. Banks aim to entice students with their first credit card, and then as time passes, ply them with student loans, auto loans, mortgages, investment accounts, retirement plans, and so on.

Each semester at high schools, universities, and colleges across the country, Citi employees would arrive on campus to sign up students as new credit card customers. It was a golden opportunity for our campaign. When Citi employees set up booths to attract fresh recruits, RAN volunteers would set up a table nearby with photos and fact sheets documenting the impact of the bank's loans on ancient redwood forests, national parks in the Amazon, and other endangered regions. (Not many applications for credit cards were submitted on the days we were there.)

But it wasn't just students who were involved. RAN staff members and volunteers would pass leaflets to Citi employees outside Citi's headquarters in New York. We quickly found insiders who were willing to give us valuable information. "I remember standing outside the Citigroup Center in January and being pleasantly surprised by how many people not only took the flyer from my frigid hands, but gave me a subtle thumbs-up, a smile, or told me how much they appreciated our campaign," remembers former RAN campaigner Dan Firger with a laugh. "Not every employee was on our side, but it was gratifying to see how many really cared about what their company was doing."

RAN had successfully reached out to employees before. Often a public campaign will inspire employees within a company to take action. These employees want to keep their jobs, but also wish to work for an employer that's doing right by people and the planet.

When we were pressuring Home Depot to stop selling wood from endangered forests, I began to receive calls from a Home Depot worker who wanted to help. He was concerned that his two daughters wouldn't have rainforests to visit when they got older. He gave me information about the sources of Home Depot's wood and one day shared the access codes to the intercom at every one of Home Depot's stores. Weeks later, volunteers could be heard on the intercom at Home Depot stores across the country saying, "Attention, Home Depot shoppers, we want to draw your attention to the doors in aisle 16 which were made from wood that has been ripped from the heart of the Amazon basin. In aisle 12 . . ."

As the Citi campaign continued, RAN placed an advertisement in the *New York Times*. The headline "Did you know someone is using your credit card without your authorization?" ran above pictures of clearcut forests, oil pipelines, and pollution-belching smokestacks. The ad informed customers that Citi was quietly using their money to fund dozens of controversial projects, and urged them to cut up their Citi credit cards and send them to RAN. We began to receive thousands of cut-up cards in the mail.

Eventually dozens of organizations were pressuring the company from all sides, including Amazon Watch, International Rivers Network, the Ruckus Society, and the Service Employees International Union. Students mocked Citi director and former treasury secretary Robert Rubin at a speech at Columbia University. Activists hung a banner at Citi's headquarters reading, "Hey, Citi, not with my money!" Local residents used civil disobedience to blockade Citi branches in Iowa, New York, Florida, California, Washington, D.C., and elsewhere. Volunteers cut up Citi credit cards and held protests at Citi branches around the country.

A group of investors led by Trillium Asset Management and Friends of the Earth represented key shareholders who wanted change. Shareholder resolutions were filed. International leaders came to speak at Citi's annual shareholder meetings. At one meeting in April 2002, Lily la Torre, a leader from the Peruvian environmental organization Racimos de Ungurahui, implored Citi to withdraw its support for an oil pipeline that would cut through primary rainforests. She invited CEO Sandy Weill to visit her community to learn directly about the effect the pipeline would have. Weill declined.

When informed that Weill would take a summer vacation in Tuscany, we placed an ad in the *International Herald Tribune* with pictures of the Citi CEO joined by President Bush and World Bank CEO James Wolfensohn. The headline read, "Put a Face on Climate Change and Forest Destruction."

A turning point came early in 2003 when Weill, a Cornell University alumnus, came to give a speech at his alma mater's business school. Cornell's students were well prepared. They arranged for RAN founder Randy Hayes to address students the night before Weill's speech and invited Weill to a "Randy versus Sandy" debate. Again, Weill declined. The next day, as Weill approached the lecture hall, three banners were unfurled, urging him to do the right thing. During his remarks, several students held signs inside the room protesting Citi's dirty investments. One read, "Destroying Old Growth Forests Isn't Cool!"

Weill finished his speech and took questions from the audience. The first student, Brihannala Morgan, stood up and thanked Weill for coming, and then challenged him on his company's lack of a responsible environmental policy. Before the audience, she introduced Weill to Hayes, who said, "I'd like to work together with you to bring environmental responsibility to Citigroup, and I'd also like to invite you to join me in an academic debate on this subject, perhaps to be held right here at Cornell." Weill declined once again to engage, but assured the audience that he took these issues seriously.

The next questioner stood up, thanked Weill again for coming, and asked another tough question. Five of the eight questions asked weren't from students eager to suck up for a fast-track summer internship. They were from kids asking why Weill's company was sacrificing their future. Eventually the chief executive admitted that his company could and should do more. He mentioned the ad in the *International Herald Tribune* the previous year, and how embarrassed he was to have his grandson ask him what he was doing to make climate change worse. He promised the audience that Citi would take quick action.

A couple of weeks later, we received word that Citi was willing to negotiate. At the time, RAN was running advertisements on cable television in New York, in which Ali MacGraw, Daryl Hannah, Susan Sarandon, and Ed Asner were pictured cutting up their Citi credit cards, interspersed with images of oil spills and blackened tree stumps. "Stop bankrolling bulldozers," growled Asner. On the eve of Citi's 2003 shareholder meeting, RAN agreed to pull the ads and suspend all campaign activities—in exchange for a commitment by Citi to set a new global standard for environmental responsibility by a bank.

Two months later, in June 2003, Citi joined with international banks Barclays, ABN AMRO, and WestLB in launching the Equator Principles—a set of voluntary guidelines that minimize or eliminate some of the adverse social and environmental impacts of the projects banks fund. All four banks had been the target of public-pressure campaigns in the preceding eighteen months. As of 2010, sixty-seven banks have adopted the principles, covering more than 90 percent of all project finance deals around the world.

In January 2004, Citi went a step further by announcing that it would deny funding for logging in tropical rainforests, enact special restrictions on extractive industries operating in critical ecosystems worldwide, stop financing illegal logging activities, and enhance consultation with indigenous communities. The announcement was covered by CNN, the *Wall Street Journal,* the *New York Times,* and other outlets. Within four months, Bank of America adopted similar standards, followed by JPMorgan Chase and the investment banking firm Goldman Sachs. "This was a great paradigm shift; today communities around the world are being given the tools to 'follow the money' if they want to stop destructive projects," says Ilyse Hogue. "Grassroots citizens stood up and together we finally got banks to admit culpability and accept responsibility for their loans and investments."

It was an important victory and a hard-earned one. We at RAN never knew what prompted Citi to change its mind and take action to help protect endangered ecosystems. It could have been a colleague who bent Sandy Weill's ear, or a shareholder. Perhaps it was the confrontation at Cornell, the ad in the *International Herald Tribune,* or the thousands of letters and e-mails the company received. I'd like to think it was all these things and more, but also that Weill and his team stepped forward because it was simply the right thing to do.

The agreements with Citi and the other banks closed a chapter, but the story continues. Each bank has acknowledged that climate change is a critical issue facing society. Each has pledged to reduce energy use at its own facilities and to study other potential solutions. However, not one bank has committed to phase out loans and investments in activities that cook the planet. Not yet, anyway. We still have some work to do.

Perverse Subsidies

Corporate banks such as Citi, Chase, and Bank of America are just one part of the problem. Public financing institutions are also bankrolling climate change by diverting taxpayer funds toward the fossil-fuel industry. For example, the World Bank Group has provided more than $8 billion to the oil industry since 1992. In the last ten years, the U.S. Export-Import Bank and the Overseas Private Investment Corporation have given more than $21 billion in loans and loan guarantees to U.S. corporate interests for refineries, pipelines, and power plants in more than forty countries around the world. The beneficiaries of these loans are companies such as Halliburton, Exxon, Bechtel, and others. Why not invest in clean energy and efficiency projects instead?

Ending corporate welfare for the world's biggest climate polluters is a topic that could unite all Americans and bring us into community with the rest of the world. Whether it's the government subsidies discussed in the preceding chapter or loans from public banks, we shouldn't use taxpayer dollars to enrich already profitable corporations, or to keep America hooked on dirty energy. In the United Kingdom, it is the right-wing Conservative Party that is calling for an elimination of such "perverse subsidies." Party leader David Cameron, who became prime minister in 2010, said, "This is a vital issue—we have a responsibility in this generation to make sure we provide a greener and cleaner planet for our children. We cannot go on as we are in terms of the way we run government and live our lives."

Pass It On

In April 2010, the World Bank approved a $3.75 billion loan to build one of the world's largest coal-fired power plants in South Africa, defying international protests and criticism from the Obama administration.

For years civil-society groups and grass-roots activists have lobbied the World Bank and other financial institutions to stop funding destructive investments. In April 2010 the World Bank approved a controversial $3.75 billion loan to build one of the world's largest coal-fired power plants in South Africa, defying international protests and criticism from the Obama administration that the project would fuel climate change. Officials from Eskom Corporation claim their coal plant will help the poor get access to electricity, but the poorest people aren't even connected to the grid. Meanwhile, South African activists say that electricity rates will triple over the next five years in order to pay for this plant and other coal and nuclear power plants proposed by Eskom.

After the Copenhagen climate talks in December 2009, the World Bank positioned itself to lead financial support for mitigating the worst effects of global warming. But how can the World Bank help fight climate change if it's financing the problem—pollution from coal plants—in the first place? The U.S. government abstained from the vote approving the South Africa loan when it should have voted no: sending a clear signal that the project violates both World Bank rules and the Treasury Department's coal-financing guidelines.

Here's another story about efforts to stop the World Bank's lending to dirty oil and coal projects—and why concerned citizens won't give up.

World Bank on Trial

Tensions were high in a crowded conference room at the World Bank offices in Prague, Czech Republic, in late September 2000. The next day the city would be filled with tens of thousands of European citizens calling for fundamental reform—or the complete abolishment—of the World Bank and the International Monetary Fund (IMF). James Wolfensohn, the World Bank president, gathered several nonprofit leaders around the table to hear their concerns. They represented a diverse network of organizations that criticized the World Bank and the IMF for deepening poverty, causing widespread social and environmental instability, and "turning slowdowns into recessions and recessions into depressions," as described by former World Bank chief economist and Nobel Prize winner for economics Joseph Stiglitz. Wolfensohn knew he had to do something.

Established in 1945, the World Bank (officially known as the World Bank Group) is a collection of five international agencies whose original mandate was to assist with postwar reconstruction. Today the bank uses public funds to provide financing and advice to countries and corporations alike, ostensibly to improve living standards and alleviate global poverty. However, the bank's loans and investments—particularly in the fossil-fuel sectors—and the conditions that they place on those loans too often produce the opposite result. In developing countries from Cameroon to Colombia, communities assailed World Bank–financed projects as benefiting only oil corporations and corrupt government officials, not the poor. Between 1992 and 2005 the World Bank Group committed over $28 billion to fossil-fuel projects—seventeen times more than its financing for renewable energy and energy efficiency.

By the time the meeting in Prague was held, discontent with corporate-led globalization was at a fever pitch. Protests criticizing the World Trade Organization in Seattle and the World Bank and IMF in Washington were generating worldwide media coverage. To the surprise of many community leaders in the room, Wolfensohn offered a radical solution. He proposed that the World Bank appoint an independent blue-ribbon panel to reassess whether World Bank investments in extractive industries were justified, given their questionable ability to promote sustainable development and alleviate global poverty. An agreement was made to move forward with this plan.

An independent team known as the World Bank Extractive Industries Review (EIR) was established, led by Emil Salim, Indonesia's former minister for the environment. "The World Bank was criticized that its oil, gas, and mining portfolio was not contributing to poverty alleviation and sustainable development," Salim told me years later. "I was to set up a multi-stakeholder process to discuss [whether this was true]."

Salim's team was given a multimillion-dollar budget and a mandate to incorporate input from all sides. Conferences involving a wide range of stakeholders were held in Europe, Africa, Asia, and North and South America in 2002 and 2003, where industry executives, nongovernmental organizations, indigenous communities, labor unions, and others gave testimony. The team also had special private meetings with numerous governments and with Royal Dutch Shell, Exxon, Chevron, and some of the world's largest mining corporations. Six studies were commissioned and site visits were conducted to examine firsthand the impact of World Bank activities on communities, local economies, and the environment.

"Many of us were skeptical from the outset. No one knew what the EIR's recommendations would be, nor even whether they'd be accepted in good faith," recounts Oil Change International's Steve Kretzmann. "But that misses the point. The World Bank essentially agreed to put the fossil-fuel industry on trial, and created a process where all the evidence could be carefully considered."

For many people, this was an extraordinary opportunity to share their views in an official forum. Representatives from Indigenous organizations around the world met in Oxford, England, to formulate a collective response. The Indigenous Peoples' Declaration on Extractive Industries stated, "Our futures as indigenous peoples are threatened in many ways by developments in the extractive industries. . . . Our experience shows that exploration and exploitation of minerals, coal, oil, and gas bring us serious social and environmental problems, so widespread and injurious that we cannot describe such development as 'sustainable.' Indeed, rather than contributing to poverty alleviation, we find that the extractive industries are creating poverty and social divisions in our communities, and showing disrespect for our culture and customary laws."

In December 2003, more than three years after Wolfensohn agreed to conduct the review, the EIR released its official report, *Striking a Better Balance*, which strongly recommended that the World Bank improve its governance and accountability, respect human rights, and strengthen social and environmental performance standards. The fourth and final recommendation asked the bank to phase out all oil and coal activities: "The WBG should phase out investments in oil production by 2008 and devote its scarce resources to investments in renewable energy resource development, emissions-reducing projects, clean-energy technology, energy efficiency and conservation, and other efforts that delink energy use from greenhouse gas emissions. . . . The WBG has for the last few years not invested in new coal mining development. This should continue."

The World Bank's managers were in a tough spot. They had created this independent team, after all, but were hesitant to follow its strong recommendations. A collection of Nobel Peace Prize winners turned up the heat in a letter to the bank, saying, "War, poverty, climate change, greed, corruption, and ongoing violations of human rights—all of these scourges are all too often linked to the oil and mining industries. Your efforts to create a world without poverty need not exacerbate these problems."

Nine months and countless meetings and conference calls later, the bank's management officially responded. They chose to disagree by agreeing, stating that the bank "welcomes the Review" and agrees with "the majority of its recommendations." The bank announced, however, that it would not accept the recommendation to phase out oil and coal investments. Instead, it promised: "Our future investments in extractive industries will be selective."

One wonders what the bank's definition of "selective" might be. Wolfensohn continued making loans to the fossil-fuel industry in the last year of his presidency. After leaving the bank in 2005, Wolfensohn was replaced by Paul Wolfowitz, one of the architects of the Iraq War. Appointed by the Bush administration, Wolfowitz certainly didn't change the bank's policy on extractive industries. According to the Bank Information Center, the International Finance Corporation, which is part of the World Bank, increased its loans to corporate oil and gas companies by 35 percent from 2005 to 2007. "A significant portion of these investments are for projects involving export of oil and gas to Europe and the US, thereby subsidizing these countries to prolong their dependence on fossil fuels," says Bank Information Center's Heike Mainhart-Gibbs. In early 2008, the International Finance Corporation approved $450 million in loans to a massive, 4,000-megawatt coal plant in India.

Robert Goodland, an advisor to the EIR team, believes the World Bank missed an unusual opportunity: "We . . . strongly recommended the WBG extend their then-current moratorium on lending for coal, to phase out of oil lending by 2008, and to ramp up the transition to renewables." Instead, the World Bank went in the opposite direction by significantly increasing its loans to the oil and coal industries. Goodland called the bank's response to the EIR a "monumental blunder" that would impact the developing world most, as increased loans to the oil and coal industries intensified the climate change risks on the world's poorest people.

"I have been disappointed in the way the World Bank responded," says Salim. "Oil and coal industries are rich and strong enough to finance their own activities. The World Bank should not make the strong stronger, but should instead push renewable energy, which is very behind in its development."

In the end, the EIR gave a guilty verdict on World Bank financing of extractive industries—but the bank's managers have suspended the sentence. Actually, that's not true. They've thrown out the verdict, absolved the accused, and added an extra billion or ten to make sure there were no hard feelings.

Funding a Better Future

Undeterred, citizens groups and grassroots leaders have renewed their efforts to end public giveaways to the fossil-fuel industry. In coordination with allies working to secure climate-friendly policies at corporate banks, an international movement on financial activism is emerging, perhaps even led by the president of the United States. In a speech during the 2009 G-20 Summit in Pittsburgh, President Obama called on world leaders to phase out the many billions in subsidies to the fossil-fuel industry. "This reform will increase our energy security," he said. "It will help transform our economy, so that we're creating the clean energy jobs of the future. And it will help us combat the threat posed by climate change.... All nations have a responsibility to meet this challenge, and together, we have taken a substantial step forward in meeting that responsibility." As of late summer 2010, G-20 countries have not yet made firm commitments to substantially reduce those subsidies.

In 2007 Congressman Maurice Hinchey (D-NY) introduced the End Oil Aid Act (H.R. 1886) to prohibit the use of taxpayer dollars to subsidize the overseas operations of the oil industry. That bill didn't go far, but Hinchey has supported every opportunity in Congress to rein in fossil-fuel subsidies abroad. And in the U.K. Parliament, a petition signed by fifty members calls on the government to produce a climate-change strategy that phases out support for oil and gas projects.

Activists continue to pressure corporate banks in creative ways. In Washington, D.C., two Bank of America customers dressed up as polar bears and withdrew their life savings of $27,000 in protest of their bank's role in accelerating climate change through its loans to the coal industry. At Kayford Mountain, West Virginia, local residents held up a giant banner adjacent to a mountaintop-removal site, reading, "Mountaintop Removal—Funded by Bank of America." In all, demonstrations were held at more than a hundred Citi and Bank of America locations in November 2007 to protest the companies' financing of coal and other "investments of mass destruction."

Three months later, in February 2008, Citi, JPMorgan Chase, and Morgan Stanley released the "Carbon Principles," a new set of lending guidelines on coal-plant financing. The principles don't ban funding for new plants outright, but they do make it more difficult by forcing utilities to justify building a plant in a time of rising coal prices, pending climate legislation, and demand for carbon sequestration.

Grassroots pressure clearly is having an impact, but people don't have to wear polar bear suits to promote clean-energy financing. Pinstripes work just as well. Meeting the demand for environmentally conscious lenders are banks such as ShoreBank Pacific, which bills itself "the nation's first environmental bank." ShoreBank Pacific loans money from its "EcoDeposits" program to businesses and organizations seeking to reduce their environmental footprint. All loans are evaluated by an internal science team that helps the bank's clients improve their environmental performance.

New Resource Bank, founded in San Francisco by Peter Liu, seeks to define full-service environmental banking. Its offices have achieved "gold" status in the Leadership in Energy and Environmental Design program (LEED); its employees are reimbursed for using mass transit; and the firm has made loans to organic farmers, green-home builders, clean technology firms, and other environmental entrepreneurs. "There was a real need in the business community for a green lender, and also for a bank to make a difference," Liu says. New Resource Bank has no coal- or oil-company clients, and it partners with homeowners and solar providers to help install residential solar arrays with no money down. To attract depositors from the Bay Area and beyond, New Resource Bank refunds fees from any ATM in the country.

Credit unions are another important alternative to commercial banks that finance climate change. A credit union is a nonprofit, cooperative financial institution that is owned and operated by its members. Most have some common bond that unites all members, be it a profession, geographic location, or religious affiliation. Credit unions don't have the same quarterly financial pressures as do most corporate banks, and do not provide corporate financing or financial services to companies such as Exxon, Peabody Coal, Shell, or others. They are bound by mandate to give lending preference to their members and are better structured to finance small-scale renewable energy projects and small-business ventures that are too early-stage or localized for the commercial banks.

"Follow the money" is more than a catchphrase. It's how you can predict the future. "The surest indication of what kind of energy infrastructure our country will have in the next ten to fifteen years is to look at where commercial banks are directing their corporate financing," says Bill Barclay, a finance expert at Rainforest Action Network. It won't do to have the world's largest financial institutions continue to bankroll dirty energy. Literally trillions of dollars of investments in transportation, energy, and other sectors need to be redirected to clean and sustainable technologies. We need our banks to help lead the clean-energy revolution or get out of the way.

Take Action

Take it personally

Tell your bank to fund the future:

1. *Stockholders:* If you own shares in Citi, Bank of America, JPMorgan Chase, or other banks, exercise your authority: you're an owner of the company. Contact your bank's managers and urge them to redirect bank financing in the energy sector to clean businesses. Attend your bank's annual shareholder meeting to tell its officers what you think in person (or send a proxy). Contact As You Sow, Trillium Asset Management, and other shareholder advocacy groups for more information.

2. *Investments:* Are your mutual funds, cash investments, or private banking accounts managed by Citi, Chase, Bank of America, or even Goldman Sachs, Merrill Lynch, or others? Contact these institutions and tell them to stop investing in oil and coal, or you'll move your money to someone who will. Find some friends who invest with such banks as well, and multiply your leverage. Visit www.ran.org for more information.

3. *Credit cards, mortgages, and loans:* Banks have an opportunity, and responsibility, to prohibit any investment in industries that threaten to destabilize our climate. Compare your bank's social and environmental performance with those of New Resource Bank, ShoreBank Pacific, and other green financial institutions and consider which deserves to manage your accounts.

4. *Credit unions:* To find a credit union near you, visit www.creditunionsonline.com.

Express yourself

We can't reduce our dependence on oil and coal if the world's largest banks supply those industries with whatever financing they need, for any project, anywhere. Regardless of where your personal accounts are held, make your views heard:

1. If the World Bank had heeded the recommendations of its own Extractive Industries Review, we wouldn't still be giving billions in taxpayer dollars to some of the world's richest corporations. Join the campaigns of Oil Change International and the Bank Information Center to end aid to the oil and coal industry.

2. Want to know who's funding climate change? Take a look at America's three largest banks: Citi, Bank of America, and JPMorgan Chase. Join the campaigns of Rainforest Action Network, Sierra Club, Friends of the Earth, Co-op America, and others to bring ethics to the banking industry.

3. Sixty-seven banks have signed the Equator Principles establishing social and environmental guidelines that help protect endangered ecosystems and community

rights. However, there is no similar code of conduct regarding climate change. Check out what the international coalition Bank Track is doing to redirect the global banking industry to put clean energy first. More information can be found at the group's Web site, www.banktrack.org.

Stay engaged

Let's put our money to work creating a sustainable energy economy. For an elaboration of what that economy might look like, check out the International Forum on Globalization's (IFG) *Alternatives to Economic Globalization,* a summary of which can be found at the IFG Web site, www.ifg.org/alt_eng.pdf. In the resources section here you'll find more organizations to support and other sources of information.

CHAPTER 5

Redesigning Mobility
Moving America in a Post-Oil Economy

My other car is a bus.

— BUTTON CREATED BY THE AMERICAN
PUBLIC TRANSPORTATION ASSOCIATION

There are people who like trains, and then there are Train Lovers. I'm probably in the former camp. I didn't have train sets growing up, nor did I harbor dreams of being a conductor someday. I mostly ride commuter trains to and from work, and as long as they run on time, are relatively clean and comfortable, and get me to where I need to go, then they're all right with me.

But that was before I got on board the *shinkansen,* a high-speed bullet train that links Japan from north to south. After my former colleague Brant Olson and I took the train from Tokyo to Kyoto in August 2006, I became a convert: bullet trains are the most technologically sophisticated, stylish, and efficient way to travel. We simply must get them here in the States.

The *shinkansen* isn't your grandfather's locomotive. Painted a pristine white, with sleek aerodynamic noses, the trains reach speeds of more than 180 miles per hour. New trains entered into service in mid-2007 improve speeds by inclining at turns and also use 19 percent less power. On the horizon are magnetic levitation trains—which float several millimeters over the railways, held by an electromagnetic force. These trains have safely traveled over 350 miles per hour in Japanese test runs. A nineteen-mile demonstration line is currently in operation at the Pudong International Airport in Shanghai, China.

Overall, Japan's rail system is among the best in the world, with trains that are quick, clean, and convenient. For an island nation smaller than California,

Japan has more than twelve thousand miles of tracks and more than twenty-six thousand runs daily, connecting Japan's biggest cities to its most remote towns. Introduced in 1964 for the Tokyo Olympics, the *shinkansen* is wildly popular: it has more than eight hundred thousand riders *every day*. Compare those figures with those of Amtrak, the twenty-one-thousand-mile intercity rail system in the United States, which had a daily ridership of more than seventy-eight thousand in 2008. Japan's high-speed railway is also the safest form of transport in the world: in more than forty years of operation, not a single fatality has occurred.

China is coming up fast, at first under Japan's tutelage. China opened its first high-speed rail line in 2007, and it is on track to complete nearly ten thousand miles by 2020. Starting in 2011, 236-mph trains will operate between Beijing and Shanghai. And by 2012, just four years after launching its first high-speed passenger service, "China will have more high-speed train tracks than the rest of the world combined," according to a *Washington Post* report.

And traveling this way is a breeze, from start to finish. Unlike the airport experience, with its long lines, boarding passes, frequent delays, and baggage hassles, getting on and off Japan's trains is as smooth as can be. We arrived at Tokyo Station about eight minutes before our scheduled departure and quickly bought tickets that identified our car number and assigned seats. Clear signs (in Japanese and English) directed us to the correct track; another set of signs pointed out where to stand to board our particular car. At the precise minute it was due, the train quietly sped into the station. Also impressive was the boarding process: even though these trains can hold more than one thousand passengers each, the boarding process at any particular stop takes no more than ninety seconds, as passengers board fifteen separate cars, each with a door at the front and back.

On the train, unlike being in an automobile, there was no fighting traffic and getting tense behind the wheel. Here, we could walk around, go to the dining car, play cards, read, listen to music, or get a beer—it was good times on the rails! The biggest challenge to riding the *shinkansen* is learning how to look out the window. The ride is super smooth, and you don't realize how fast you're traveling until you look outside. If you look at the ground immediately outside the train, you can get dizzy as it zooms by at a couple hundred miles per hour. The secret is to look a ways into the distance, where your eyes can adjust and you can relax and watch the world go by.

We sped past Mt. Fuji and the bright lights of Nagoya on our way south. A little more than two hours after leaving Tokyo, we pulled into Kyoto Station, a postmodern wonder of glass and steel, complete with an eleven-story hotel, an amphitheater, a public park on the roof, and more than a dozen restaurants, which, on this summer night, were packed with young people. First unveiled in 1997, the station has become a social and commercial center for the entire city.

After checking into our hotel across the street, we headed into town rested and relaxed. Our plan was to down a few beers and see if we could find that Kyoto Protocol on climate change somewhere. We'd heard they needed an American to sign it.

Step Out of the Car, Please

More than 70 percent of the oil that is consumed in the United States each year is devoted to transportation. If America is to ever have a real shot at breaking its fossil-fuel addiction, we'll need to get around much more efficiently. Certainly, a component of that is pushing automakers to manufacture fuel-efficient vehicles, which I'll discuss in the following chapter. It won't be sufficient to build better cars, however. We'll also need to find elegant and effective ways to get people out of those cars whenever it's appropriate, without sacrificing the comfort and convenience to which we've grown accustomed.

Let me first calm any unfounded fears. This chapter isn't pushing some kind of utopian dreamworld in which our energy problems would be solved if everyone could pedal their bicycles to Home Depot and strap sheets of drywall to their backpacks. Nor am I suggesting that if people in rural Utah or western Pennsylvania would just take a bullet train to the office, life would be dandy. Rather, this is about giving ourselves more options to get from one place to another. And it's about making those and other options more practical and attractive at the same time. Some of the solutions are reachable in the long term, others right away.

Let's start with some givens. Convenient public transit is not yet available to many Americans or just isn't practical where they live and work. Americans in twenty, thirty, or more years will most likely still have cars in many areas. And let's face it, cars can be fun. They not only symbolize freedom; for many people, they *are* freedom. Jack Kerouac captured this in his classic book *On the Road,* and when Bruce Springsteen sings, "Just roll down the window and let the wind blow back your hair," he's referring to the distinctive pleasures of someone savoring life—in a car. Learning to drive is a formative experience for many Americans. How many of us can remember when we first got our license, or the first car that was truly our own, when we could finally go anywhere we wanted, anytime?

But if we're a car culture, some things about that culture must change, as climate change becomes a greater threat, oil dependence deepens, and Americans spend more time in traffic with each passing year. We can't eliminate cars in the near future, but we can definitely create more attractive alternatives. This is the challenge: finding a way to decrease our need for cars and increase our quality of life at the same time. Put another way, how do we make other transportation options more attractive than the automobile, so that everybody wins?

We'll look at some practical solutions in this chapter. Some of these fixes will be immediate, such as embracing car shares or increasing funding for buses, bike paths, sidewalks, and light rail. Others may take up to a decade or more, such as rejuvenating Amtrak by establishing a new, homegrown system of American trains. Still other remedies—such as rethinking the layout of our communities so that jobs, recreation, and amenities are accessible by rail, bike, and foot—could take even longer. Each solution will require significant investment from the public and private sectors—but isn't that a better way to spend our dollars than on corporate handouts for oil and coal?

How to Run a Railroad

In the end, you get what you pay for. The reason Japan's trains are so efficient and popular is that the Japanese government has invested heavily to modernize its railway infrastructure. Beginning in the 1950s, Japanese citizens saw the development of a rapid public train system as integral to uniting the country and accelerating its economic growth. Although the operation of Japan's trains has been privatized since 1987, the government owns the tracks, leases them to private companies, and reinvests the revenues into research to make the trains even faster, safer, more energy efficient, and—along with Europe's railways—the envy of the world.

In contrast, U.S. transportation priorities have heavily favored the automobile over the last seventy years, starting with massive investment in the interstate highway system. Amtrak received about $1 billion in federal funds in 2003; adjusted for inflation, this is less than two-thirds of what the rail agency received twenty years earlier. Compare that with federal spending on highways and aviation, which has more than doubled in the same time period. Congress earmarked more than $49 billion for the Federal Highway and Federal Aviation Administrations in 2007.

> **Pass It On**
>
> Budgets matter. Passenger rail funding in 2003 was just two-thirds the amount spent in 1983. In the same period, federal outlays for planes and automobiles doubled. Even with some stimulus funds going to high-speed rail, those investments are a tiny portion of total transportation spending.

Total federal budget outlays for high-speed rail in 2006 and 2007 combined: $0. In a welcome shift, the Obama administration pushed for $8 billion in funding in the 2009 American Recovery and Reinvestment Act to launch this country's high-speed rail network. In 2010, an additional $2.5 billion was appropriated for high-speed rail.

Most of the stimulus money went to three major projects: a high-speed rail line linking Tampa and Orlando, Florida; a high-speed line between Southern and Northern California; and upgrades to existing lines connecting Chicago with St. Louis, Milwaukee, and Detroit. Some $2 billion was designated for incremental upgrades to existing Amtrak passenger rail service in twenty other states or for preliminary work on future high-speed rail lines. It's a start, but we need to make a long-term investment in a systemwide upgrade.

We also have to be smart about how we incorporate trains into our transportation mix. My enthusiasm for high-speed trains doesn't mean they're appropriate everywhere, though they certainly make for a wise investment in many high-traffic transportation corridors. But Amtrak opponents argue that the government has no business running a railroad at all. They say that all subsidies should be cut, the system handed over to corporations, and unprofitable runs shut down. They even point to Japan, arguing that after its railways were privatized, ridership continued to increase, earning corporate profits approaching $2 billion annually.

This argument ignores an important truth, however. Japanese taxpayers and those of other countries with advanced systems, such as France, Switzerland, Germany, and others, set a goal of having world-class railway systems. Each country made significant investments into their systems over several decades and are now enjoying the dividends. Even after privatization, Japan continues to invest billions each year into railway infrastructure and safety and design improvements.

America's big investments in infrastructure have historically provided a foundation for economic growth. We still enjoy the benefits of public works projects in the 1930s, 1940s, 1950s, and 1960s that gave us hundreds of buildings, public pools, trails in our national parks—and, yes, our interstate highway system and nearly every airport in the country. A similar investment in a national rail system today would reconnect and revitalize American cities. China invested $88 billion in railroad construction in 2009, an 80 percent increase over 2008 totals, and this will rise to $120 billion in 2010—much of it spent on the expansion of China's high-speed passenger rail. France and Germany each devote 20 percent of their entire transportation budget to rail. Even with the one-time injection of stimulus funds, Amtrak's budget is a tiny portion of our annual transportation outlays.

Trains can be an elegant way to travel and reduce gridlock, but they're also a climate-friendly mode of transport. A study commissioned for the Department of Energy by the Oak Ridge National Laboratory shows that domestic airlines consumed on average 20.5 percent more energy per passenger mile than Amtrak, while cars consumed 27.2 percent more energy. To the extent that we succeed in reducing our dependence on coal and greening our electricity grid, Amtrak's trains will become an even more efficient way to travel. And since some trains still run on diesel fuel, those engines need to be updated and more rail electrified.

In the end, it's a question of values and priorities. America deserves better than a third-rate rail system with technology several decades out of date. An ambitious public works program to rejuvenate the nation's passenger rail system and bring state-of-the-art high-speed rail to the United States could be one of the more effective long-term strategies to fight climate change. The alternative is to penny-pinch Amtrak and continue to devote billions in taxpayer funds to build more highways, airports, and parking lots, and hire more traffic cops.

If we choose that path, however, we might choke ourselves, literally. In the summer of 2008, 127 million Americans lived in counties that were in violation of federal Clean Air Act regulations. As the U.S. population grows and pollution levels increase, our roads will continue to be more and more crowded. According to the Texas Transportation Institute's 2009 Urban Mobility Report, traffic congestion is worsening in all of the nation's 437 urban areas. Heavy traffic caused 4.2 billion hours of travel delay in 2007 (the most recent year for which complete data were available). The typical commuter spent nearly a full workweek— thirty-eight hours—suffering through traffic congestion. Nationwide, this lost productivity costs the economy $87.2 billion annually. Put another way, 2.8 billion gallons of gas were wasted, enough to fill fifty-eight supertankers.

Ask yourself, isn't there a better way to get where we need to go? If Japan, France, Germany, Switzerland, and other countries can have modern, comfortable, and super-fast trains, why can't we? China is investing in high-speed trains. So is Mexico, with a planned 360-mile route from Guadalajara to Mexico City. Trains of all types can help America to decrease its oil consumption, relieve gridlock, and travel in a more relaxed and convenient style. By reinvesting in a beleaguered transportation sector, we can create new jobs and once again unleash the power of American ingenuity.

Transit-Oriented Development

The secret sauce for sustainable transportation and vibrant, convenient, walkable neighborhoods is diversity. "There is no 'magic' technology or solution on the horizon because there is no single cause of congestion," notes Tim Lomax, a research engineer at the Texas Transportation Institute. "The good news is that there are multiple strategies involving traffic operations and public transit available right now that if applied together, can lessen this problem."

Americans are far less likely to use public transportation than people in other countries, according to a 2009 report. Just 5 percent of Americans surveyed report daily use of public transportation, and only 7 percent report taking public transportation at least once a week. Only 18 percent of Americans say that public transportation is easily available to them, a far lower percentage than the international average, and 61 percent say that they never use public transportation. Only 26 percent of Americans regularly walk or bike to destinations, the survey found.

Promoting walking, biking, and transit use begins with the design and layout of our cities and towns. For much of the past seventy-five years, cheap gas and the rise of the automobile have made it possible for more Americans to move farther away from their jobs, resulting in the segregation of homes from offices and shopping, making the automobile central to daily existence. In many communities the corner store no longer exists, replaced by a strip mall supermarket with plenty of parking. Streetcar lines in hundreds of cities were ripped up long ago, with the encouragement of tire manufacturers and automobile companies. Commute distances to work lengthen for more Americans every year. In many communities, sidewalks don't even exist and bike paths are few and far between. Sprawl continues to devour agricultural land and open space. This growth in suburban development is dramatically but rightly characterized by author and vocal critic of American development James Howard Kunstler as "the greatest misallocation of resources in the history of the world."

A reformist philosophy of traditional neighborhood design known as the New Urbanist movement has emerged in the past few decades, primarily in response to sprawl and related trends. The movement seeks to "reestablish the relationship between the art of building and the making of community," according to the Congress for the New Urbanism. Its intention is to restore urban centers and towns as the true hubs of commercial and residential life and to foster a shared sense of community. New Urbanist planners favor compact, mixed-use neighborhoods, reducing dependence on the automobile by slowing down traffic, creating more local parks and public spaces, and making it easy to run errands on foot or by bike. Walkable, bikeable neighborhoods with public transit also reduce transportation costs and make housing more affordable.

I asked Shelley Poticha how this approach could help to promote greater transit use. Poticha has been the director of the Congress for the New Urbanism, president and CEO of Reconnecting America (a national organization working to integrate transportation systems and the communities they serve), and senior advisor for sustainable housing and communities at HUD. "It starts by making streets walkable," she answered. "Basically, unless a place is walkable, it's never going to be transit-friendly."

The idea is catching on. Maryland has adopted New Urbanist principles as a core element of its town planning. Towns such as Kentlands, Maryland; Seaside, Florida; and Austin, Texas, all have examples of New Urbanist design. Although New Urbanism has its critics—many argue that its standards are too prescriptive and its designs too homogeneous—planners are increasingly designing more compact urban and town centers.

Making a town or city friendly to pedestrians is just the beginning. Urban planners increasingly favor "transit-oriented development," or TOD, around streetcars and light-rail systems as a way to increase transit ridership, decrease traffic, and generally improve the quality of life in urban areas. TOD has been shown to increase property values around high-quality train systems, leading to a U.S. renaissance in light-rail systems, and particularly streetcars, in recent years: more than a hundred cities around the country have recently installed or are planning new streetcar lines, which are "a very low-cost way of developing high-quality transit," Poticha says.

One metropolitan area making great progress in promoting TOD is Denver. In 2004 its voters passed a $4.7 billion "FasTracks" ballot measure that will fund six new transit lines with 119 miles of track and seventy new transit stations in the next fifteen years. The Mile High city will also develop transit villages around these stations to provide a variety of housing and shopping choices within easy walking distance. "We're really focused on getting each stop to become a little village so there's not a sea of parking spaces," says Denver mayor John Hickenlooper. "People will actually be able to walk right from their home to the light rail and take [it] to work. . . . More families will be able to be a one-car family, instead of being a two- or even a three-car family."

In addition to states and municipalities, federal policymakers can play an important role in establishing priorities that will help reduce gridlock and emissions at the same time. The government funnels hundreds of billions of dollars each year to a range of transportation projects, from highways, bridges, and airports to bike paths and light rail. How those dollars are apportioned determines how efficient our transit systems can become. All too often, however, lawmakers have forgotten a key purpose of transportation funding: to make our towns and cities livelier, healthier, and more affordable. "We ought to be evaluating all our transportation investments against better standards: are those investments going to help us reduce our dependence on foreign oil, or reduce greenhouse gas emissions?" Poticha says. "Will they give people greater choice about how to get around? Will the investments stimulate local economic development?"

Congress failed to reauthorize the national transportation bill before it expired in 2009, instead allocating billions in funding to keep a broken system going. The next time Congress takes up the transportation challenge—still not on the horizon as this book's second edition came out—lawmakers should establish national goals for reducing oil consumption and pollution and hold states and local governments accountable. We need to invest in transportation choices that enable Americans to live and travel affordably and without oil. If all Americans recognized that transportation is about oil—and the $1 billion drained from our economy daily to pay for it—we would demand a system that keeps those dollars in our economy and moves us safely and efficiently without oil.

Pedal Power

Remember when you first learned how to ride a bike? Close your eyes, and you can probably remember the combination of nervousness and delight, wind blowing your hair, someone shouting encouragement behind you, handlebars shaking erratically. Learning to ride a bicycle is exhilarating and evokes strong feelings of autonomy and freedom. Making it easier for people of all ages to ride more frequently could also help bring us freedom from oil.

Getting into gear are some of America's largest cities, which see a win-win in reducing greenhouse gas emissions and other pollutants, as well as relieving gridlock. Mayor Michael Bloomberg has committed to have two hundred miles of bike trails in New York City by 2010. This total includes bike paths that are separate from road traffic, as well as bike lanes painted onto city streets. Similarly, Chicago is planning to have five hundred miles of bike trails by 2015. "We want to make Chicago the most bicycle-friendly city in the United States," says Chicago mayor and avid rider Richard M. Daley. Austin, Texas, will spend $250 million for new bike trails, including thirty-two miles through the town center. Also in Texas, Dallas/Fort Worth has $900 million in bicycle paths planned. "Texas is reaching out to embrace biking like never before," says Robin Stallins of the Texas Bicycle Coalition. "That says a lot about a shift of cultural values." Even the nation's capital is adding bike lines, including a new path down Pennsylvania Avenue.

> **Pass It On**
>
> New York and Chicago are planning two hundred and five hundred miles of bike trails, respectively. Austin is investing $250 million in bike transit; Dallas/Fort Worth, $900 million.

It also says a lot about the effectiveness of organizing by local citizens who seek to promote safe and clean transit. "The most important thing you can do to promote clean transit is to be an advocate," says Kristen Steele, communications director for the Alliance for Biking & Walking (formerly known as the Thunderhead Alliance), an organization that supports local bicycle-advocacy groups nationwide. Many of these groups, along with the AARP (formerly the American Association of Retired Persons) and others, are coordinating a "complete the streets" campaign, advocating more walkable and bicycle-friendly communities.

If you don't ride a bike, you can still help. One of the most effective ways to support both public transit use and cycling is to advocate for making them better integrated. Most people will walk to public transit if there is a bus or train stop within a half-mile radius—basically a ten-minute walk. Cyclists riding at a safe, easy speed can cover three to four times that distance in the same amount of time, increasing by up to ten times the total area in which commuters can conveniently take advantage of public transportation. An obvious solution, then, is to make it easier for people to ride their bikes to the bus or train.

Cyclists need to be able to either bring aboard or store their bikes securely at the train stop, or to rack them on a bus. It costs $10,000 to $12,000 to construct each auto parking space at a transit facility, compared with a few hundred for a rack or bike locker. Knowing this, some cities have made aggressive investments in racks and lockers and are enjoying the dividends of increased ridership. In Vancouver, for example, bicycle commuting increased by 30 percent following the installation of bike storage lockers at bus and train stops. In 1994, Seattle put bike racks on every bus, helping transit use to increase by 17 percent. A bike station installed at Washington, D.C.'s Union Station in 2010 provides rentals, safe locking, and other services. But only a third of all buses in North America currently have bike racks installed.

Storage is important, but safety is imperative. While in most American cities less than 4 percent of residents bike to work each day, in Copenhagen 35 percent do so. In Beijing, it's a shade over 30 percent; in Amsterdam, 40 percent. In the United States, Boulder leads with 21 percent. These cities promote cyclist- and pedestrian-first policies, with hundreds of miles of bike lanes—lanes that are raised, colored, or otherwise removed from oncoming traffic to separate motorists and cyclists. Other advantages include bike-only bridges, bicycle parking facilities, and special mirrors to avoid accidents at dangerous intersections.

In another move to reduce vehicle traffic and greenhouse gas emissions, cities in Europe, including Brussels, Lyon, Vienna, and Paris, make bicycles available for free or at a very low cost to tourists and residents alike. Paris has more than twenty thousand bikes available at nearly fifteen hundred locations across the city, or approximately one bike station every 250 yards. The first half-hour of usage is free. Parisians use them like cars to run errands around town. The city estimates that each bicycle will be used about twelve times a day, for a total of about 250,000 daily trips across the city, or 91 million per year. And we've made some progress on the home front: besides adding bike lanes, D.C. initiated the first U.S. public bike-sharing program in 2008, which is growing apace.

Cycling keeps you healthy, saves money, and means less grit and grime in the air. It also helps make cities quieter, more peaceful, and to many, more beautiful. "Look, I know that promoting bike use is good for the climate and reduces pollution and all that," says Leah Shahum, executive director of the San Francisco Bicycle Coalition. "But I just love my city, and I know that getting more cars off the road makes San Francisco a more beautiful and civilized place to live."

Get on the Bus

Let's face it: there aren't many bus groupies out there. Some people visit Japan, Germany, or France and remark about the beauty and sophistication of the country's trains. Others wax poetic about the elegant simplicity of the biking cultures of the Netherlands and China. But how frequently do you hear people purr with delight about a city's bus system? Buses are the workhorse of transportation networks. They don't get the glory, but they do get the job done—and help those who need transit options the most. For millions of Americans, buses are the most convenient form of transportation. And for millions of others who are disabled, elderly nondrivers, or too poor to own a car, bus transportation provides vital access to food, medical care, and the outside world. Since they don't require an airport or rail lines, buses are also the most flexible. All you need are passengers and roads (and a bus, of course).

OK, so you might not regularly subscribe to *Bus Transit Quarterly,* and *Innovations in Public Transportation* rarely finds itself on your bedside nightstand. That's all right.

Pass It On

As of 2008, hybrid buses and those fueled by natural gas or biodiesel made up nearly 30 percent of all transit buses. Raising that number still higher will make our cities better places to live.

Just remember this: BRT. The increasing utilization of Bus Rapid Transit systems (BRT) is easily the most promising innovation in the world of inner city transit.

What BRT does is revolutionize the bus-riding experience. Gone are the days of slow, bumpy, lurching rides in buses belching smoke. BRT has low-riding, comfortable coaches (many, like the bus I ride, with wireless technology). They are cleaner-burning and make fewer stops; many run in lanes designated for buses only; some also have the ability to switch stoplights from red to green

Pass It On

Public transportation currently saves 4.2 billion gallons of gasoline each year, enough to fill a supertanker leaving the Persian Gulf every few days, even though highways and roads continue to get the lion's share of transportation dollars.

as they approach. BRT lines typically cut trip times in half and have increased ridership by more than 50 percent in many areas, enticing ever more commuters out of their cars. Further, many mass transit systems are purchasing hybrid-electric buses, which reduce gas consumption and cut down on soot by as much as 90 percent. As of 2008, hybrid buses and those fueled by natural gas or biodiesel were common in public transit systems, making up nearly 30 percent of all transit buses, according to the American Public Transportation Association.

When you add it all up, U.S. public transportation currently saves 4.2 billion gallons of gasoline each year and reduces our carbon footprint by 37 million metric tons of emissions. Yet highways and roads continue to get the lion's share of transportation dollars. This must change when Congress gets moving on the next (overdue) transportation bill. We need to maintain the infrastructure we currently have, but it's critical to begin building out the new infrastructure we'll need to move beyond oil. You'll find ways to help modernize America's transportation systems in the "Take Action" section at the end of this chapter.

One Car, Many Drivers

Redesigning mobility isn't just limited to public transportation; it also includes, yes, cars. Cyclists might teach us to share the road, but we can also share our cars.

If you live in a major city, you've probably seen gas stations and corner parking lots become home to small cohorts of snazzily marked cars. A "car share" is a membership club that gives people access to a fleet of vehicles located throughout a city or region. They're different from rental agencies in that the cars are often used for just a few hours and are located in the middle of city neighborhoods, rather than in airports or other, often remote, locations. "We are trying to replace car ownership," said Scott Griffith, Zipcar's chief executive. "It's a business model that locates cars in neighborhoods and uses twenty-four-hour technology to locate the car."

Car shares are easy and cheap, for short trips. Members can reserve a car online for a couple of hours, a day or weekend, or longer. They can rent a truck for moving, a convertible for the weekend, or a hybrid just because. Most members join a car share because they realize that they can walk, bike, or take transit for work and most errands, and then get the car for weekend trips, grocery shopping, or whatever. There's no hassle: the company cleans the car and takes care of oil changes, repairs, car insurance, and all maintenance. Even the gas is included in the fee.

Car shares can be an important way to reduce reliance on the automobile. Think of them as a kind of halfway house for auto addicts. There are more than a dozen nonprofit car-share organizations located throughout the United States, as well as at least one for-profit business, Zipcar—which in 2010 had more than four hundred thousand members and seven thousand vehicles throughout the United States, Canada, and the United Kingdom. Car sharing has helped more than 40 percent of Zipcar members to either sell their car or forgo buying one altogether. Research by the company shows that each Zipcar takes fifteen to twenty other vehicles off the road and that 90 percent of members drove fifty-five hundred miles or fewer yearly once they had joined. The company estimates that this leaves a total of 32 million gallons of crude oil in the ground each year.

Pass It On

Getting more cars off the road makes us healthier: in the summer of 2008, 127 million Americans lived in counties that were in violation of federal Clean Air Act regulations.

Individuals joining car-share programs report a 47 percent increase in public transit trips, a 10 percent increase in bicycling trips, and a 26 percent increase in walking trips. The cars are currently available in hundreds of locations: mostly urban centers but also smaller towns and college campuses. If you live on a farm or out in the country, car shares probably aren't for you. But if you live in a city or town that has one, then you might have the best of all worlds by saving money and hassle while having access to a car when you need it.

Essentially, car shares can help fill in the gaps as America shifts to a more sustainable transportation system. Although we have a long way to go in building such a system, we'll know we're getting close when getting in the car starts to seem less convenient than other options. We'll no longer be solely dependent on personal vehicles to shop, work, and play. We'll have more choices that are efficient and that work well together, so that we can pick the best form of transportation for a particular task, whether it's walking to a nearby store or place of work; taking a bullet train to a city a few hundred miles away; hopping on a bus, subway, or ferry; riding a bike; or using car share. The genius will be in cultivating an easy complexity. It may be a long journey, but it'll be a great ride along the way.

Take Action

Take it personally

1. Each of us decides where we live and work. Some have fewer options; others have more flexibility. If you do have a choice, make it a conscious one. By living near mass transit or close to where you work, you'll spend less time in traffic and less money on gas, use less oil, and create fewer emissions. Try calculating the walkability of your neighborhood—or of a place you're considering moving to—at www.walkscore.com/.

2. Once you're settled, resolve to walk, bike, or take transit when you can and drive only when you must. Dust off your bike, inflate the tires, and hit the road. Join a car share. Grab your iPod or a book and hop on the bus. Even one day a week makes a difference.

3. Get involved. Your town's planning commission makes important decisions about whether we have more strip malls or walkable communities. Our federal, state, and local tax dollars are spent on a long list of transit projects (and a lot more on highways). Should we invest more transportation dollars in trains, bike paths, and rapid-transit systems? Explore the groups listed in the Resources section, follow the news, and share your opinions with officials and candidates for office.

Express yourself

1. *At your workplace.* Some states and cities allow employers to offer incentives to take mass transit, such as pretax vouchers. Does yours? Is there space available for employees to store bicycles? Make sure that your company is part of the solution.

2. ***At your school.*** Help create walkable communities by signing up your school for the International Walk to School Day. (See www.walktoschool.org/downloads/WTS-report-2009.pdf.) In 2007, more than twenty-seven hundred schools from all fifty states participated. You can also initiate a Safe Routes to School program—see www.saferoutesinfo.org.

3. ***Take the train.*** We can start by fully funding Amtrak and then make significant and strategic investments to modernize and update our train systems. Lobby your local politicians until they get on board. High-speed trains are coming to the United States; see www.fra.dot.gov/Pages/203.shtml for a list of high-speed rail corridors. Or join groups such as the Midwest High Speed Rail Association and the National Association of Railroad Passengers, which support high-speed rail lines across the country.

4. ***Get on the bus.*** Join a local bus riders' union and lobby for affordable, efficient, and environmentally smart mass transit. The Los Angeles Bus Riders Union (www.busridersunion.org) works to reduce fares and increase service to promote sustainable transit for all. Help bus systems in other cities secure a greater share of state and federal financing. Don't have a union in your area? Start one, or at least ask friends to join you in writing to local officials for more balanced financing. Transit and buses face big recession-linked cutbacks; we need to engage now to sustain operating support for transit.

5. ***Hop on a bike.*** Use your own bike, but don't stop there. You can support local cycling organizations and lobby officials for more bike-friendly transit, safe bike trails and lanes, and storage at train stations and on buses. An effective national group is the League of American Bicyclists (www.bikeleague.org).

6. ***Tell your representatives in Congress*** that it's time to pass a transportation bill that moves us beyond oil; creates choices for Americans in rail, transit, biking, and walking; and invests in fixing the roads and bridges we have. Remind them that we waste billions every day they delay action. Also ask officials in your state department of transportation and your regional or metropolitan planning organization what they are doing to help create a twenty-first-century transportation system.

Stay engaged

Adopt a project. What do you care about most? If you're inspired by the idea of a modern train system in the United States, then make that an effort in which you stay active for the long haul. Have fire in your belly about buses or bikes? Lobby for better service, a street path, bike lane, bike racks, or other project; find a local group or start your own. And if you want to influence the next national transportation bill when Congress takes this up, join one of the organizations listed in the Resources section to stay involved.

CHAPTER 6

Jump-Start Detroit

How Automakers Can Save Themselves, and the Planet

*If we are going to create jobs—good, family-sustaining
manufacturing jobs—we are going to do it with clean
vehicles, mass transportation, and renewable power.
There are no other markets with this potential.*

— Lynn Hinkle, United Auto Workers,
Local 879, Minnesota

The woman's voice on the voice mail at Rainforest Action Network was anxious but determined.

"Jennifer, this is Heather. Ford wants its truck back—and the representative is getting pretty insistent. I think we need to do something."

Heather Bernikoff-Raboy and her husband, Dave Bernikoff-Raboy, live on a 160-acre ranch in the foothills of the Sierra Nevada. Dave is a software engineer turned rancher, and Heather, a former health care professional. They're both passionate about electric vehicles and how they help reduce American oil consumption.

"We use the Ranger for just about everything on the ranch—we've even towed a forklift out of the mud with it," says Dave. "It's all-electric, and with our solar panels, the cost to run the truck is almost nothing. It requires hardly any maintenance, no oil, and no gas. Nothing. People stop me on the street all the time and ask me how they can get one of these trucks for themselves."

The Bernikoff-Raboys acquired their electric Ford Ranger in April 2001 through Ford Motor Company's GreenLease program. In January 2004, the company sent the Bernikoff-Raboys a letter giving them the option "to make arrangements to purchase the leased vehicle," adding, "Ford Credit can finance the purchase." Dave sent a certified letter to Ford accepting its offer of sale, and after the lease expired he continued to send payments, which the company deposited.

Then they were told that a mistake had been made. On November 18, 2004, Ford sent another letter to the Bernikoff-Raboys, this time reneging on its sales agreement: "Unfortunately, there is no possibility to extend your lease or for you to purchase your vehicle."

The Bernikoff-Raboys had driven the Ranger on the ranch for three and a half years and didn't want to go back to another gas-guzzler. They thought it was strange that Ford was refusing to sell them the Ranger EV, but they weren't surprised. The company wasn't quite pulling out all the stops to market these vehicles. "We had to search online to find this truck, and when we went to lease it, the salesman was not enthusiastic," Heather recalls. "The truck was practically hidden at the back of the lot. And they couldn't even find the key! We had to wait an hour while the dealership got a locksmith to come out and make us a new one."

The Bernikoff-Raboys' experience was not unique. Some research revealed that other Ranger EV owners were also being asked to turn in their trucks, as were the owners of Ford's electric Th!nk vehicles. At the same time, Toyota, Honda, and Nissan were reclaiming their electric vehicles, and GM was taking back its EV1, as depicted in the movie *Who Killed the Electric Car.* The automakers' plan was to take all the electric vehicles off the road, crush them, and turn them into scrap.

Here's a little background on this story. In 1990, the California Air Resources Board, in an attempt to reduce smog and other pollutants, mandated that 5 percent of all vehicles made for California produce zero emissions by 2001. The auto industry vigorously opposed the rule, arguing that (a) the technology for zero-emission vehicles wasn't ready, (b) even if it was ready, the vehicles would be too expensive, and (c) there wasn't enough demand for pollution-free vehicles anyway. Reluctantly, however, automakers began manufacturing thousands of electric cars and trucks to meet the mandate, all the while arguing that the burden of producing them was too onerous. The vehicles were a hit with customers, but the automakers weren't interested in expanding their electric-vehicle programs. Once the Air Resources Board rescinded the zero-emission-vehicle mandate, the auto industry moved quickly to pull its electric cars off the road.

"It didn't make sense to us," says Heather. "Electric vehicles don't have a tailpipe and don't emit any smog or greenhouse gases. The Central Valley of California has some of the highest asthma rates in the state. We thought it was criminal that Ford and everyone else would forcibly take these vehicles off the road."

The Bernikoff-Raboys were ready to take action. They contacted Jennifer Krill and Jason Mark, program directors at Rainforest Action Network and Global Exchange. Krill and Mark had recently helped to prevent several dozen all-electric Th!nk vehicles from being crushed and would later help protect more than a thousand Toyota electric RAV4s from the same fate—all part of a national campaign to compel Ford and other automakers to build zero-emission vehicles nationwide.

Dave and Heather didn't consider themselves protesters, but they wanted to do something to keep their truck on the road. Together with Krill and Mark, they hatched a plot to stage a literal auto "sit-in." Think of it as a Charlton Heston–inspired demonstration: they'd drive to the Ford dealership, alert the media, and dare the company to pry the truck from their cold, well . . . maybe not dead, fingers. The gamble was that Ford would blink—that the company couldn't possibly be so determined to crush these vehicles that they'd risk such negative publicity. When Heather received a call from Ford in January 2005 that their truck would soon be seized, the plan went into motion.

Joined by Bill Korthoff, who brought his own Ranger EV, and some other supporters, the Bernikoff-Raboys staged a round-the-clock vigil in their truck outside the Downtown Ford dealership in Sacramento. "That first night was pretty cold and lonely," Heather said, recalling how they shivered in the foggy, freezing winter weather. But the media coverage made the sacrifice worthwhile. An article in the *Los Angeles Times* quoted Dave: "If this truck was good enough that Bill Ford drove it to work every day, how come it's not good enough for me to buy? How come they're not going back and getting all the Pintos? How about the Excursion—it's being discontinued. It gets 12 miles per gallon. Why not go back and crush all of those?"

News reports on television soon made the group minor celebrities. As the days passed, local residents came to share a drink, deliver hot coffee and home-cooked meals, and take pictures with their kids under the "Declare Independence from Oil" banner that hung from the trucks.

On the seventh day, Ford relented, offering to sell Ranger EVs back to their lessees for $1. The Bernkikoff-Raboys and other EV owners were happy to purchase their vehicles but amazed that Ford needed to be pressured at all. "It's unfortunate it took this level of effort to get them to do the right thing," Dave told a reporter.

By the time Ford reconsidered, only a few hundred electric Rangers were still on the road. More than a thousand electric Ford Th!nk, Toyota RAV4s, and other electric vehicles were also saved, but thousands of others were crushed. "I wish every single one of our products generated as much customer passion," said Niel Golightly, Ford's director of environmental strategies. If Ford produced more electric vehicles, maybe that would be the case.

In the end, Ford and other automakers had made a big mistake: they had infuriated loyal customers and inspired them to get organized. The former drivers of those vehicles know what it's like to have cars and trucks that don't run on gas. They've continued to pressure the automotive industry, and the impact is starting to be felt—along with uncertain gas prices and the fact that Congress and the EPA have finally acted to raise fuel economy and greenhouse gas standards. Automakers, including GM, Nissan, BMW, VW, and Toyota, are all bringing electric vehicles to market in 2010 or 2011. The question is how fast the market will grow. With any luck, you may soon be driving an electric car.

Internally Combusting

It's exasperating. One of the best opportunities to fight climate change and beat America's addiction to oil was completely ignored by federal policymakers and major automakers for almost three decades: namely, raising fuel economy (mileage) standards for new cars and light trucks. Standards set back in 1975 mandated a goal of 27.5 miles per gallon, but once that average was reached in the late 1980s, automakers successfully resisted further improvements until 2007. Passage of the Energy Independence and Security Act that year got the ball rolling, calling for new vehicles to average 35 miles per gallon by 2020.

The Obama administration pushed things along, with goals of 35.5 miles per gallon by 2016 and first-time-ever improvements for medium and heavy trucks. The administration will soon set mandates for fuel economy for vehicles produced all the way through 2030. Raising greenhouse gas standards for all vehicles, part of the administration's package, would be one more step to ushering out the internal combustion engine and ushering in advanced hybrids and electric vehicles.

Still, 2030 is a long way away, and we're still just tinkering when what we need is a breakthrough strategy. Here's the reality that we face: one out of every seven barrels of the world's oil is consumed on American highways. When you factor in trucking, shipping, and airlines, 70 percent of the nearly 20 million barrels of oil we consume daily is used for transportation. America's cars and light trucks alone emit more greenhouse gases than any country in the world except China, the United States, Russia, and Japan.

The problem will get worse before it gets better. In 1950, there were 50 million cars and trucks on the planet. In 2008 there were about 668 million. Within twenty years, there will be more than 1 billion.

Here's the kicker. Technology available today could make a huge dent in this problem, but it's barely being utilized by automakers. An analysis done by the Union of Concerned Scientists and the Center for Auto Safety in 2001 showed that a national fleet average of fifty-five miles per gallon was achievable using technologies in existence back in 2001, including hybrid-electric engines. Hitting this average would save more oil each year than the United States uses from the entire Persian Gulf and California coast, as well as the oil believed to be in the Arctic National Wildlife Refuge. Notably, that report was released way back in 2001, but its point remains valid: technology is the key to swapping our gas-guzzlers for gas-sippers or not using gasoline at all. Since then, hybrid and electric battery technologies have advanced considerably. Plug-in hybrid electric vehicles—where no gas is used for the

Pass It On

There are 670 million cars on the road globally, up from 50 million in 1950. By 2025, there will be more than 1 billion. Transportation accounts for 70 percent of U.S. oil consumption, and today's automobiles are 97 percent reliant on oil as a fuel.

majority of trips—can boost fuel efficiency to more than a hundred miles per gallon. That's utilizing existing technology—no new inventions required. Using lightweight materials as recommended by the Rocky Mountain Institute can yield even greater increases, while not sacrificing safety or performance.

And the rebirth of electric vehicles might change the automotive industry completely. General Motors' Volt will debut late in 2010. Nissan has staked its reputation on the Leaf, an all-electric car that will travel one hundred miles or so on a single charge. Other automakers are rushing to add gas-optional offerings to the mix. Toyota's first plug-in hybrids are due in 2012. Ford will sell ten thousand versions of its electric Focus in 2011. Mitsubishi's four-door electric hatchback will be sold to fleet customers late in 2010. The number of vehicles will be small to start with, but the future could bring us an oil-free option.

"Clearly, the entire industry could build nothing but zero-emission cars today if it wanted to," said Ford's Niel Golightly way back in 2004. But besides a handful of electric and plug-in hybrid electric vehicles that exist now or that the major automakers promise are just around the corner, the industry continues to churn out gas-guzzling cars and SUVs by the millions. What's preventing change? The same list of reasons that the industry used in California: that the technology isn't ready, it's too expensive, and customers don't really want fuel-efficient cars (even though they say they do).

Let's put the old objections of automakers into perspective. This is the same industry that fought taking lead out of gasoline and using catalytic converters to reduce toxic emissions in the 1970s. America's automakers also fought mandatory seat-belt laws, resisted making air bags standard in all vehicles, and insist on using manual typewriters instead of computers in all their offices.

OK, that last part isn't true. But seriously, domestic automakers are rarely accused of being enthusiastic innovators when it comes to safety or fuel economy. Some automakers have attempted to deflect criticism with the promise of hydrogen-fueled vehicles. But those vehicles remain on the horizon; they would require both generating a fuel and retrofitting every gas station in the country.

We deserve better. Remember, the top-selling truck in America, the Ford F-150, gets lower gas mileage today than did the Model T in the beginning of the twentieth century, even with today's new engines. When automakers came

Pass It On

The average fuel economy for passenger vehicles has hovered around twenty-five miles per gallon for more than twenty years. The Ford F-150, America's best-selling truck, gets less gas mileage today than did the Model T from early in the twentieth century.

to Washington in June 2007 to discourage senators from raising fuel-economy standards, they met a cool reception from some. "I think the issue is over. I think you've lost that issue," said Senator Byron Dorgan of North Dakota. "I think your position is 'yesterday forever.'"

The industry's stubbornness was compounded by the unwillingness of federal regulators to give it tough love. Led by the congressional delegation from Michigan, lawmakers routinely blocked legislation that would boost mileage standards significantly. That changed somewhat with the 2007 energy bill and, as noted, the Obama administration is also moving ahead to set the bar through 2025 and take on heavy-duty trucks as well. But the time to drive automotive technology out of the oil age is now. Even with the progress we've made, we lag behind Japan, the European Union, and even China when it comes to fuel economy or greenhouse gas standards.

The American auto industry paid the price for its inflexibility, having hemorrhaged money and workers. GM lost $2 billion in 2006; Ford lost $12.6 billion, or the cost of a $25,000 Mustang nearly every minute. In the late 1990s, GM had 225,000 workers; by 2007 there were only 73,000. In 2008, GM and Chrysler hit rock bottom and required a massive taxpayer-funded bailout. Ford, which avoided bankruptcy and bailout, also laid off tens of thousands of workers; among those were nearly two thousand employees at Ford's Twin Cities Automotive Plant in St. Paul, Minnesota. The plant, which operated on clean energy from the 18-megawatt hydroelectric plant on the Mississippi River, made Ranger pickups and EVs like the one the Bernikoff-Raboys drive. In late 2005, Ford revealed that the plant was to be shut down, part of the company's massive layoff and restructuring plan, which management perversely named "The Way Forward."

One of the Twin Cities plant workers, Lynn Hinkle, flew with others to Ford's headquarters in Dearborn, Michigan, to propose converting the plant to produce hybrid or other fuel-efficient vehicles or trucks that would run on biofuels (so-called flexible-fuel vehicles, discussed in the next chapter). Given the strong demand for Toyota's hybrids, Hinkle was optimistic. "We felt that if Ford would capitalize on this market, it would be a win-win for everybody. A green plant producing green cars ... the impact on Ford's brand would have been enormous," he told me. However, the plan was quickly rejected. The St. Paul plant is still turning out Rangers, but Ford plans to close it in 2011.

American autoworkers used to be the backbone of the U.S. economy, part of a proud and prosperous working class. They could be so again. One study calculated that reaching an average fuel efficiency of just forty miles per gallon by 2015 would lead to 161,000 more jobs, including 40,800 in the auto industry, and save consumers an annual $23 billion to boot. Progress has been made, but the historic resistance of federal lawmakers to push for strong standards that would modernize the industry set a pattern that *New York Times* columnist Thomas Friedman was fond of calling an "assisted suicide."

It's time to stop playing small ball over tiny increases in fuel economy and greenhouse gas standards when a complete automotive revolution is not only required but achievable. We don't need dramatic breakthroughs or new inventions to rescue the United States from its oil dependence. Game-changing solutions are available today. Our country has the technology, the resources, and the know-how to build clean cars and to dramatically reduce our use of dirty oil. The only thing we lack is the political courage to make the profound changes that the industry needs to thrive in a world with climate change and dwindling oil supplies.

In the sections to come, I'll discuss the innovators and advocates who will soon take plug-in hybrid and electric vehicles to the mainstream, and the Silicon Valley entrepreneurs who are making some of the fastest—and cleanest—cars on the planet. I'll also describe the policies that could help kick-start an automotive revolution, and suggest ways to make sure that revolution actually happens. First let's meet the godfather of the plug-in hybrid engine: a professor from California's Central Valley.

Plug It In!

It's said there are two ways of teaching people to swim: give them lessons or just throw them in the water. Professor Andrew Frank learned about automobiles the harder way.

"My father bought a car for me in 1948 for about $25," Frank recalls. "It was a '29 Nash, but it didn't run. My dad said, 'Well, son, you're kinda interested in cars. Why don't you fix it? Make it run, and it's yours.'"

Frank chuckles. "I was up for the challenge. I not only fixed it but turned it into a hot rod. Chopped the engine out, replaced it, took the top off, the whole thing."

Having first taught himself, Frank has been teaching others for more than forty years, first electrical engineering at the University of Wisconsin, then mechanical engineering at the University of California at Davis. He's also been watching—and trying to work with—the auto industry. "I remember that when Toyota first introduced the Prius in 1997, American carmakers were ecstatic. They said that if Toyota really pushed their hybrid program, they'd go out of business!" Frank laughed.

In April 2007, Toyota overtook General Motors as the world's largest, and most profitable, automaker. A year later, the company announced it had sold its millionth hybrid vehicle worldwide. Sixty percent of those were sold in the United States.

Frank is working to promote the next generation of efficient vehicles, plug-in hybrids. Hybrid engines like those used in the Toyota Prius, Honda Civic, or Ford Escape use a combination of gas and electric power. Plug-in hybrids, by contrast, use electric power for a range of thirty to sixty miles and rely on a combination of gas and electric power for longer trips. Moreover, a study from the U.S. Department of Energy showed that plug-in hybrids reduced greenhouse gas emissions in forty-nine states across the country—even in states that were heavily dependent on coal to generate power. States that use large amounts of hydroelectric power, such as Washington and Idaho, produce emission savings of more than 80 percent with plug-in hybrids. North Dakota, which relies upon coal that is particularly low in energy output, won't enjoy any savings from plug-ins until it cleans its electricity grid.

Chelsea Sexton, a former GM employee featured in *Who Killed the Electric Car?* promoted the electric EV1 until it was discontinued. She says that plug-in hybrids are "the best of both worlds" between hybrids and electric cars. "Maybe your first forty miles of the day are all electric," Sexton says. "Monday through Friday you may never use gasoline. But if you want to drive to Vegas on the weekend, you have gasoline in the tank as a backup. We call plug-in hybrids 'electric cars with a safety net!'" In ironic accord with Sexton is former GM CEO Rick Wagoner, forced to resign during the federal bailout of GM: asked to name his worst decision during an interview with *Motor Trend* magazine, Wagoner said, "Axing the EV1 electric-car program and not putting the right resources into hybrids."

A typical hybrid gets twice the gas mileage of your average gas-powered car, and plug-ins get about twice the mileage of a typical hybrid. Since 78 percent of all commuters live within twenty miles of their employers, plug-in hybrids would produce zero emissions from the tailpipe and use not a single drop of gasoline for most trips. Most of the converted plug-in hybrids on the road today exceed a hundred miles per gallon. On longer voyages, to go camping or to visit grandma for the weekend, a combination of gas and electric power gives plug-in hybrids a range of four to five hundred miles on a tank of gas. After that, drivers can just pull into any gas station, fill up, and go. Frank estimates that a plug-in vehicle would cost about $4,000 to $6,000 more than a conventional car. "That's what some people pay for a sunroof, leather seats and a fancy navigation system," he says.

Pass It On

Plug-in hybrid vehicles can travel more than a hundred miles per gallon of gas. Vehicles can drive up to forty or fifty miles on a single charge, and they can recharge the electrical battery at the equivalent of $0.75 to $1.00 per gallon.

Frank has been advancing plug-in hybrid automotive technology for years. He built his first plug-in hybrid in 1971, as part of a Department of Transportation contest on the future of urban driving. In the mid-1990s Frank and his UC Davis students designed a series of improved plug-in hybrid vehicles that achieved far better mileage than anything Detroit was putting on the road. Frank offered the technology to major automakers, but everyone passed.

Several years ago, Frank and his team made further advancements. They modernized a 2002 Ford Explorer, producing a 325 horsepower vehicle that could go fifty miles on a single electric charge and get twice the gas mileage of a hybrid vehicle. Once again, Frank offered the technology to major automakers. Once again, everyone passed—except Toyota. The automaker sent a team to

Davis, California, that packed up the entire vehicle, shipped it to Japan, put it through a battery of tests, and returned it a few months later.

On a hot summer day in late June 2007, Frank told me he had recently formed his own company, Efficient Designs. He had spent the morning with an official from India and much of the afternoon with officials from China. He was planning a presentation on plug-in hybrid technology for the Chinese government later that year. "We're talking about a mandate to increase production volumes for plug-in hybrids in the near future," he said. "China could do it, and do it quickly, and if a 'low-tech' country such as India or China leapt ahead of the United States, then maybe then U.S. car companies would pay attention."

It could be a Sputnik moment.

Taking Plug-Ins Mainstream

Fortunately, we are no longer left waiting for Detroit to voluntarily mass-produce vehicles that sip rather than chug gasoline. The constellation of individuals, entrepreneurs, and organizations that emerged to pressure automakers and regulators to get moving spanned the political spectrum. The effort boasted support from Hollywood celebrities and businesses alike. "I call this a coalition of the tree huggers, do-gooders, sod-busters, cheap hawks, evangelicals, utility shareholders, mom and pop drivers . . . and Willie Nelson," says R. James Woolsey, former CIA director, conservative war hawk, and plug-in hybrid enthusiast.

Plug In America is one organization leading the way. Founded by ex–GM employee Sexton and other electric-vehicle enthusiasts, it held one of its first meetings in Dave Bernikoff-Raboy's living room. The organization lists ways for its members to take action to accelerate the transition to oil-free vehicles. "I think it is important for government to set standards making cleaner cars because what we know for sure is that Detroit doesn't have a history of wanting to do it on their own," Sexton observes.

Plug-In Partners, an organization founded by the city of Austin, Texas, has organized hundreds of cities, states, and businesses to push for the rapid production of plug-in hybrid vehicles. The coalition—which includes the cities of Anchorage, Chicago, Miami, Chapel Hill, and Salt Lake City; organizations such as Goodwill and Meals on Wheels; major utilities such as Pacific Gas and Electric; and companies such as Advanced Micro Devices and Auto Nation (the country's largest auto dealership)—is collecting vehicle orders to demonstrate the growing demand for plug-ins. "We believe that the 50 largest cities in the United States, united in purpose, can build a groundswell in demand sufficient enough to entice automakers to mass produce" these vehicles, says Will Wynn, Austin's mayor.

Unwilling to wait for the automakers, several groups began helping people to convert existing hybrids into plug-in ones. Felix Kramer founded CalCars in 2004, soon after buying his Toyota Prius. Like many Prius owners, he wondered about the purpose of the nonfunctioning, unmarked button just to the right of the steering wheel. A little online research revealed that in Japanese and European models, pressing the button allowed the car to run exclusively on electric power. However, since the U.S. Prius batteries were so small, the car could drive only one to two miles on the electrical charge.

An engineer in Texas had figured out how to program U.S. vehicles to use the electric power in a way similar to the Japanese and European models. CalCars soon published a manual on how to convert the Prius into a plug-in hybrid that travels a hundred miles per gallon or more. Other than devoting a small portion of the trunk's space to a pack of batteries, the car looks and rides like a typical car, only one that gets four times the mileage of your everyday sedan. The biggest challenge remains convincing Detroit to bring these vehicles to market quickly, says Kramer. "How do you take an idea that makes sense into something real? Plug-ins are cleaner, cheaper, and domestic. We can electrify transportation, and then clean the grid. This will do more than anything to solve global warming."

Lithium ion battery manufacturer A123 Systems began marketing battery packs and training third-party mechanics to perform plug-in hybrid conversions in 2008. The company's CEO, David Vries, then estimated that a typical conversion would take two hours and cost $10,000. For an average commuter driving a vehicle eleven thousand miles per year, the time needed to realize that amount in savings would be 5.5 years (with gas at $3 per gallon). A federal tax credit established in the 2009 stimulus bill covers up to 10 percent of the conversion cost—at most $4,000—cutting the payback time considerably. Most important, the costs are expected to drop significantly as economies of scale are achieved. "We estimate a fivefold increase in demand from an increasingly responsive American public," Vries said. The Silicon Valley Leadership Group announced in September 2007 that a hundred of its CEOs pledged to buy converted plug-ins in 2008.

Another company that did not wait for Washington or Detroit to show the way is California-based startup Tesla Motor Company. Backed by deep-pocketed investors such as Google founders Larry Page and Sergey Brin, PayPal founder Elon Musk, and eBay founder Jeffrey Skoll, in 2007 it was a small firm with some big goals. "Whether it's because of high oil prices or climate change, we essentially have to retool the entire automotive industry," says JB Straubel, Tesla's chief technical officer. Tesla got off to a good start with its first electric vehicle: the Tesla Roadster can travel about 220 miles on a single charge. It beats the Lamborghini Murcielago and is quicker than any Porsche currently in production, traveling from zero to sixty in under four

Pass It On

The Tesla Roadster is an electric car that can go from zero to sixty in four seconds and travel 220 miles on a single electrical charge.

seconds—without a drop of gas. The original price was a cool $92,000, yet the company's first edition of one hundred Roadsters sold out in weeks.

I went for a test ride at the company's headquarters in San Carlos one bright February morning. As we cruised through the hills above Silicon Valley, the company's strategy became perfectly clear: Tesla wanted to help "retool" the auto industry by getting people excited about cars again. Because this car was fast. I felt like a pilot on *Battlestar Galactica* as the car accelerated, pushing me back in my seat. Tesla employees have a favorite trick to pull on passengers taking their first rides: he or she is asked to turn on the radio—and simultaneously the driver hits the accelerator. The passenger can't sit forward enough to reach the dials.

Tesla took a big step forward in May 2010, when it purchased the NUMMI auto manufacturing plant in Fremont, California. Its partner in the purchase, Toyota, formerly shared the plant with GM. As the company stated to the press,

"Tesla's goal is to produce increasingly affordable electric cars for mainstream buyers—relentlessly driving down the cost of EVs."

Tesla plans to develop a new electric RAV4 with Toyota, along with its three-hundred-mile range Model S sedan for the family car market, slated for 2012. "We've always envisioned the company to be more than a high-end niche sports-car manufacturer," says Straubel. "It's a great way to change the world's perceptions of EVs and to show what electric cars can do, but we want to make affordable vehicles in much greater quantities." Adds Musk, Tesla's chairman, "Climate change is the biggest challenge that mankind has ever faced. If we can't change such a simple thing as the cars we drive, we're going to be in trouble."

Mobile Power Plants

On a sunny California afternoon in June 2007, about two hundred staff, guests, and media stood in the parking lot of Google's headquarters. Google's nonprofit division, Google.org, had just finished a press conference to announce several new climate-change projects as part of its new RechargeIT program. The search-engine giant had recently made plug-ins from four Toyota Priuses and two Ford Escape hybrids, and had committed to converting up to a hundred more cars. They also had installed the country's largest commercial solar array, 1.6 megawatts, so that the new plug-in cars—and a substantial portion of Google's headquarters—could be powered by renewable energy.

But perhaps the most visionary demonstration that day was to showcase a technology called vehicle-to-grid power, or V2G. Envisioned by Willett Kempton at the University of Delaware, this technology helps plug-ins and electric vehicles address a fundamental problem with the power grid: "The electrical system has no way of storing energy. When you turn on a light switch, somebody has to turn on a power plant somewhere to create the power," describes Frank.

There are various ways to store electricity for the power grid. One is with batteries, which are limited by high costs and relatively short life spans (although experimental sodium-sulfur batteries hold some promise). There are also mechanical processes, such as compressing air or pumping water up a hill when excess electricity is available. These methods are also expensive, however, and lose at least 25 percent of the stored energy. Instead, the grid often uses "peaker plants," some of the oldest and most inefficient power facilities in the country. Peaker plants are fired up only to meet excess demand, typically on hot summer days and evenings.

If they were produced on a large scale, plug-in hybrid and electric cars could offer an excellent alternative. The development of large, rechargeable batteries in these vehicles offers a way to extend the power of solar and wind by storing, at high efficiency, the excess electricity that they produce. "The sun doesn't always shine, and the wind doesn't always blow," says Frank. "To help out solar and wind, you need electricity storage, and that's where plug-in hybrids come in. They provide batteries to store energy, whether it's to drive your car or power your home."

"For alternative energy sources like wind and solar, where you might not necessarily be generating the power exactly when you need it, you can store this power and delay when it's used by holding it in the battery," says Alec Proudfoot, a mechanical engineer at Google. The batteries in plug-in hybrid and electric vehicles become short-term energy banks. They can plug in at night, when demand is lowest, and then put some of the energy back into the grid during the daytime, when demand typically hits its peak.

I don't want to sugarcoat this: there are some significant obstacles to wide adoption of vehicle-to-grid technology. First, automakers need to build hybrids and electric vehicles in significant quantities. Given the industry's poor track record on zero-emission vehicles, one might be skeptical that the automakers will make good on these plans. The challenge will be to make sure that automakers move as quickly as possible to scale up production.

Further, some new infrastructure would be required. Although plug-in hybrids or electric vehicles need only a standard 120-volt plug to charge up their batteries, plugging electricity back into the grid is more complicated. Drivers would need to estimate how much electricity they needed before the next recharge. To sell the rest back to the grid, they'd park in lots or garages outfitted with computer technology to monitor the energy drained from each battery and credit the vehicles' owners. Although this technology currently exists and can be installed cost-effectively, it's a bit complicated and would require voluntary participation from drivers.

All things considered, it's best to think of plug-ins and electric vehicles primarily as an excellent way to reduce emissions and win freedom from oil. Any future use of these vehicles to supplement the electricity grid would be a bonus.

And some of the world's best engineers are working to turn that promise into a reality. At Google's headquarters, the crowd gathered to watch a car act as a mobile power station. Larry Brilliant, Google.org's executive director, flipped the switch and . . . nothing. A few seconds passed as Brilliant grinned mischievously and Proudfoot's brow furrowed in anticipation. Suddenly, the monitor came alive and there was a vehicle-to-grid transmission. The plug-in hybrid car in front of us had just become California's newest power source. Brilliant said, "You can recharge the car from the sun, you can recharge the grid from the car, and you can recharge our enthusiasm for trying to tackle the problems of global warming all at once."

Rescuing Detroit

Engineering innovators and passionate consumers are playing key roles in helping to create a sustainable future for the automobile, but they need much more help on the policy side. Rather than assist the auto industry's suicide, the federal government must broaden its role as life coach. Lawmakers should regulate the industry and continue to hold it to much higher standards for both fuel efficiency and greenhouse gas emissions.

Other policy measures that could be implemented by Congress and the White House include the following:

- Convert the U.S. government's fleet to gas-optional vehicles. The federal government buys more than sixty-five thousand new vehicles each year. In 2009, the economic recovery act provided $300 million to replace older, inefficient clunkers with more-efficient vehicles. While vehicles purchased with ARRA funding were on average 40 percent more efficient than those they replaced, virtually none were plug-in hybrids or electric vehicles. Dedicating approximately half of federal fleet purchases to advanced automotive technology such as plug-in hybrid or electric vehicles would offer a powerful incentive for change.

- Maintain tax credits for high-efficiency vehicles. Currently available tax credits of up to $7,500 for buyers of the first million plug-in hybrid and electric vehicles will help offset the cost of the technology and encourage economies of scale that will lower costs. This tax credit would cost $10 billion over several years but could be paid for several times over by eliminating subsidies to the oil industry.

- Allow owners of plug-in hybrids and electric vehicles to use carpool and high-occupancy-vehicle lanes at all times. A similar law in California for traditional hybrid vehicles helped jump-start the hybrid market.

- Send a strong price signal to automakers and car buyers alike that the days of cheap oil are gone forever by enacting a gas tax or creating other fees on driving such as a fee for miles traveled. Gas taxes are regressive, so the revenues would need to be rebated to low-income taxpayers.

There's plenty more that federal and state policymakers could do, such as enacting "feebate" legislation: adding one-time fees to the purchase price of inefficient vehicles while reducing by a similar amount the cost of the cars earning the best fuel economy. At some point, though, the auto industry will need to become a willing partner in its resurrection. Industry executives would be wise to hire fewer lawyers and lobbyists and more engineers. Cars will need to play a smaller role in our transportation mix, but that doesn't mean we can't get excited about them again. Major automakers have a powerful new opportunity to respond to Americans like the Bernikoff-Raboys, who know that cars can be part of the solution. In doing so, they can also meet the challenge of innovators like Tesla who understand that we still want to love our cars as well.

Take Action

Take it personally

1. It's important that automakers build more fuel-efficient vehicles, but it's also important that we drive less. Join a carpool if you can. Hop on a bus or a bicycle, or telecommute. There are plenty of ways to reduce your dependence on the automobile.

2. Even so, most American households will still need a car. Some 11 million new cars and trucks are sold in the United States each year. If you need a new car, your responsibility couldn't be clearer: vote with your dollars. Don't buy gas-guzzlers and enable America's oil addiction. If you can put off a purchase, let the automakers know that you won't buy a new vehicle until they produce plug-in hybrid or electric vehicles. Otherwise, buy the most fuel-efficient model for the size and class that you need. And when you rent a vehicle, ask for a hybrid.

3. If you already own a hybrid, convert it to a plug-in if you can afford to. Your car could travel thirty to sixty miles without using a drop of gas, and earn up to a hundred miles per gallon or more. Contact CalCars or A123 Systems to find an auto shop near you that does conversions.

Express yourself

1. California regulators set the standard for the rest of the country. Ask the California Air Resources Board to set a high bar for the zero-emission vehicle mandate and its second round of greenhouse gas standards for cars and trucks. California can help bring more plug-in hybrid and electric vehicles to market. Visit www.calcleancars.org/ for more information.

2. Tell President Obama that we must move beyond oil now, setting standards for vehicles to be sold through 2025 at a minimum 60 mpg and 137 grams per mile of CO_2 emissions. Urge automakers to build plug-in hybrid and electric vehicles and revitalize our manufacturing base. You'll find a list of organizations working on this issue in the Resources section.

3. Contact your representatives in Congress and urge them to get real on oil and climate. We need comprehensive climate and energy legislation that will drive out dirty coal from our grid and set targets for oil savings that will demand continued improvement in vehicle standards, a shift in how we invest in our transportation system, and a real price on carbon.

Stay engaged

Explore other effective, creative ways to help automakers stay viable in an era of climate change and volatile oil prices. Join Global Exchange and visit your local dealership and ask that it become part of the effort to push the industry to provide cars that don't pollute. If you own stock in any of the major automakers, contact the Interfaith Center on Corporate Responsibility or other shareholder advocacy organizations to use your leverage as an owner of the company. Review the resources section at the end of this book for other ways to take effective action.

CHAPTER 7

Growing Gas

Are Biofuels Fueling or Fooling America?

The only way to reap the benefits of biofuels
without squeezing the food supply is to take food
out of the picture.

—Joel K. Bourne, Jr.

I magine the wonder of seeing an orangutan in the wild for the first time," Birute Galdikas told me. "You're walking on the forest floor, you can hear and feel an orangutan's presence, and then you spot one moving in a shaft of sunlight in the rainforest canopy. Orangutans are very gentle and quite large—adult males weigh over three hundred pounds. When you see these animals move with such grace, it takes your breath away."

I had the chance to speak with Galdikas as she traveled in the United States to raise awareness about the threat to orangutans posed by the expansion of the palm oil industry. Galdikas has been an advocate for orangutans for decades. She arrived on the remote island of Borneo at the age of twenty-five to study wild orangutans in Indonesia's tropical rainforests. With Jane Goodall and Dian Fossey, who studied and lobbied for the protection of chimpanzees and mountain gorillas in Africa, Galdikas was a fellow protégé of the famed paleontologist Louis Leakey. She established a research facility—Camp Leakey—near Indonesia's Tanjung Puting National Park and has maintained a presence there for more than thirty-five years, tirelessly defending orangutans and other endangered species in Indonesia's lush forests.

"Orangutans really are our cousins," Galdikas says. "They share approximately 97 percent of their genetic material with human beings. In their emotions and perceptions—even in their cognitive abilities—they're very much like humans." Indeed, the name *orangutan* comes from the local Malay, meaning "person of the forest." And it's a "person" with a big brain on its shoulders: a recent study led by Harvard University psychologist James Lee identified orangutans as the most intelligent animal (other than humans, presumably). Of the twenty-five primate species, orangutans have the greatest ability to learn and solve problems. They've been observed weaving leaves together to make hats to shelter themselves from the rain, building roofs, and teaching each other how to build simple tools to get food. Orangutans are also noted for their intense maternal instincts; mothers typically are inseparable from their offspring for the first eight to ten years.

Yet the biggest problem orangutans face is outside their control. Indonesia and Malaysia produced 87 percent of the world's palm oil in 2006. To achieve this production, more than 6.5 million acres of irreplaceable tropical forests have been cleared for massive palm oil plantations. "Palm oil is the worst enemy of orangutans," declares Galdikas.

How does the fate of orangutans relate to America's fossil-fuel addiction? Just this: although it has typically been used in processed foods and for soaps and cosmetics, palm oil has recently become a lucrative feedstock for the exploding biofuels market. Each year, plantation owners set huge fires to clear forests and expand their holdings, often directly in orangutan habitat. While the forests burn, airline flights are routinely canceled or delayed, and smoke from the region can often be seen from outer space. The fires in Borneo in 1997–98 alone destroyed 5 million acres of rainforest and led to the deaths of an estimated one-third of the world's remaining orangutan population.

Without a dramatic turnaround, orangutans face a brutal fate. Millions more acres of palm plantations are planned to meet the booming biofuel demand. Sadly, orangutans are threatened not only by habitat destruction. Since they eat the young palms that produce oil, many plantation owners offer a bounty on them. "We find orangutans burned, or their heads cut off. Hunters are paid 150,000 rupiah (about 20 bucks) for the right hand of an orangutan to prove they've killed them," says Willie Smits, founder and chair of the Borneo Orangutan Survival Foundation.

Biodiversity throughout the region suffers from the destruction of Indonesia's rainforests, nearly 75 percent of which has already been laid waste—mostly within the past four decades. As the world's demand for "green" biofuels grows, the pace of destruction is rapidly increasing. The United Nations Environment Program estimates that up to 98 percent of orangutan habitat may be lost by 2022, threatening not only these primates but also the Sumatran tiger, Asian elephant, and countless other species in this wondrous and diverse rainforest.

"It would be a much lonelier planet if orangutans disappeared," Galdikas says. Clearly, that is a very real risk, and the world's growing demand for biofuels will only make it worse.

Dead-End "Solutions"

The lure of biofuels is seductive. Rather than bankroll terrorists and cook the planet by burning gas in our cars, trucks, and SUVs, America can grow its way to energy independence, or so the thinking goes. Some crops, such as corn, sugar beets, and sugarcane, can be converted into ethanol, while the oil from palm, rapeseed (known as canola in this country), soy, and other plants can be transformed into biodiesel. Both are either added to gas or used to replace gasoline entirely. Plant-based fuels can be domestically grown, have the potential to clean up our air and water, and require no changes in driving habits.

Pass It On

Palm oil from tropical regions such as Indonesia and Malaysia creates up to ten times more greenhouse gas emissions than oil and causes the displacement of millions of Indigenous people.

Sounds good, doesn't it? The reality is more complex and a lot less sunny. This country's most popular fuel alternative is ethanol from corn, which might produce less energy than is used to grow and process it. Corn is also one of the most resource-intensive, environmentally damaging, and heavily subsidized industrial crops; it exacerbates soil depletion and creates "dead zones" in waterways, due to fertilizer runoff. And if dead orangutans aren't gruesome enough, consider that biodiesel from palm oil in tropical rainforests can produce up to ten times as much greenhouse gases as conventional oil.

It gets worse. Demand for plant-based fuels is growing so fast that many industrial farmers find it more profitable to grow fuel than food crops. This is causing the prices of corn, wheat, meat, and other products to rise significantly, with devastating consequences for the world's poorest people, who find they are competing with automobiles for food. All for dubious benefits: even if every ear of corn in the United States were devoted to ethanol, only 12 percent of the gasoline we now use would be replaced.

But don't go crying in your cornmeal just yet. International experts distinguish "agrofuels"—the product of highly mechanized factory farms with significant social and environmental downsides—from "biofuels," which can offer some benefits to both people and the planet. The difference is similar to that between giant industrial farms—let's call them "food factories"—and small family farmers who can grow food in a sustainable way. Our country can ill afford any further subsidies or growth in the agrofuel economy, but biofuels *may* have a small yet useful role to play, as long as strict environmental and humanitarian rules are established and enforced. We'll sort through these different approaches in the following sections.

Biofuels 101

The largest producers of ethanol in the world today are the United States, which uses corn to produce 97 percent of its ethanol, and Brazil, which relies mostly on sugarcane. Most biodiesel crops are grown either in Europe or in Southeast Asia; in 2005, Germany produced more than half of the world's biodiesel from rapeseed. However, palm oil is growing rapidly as a feedstock. Giant palm plantations are appearing throughout the tropics, from Indonesia, Malaysia, and Papua New Guinea to the African countries of Ghana, Kenya, Senegal, Nigeria, and Uganda, as well as throughout Latin America, particularly in Colombia, Venezuela, and Bolivia.

How can a plant make your car move? Let's talk about conventional ethanol first. As you might guess, sugarcane and sugar beets contain sugar. Other crops such as corn, barley, sunflower, and wheat contain starches, which can easily be converted into sugar. Once this is done, the sugar is fermented with yeast to produce the same product long used to spike the punch at college parties: grain alcohol. This alcohol is purified to produce ethanol, which is then mixed with gasoline.

Henry Ford originally designed his Model T to run on alcohol. He called it "the fuel of the future." (Oil companies had a different idea.) When you see E-5, E-10, or E-85 at the gas pump, the numbers refer to the percentage of ethanol that has been blended with conventional gasoline. If your car was manufactured since the early 1980s, you can use up to 10 percent ethanol without any modifications needed. To use fuel containing larger percentages requires driving a "flexible-fuel vehicle," which automakers are manufacturing in increasing quantities each year.

Biodiesel production is also straightforward. The process is called transesterification, in which chemicals are mixed with vegetable oils or animal fats to separate glycerine from methyl esters. Glycerine is often used for soaps and cosmetics; methyl esters is the scientific name for biodiesel. Biodiesel can be made from almost any fat or oil, from palm, soy, rapeseed, jatropha (a leafy bush found in dry regions near the equator), or even recycled cooking grease.

Finally, fuel can be generated from the cellulosic matter in grasses, agricultural waste, and even trees and algae. Researchers working on this experimental process believe that significant energy savings and reductions in greenhouse gas emissions can be achieved. Other experts doubt that this fuel will be available commercially any time soon and point out different, but significant, environmental drawbacks. We're talking about "cellulosic ethanol" here, the stuff of prairie switchgrass and State of the Union speeches. We'll examine the issue more closely later in this chapter.

Here's what the availability of biofuels means for you and me. If you own a diesel-powered vehicle that has been manufactured since 1993, you can drive on 100 percent pure veggie oil. If you have a flexible-fuel vehicle, you can power up on at least 85 percent corn. The burning question (pardon the pun) is: should you really want to?

Driving Food Insecurity

Agriculture's rapid shift from food to fuels is sending shock waves throughout the globalized food system. Ethanol production in the United States totaled 10.6 billion gallons in 2009, more than double the production as recently as 2007 yet still a small amount compared with the 140 billion gallons of gas the

United States consumes each year. Producing this much ethanol consumed 29 percent of the U.S. corn crop in 2009, yet this ethanol displaced less than 10 percent of the gasoline we used. The energy bill signed in 2007 mandates that 36 billion gallons of fuel come from biofuels by 2030.

Worldwide total production of ethanol and biodiesel has more than tripled since 2000, reaching 23.4 billion gallons in 2009, which is still a tiny percentage of the global supply of transportation fuels. In the European Union, agrofuels comprised just 1 percent of transportation fuel in 2005; the EU has committed to increase biofuel consumption to meet 10 percent of its transportation fuel needs by 2020.

An in-depth study released by Iowa State University revealed that current levels of agrofuel production in the United States have already raised retail food prices for basic staples, including cereals, eggs, milk, meat, and other essentials, by more than $14 billion. The study showed that if the United States hit projected levels of ethanol production by 2020, the U.S. acreage devoted to corn would increase significantly, further crowding out soy, wheat, and other crops. The U.S. Department of Agriculture has released advisories about rising food prices; the United Nations Food and Agriculture Organization (FAO) has issued similar warnings, citing the demand for agrofuels as a main cause.

Pass It On

U.S. ethanol production grew from about 1.6 billion gallons in 2000 to 10.6 billion gallons in 2009. By 2030, it is projected to total 36 billion gallons.

The food and energy sectors of the economy, once separate, are thus converging. The world's poor will be hurt the most, as a rush to agrofuels will increase food shortages and drive up prices. Nearly 2.5 billion people in the world live on less than $2 per day, according to the World Bank. Increases in the prices of their food—whether grown in-country, imported for sale, or distributed as aid—could be devastating. "The stage is now set for direct competition for grain between the 800 million people who own automobiles, and the world's 2 billion poorest people," writes Lester Brown of the Earth Policy Institute. "The risk is that millions of those on the lower rungs of the global economic ladder will start falling off as higher food prices drop their consumption below the survival level."

Filling the gas tank of a typical SUV with 100 percent ethanol just once requires more than 450 pounds of corn, or enough calories to feed one person for an entire year. The United Nations World Food Program estimates that 850 million people in thirty-four countries are facing urgent and persistent food shortages. The program can afford to feed just 90 million of those people, and warns that food-price increases due to the booming agrofuels market might further cut the number of people it can serve. In December 2007, Jean Ziegler, the U.N. special rapporteur on the right to food, called agrofuels a "crime against humanity" and demanded a five-year moratorium on the expansion of the industry.

More than eighteen thousand children die every day around the world due to lack of food and malnutrition. Continued growth in agrofuel production could make this tragedy even worse. If strong action isn't taken, the decision about whether food goes into children's bellies or into automobiles will be made by some of the world's largest corporations.

The ABCs of Agrofuels

The industrial powerhouses behind agrofuels are an alphabet soup of corporate plunderers. In the United States we have mainly Archer Daniels Midland Company (ADM) to thank for the development of the corn-based ethanol market. ADM's former CEO Dwayne Andreas was infamous for cutting the $25,000 check to pay for Nixon's hacks to break into the Watergate in 1972. He began peddling ethanol back in the 1970s to diversify the company's market for corn. ADM now leads the country in ethanol production, supplying more than 25 percent of the market here in the United States. A large donor to both Republicans and Democrats, ADM receives billions of dollars in federal and state ethanol subsidies. The conservative Cato Institute in 1995 called the company "the most prominent recipient of corporate welfare in recent U.S. history."

In expanding the global trade in agrofuels, ADM is joined by its agribusiness competitors Cargill and Bunge. All three companies are expanding massive soy plantations in South America's Cerrado, a vast forested savannah encompassing parts of Brazil, Paraguay, and Bolivia that is inhabited by thousands of Indigenous peoples and an extraordinary diversity of plant and animal life, including jaguars and maned wolves. Deforestation rates in the Cerrado rival that of the Amazon, where more than 15 million acres were cleared by entrenched and often corrupt businesses to feed mills operated by Cargill and Brazilian companies. Under pressure from Greenpeace and other environmental and human rights organizations, Brazilian companies and their international counterparts agreed to a moratorium of several years to prevent further deforestation in the Amazon.

No such agreement exists in the Cerrado, however, or in any of the other regions where Cargill, ADM, and Bunge operate. Furthermore, human rights abuses such as forced labor are rampant on these plantations. "Agribusiness is having a party but not inviting the rest of us," says Hiparidi Toptiro, president of the Mobilization of the Indigenous People of the Cerrado (MOPIC). When ADM, under pressure, came to the headquarters of Rainforest Action Network for a meeting in September 2007, it was the only company that had declined to sign an antislavery pact to prevent forced labor on plantations in Brazil. An ADM executive told us that the issue was "highly complex," and it would take time for the company to determine the "appropriate" response. Incredulous, I asked, "How many more meetings will it take before you decide slavery is bad?" A month later, ADM informed us that it would sign the pact.

Cargill and ADM are also profiting from palm oil throughout the tropics. Plantations owned by Cargill contribute to extensive deforestation in Papua New Guinea and Indonesia, including prime orangutan habitat near Indonesia's Gunung Palung National Park. ADM is a major investor in Wilmar, a Malaysian-owned firm that operates palm plantations to the east and west of Indonesia's Tanjun Puting National Park as well as in Malaysia, Uganda, and elsewhere.

Pass It On

It takes 450 pounds of corn to make (a) enough ethanol to fill the twenty-five-gallon tank of a typical SUV or (b) enough calories to feed an average person for a year. Even if every ear of corn in the United States were devoted to ethanol, only 12 percent of U.S. gasoline use would be replaced.

Land Grab

The explosion of agrofuel production in many tropical countries has all the makings of a human rights disaster: weak and corrupt governments, powerful corporations seeking land from poor and marginalized farmers, and the potential for enormous profits.

In Colombia, the threat of agrofuel plantations and attendant human rights violations has been added to the terror of a decades-long civil war. There are more displaced citizens in Colombia than in any other country except Sudan. Many palm plantations in the country have been established illegally, using force and without any consultation with local landowners. It's likely to get worse, as Colombian authorities try to double production of palm oil by 2011.

Milvia Días lost her land and her father, Innocence Días. Several years ago, Innocence was threatened by paramilitaries who wanted the family's land. One afternoon he went out to fix a small hole in a fence. "We stayed up all night waiting for him," Milvia recalls. The family sent out a search party early the next morning, to find that Innocence had been murdered. "He was in the field where he had been mending the fence. He had seven stab wounds and his throat was cut from ear to ear. And they ripped his throat out." The family fled, and Milvia now resides in the western Choco region of Colombia. The farm they were forced to abandon is now covered with palm trees.

It is a sad irony that, in the rush to find alternatives to oil, corporations and nations are allowing the same abuses to occur that once characterized the oil boom. "If you don't negotiate with us, we'll negotiate with your widow" is a common line used by thugs in Colombia to pressure peasants to sell their land, according to an advocate with Christian Aid.

In a globalized world, however, the rights and dignity of people can no longer be violated in secrecy. Organizations such as Food First, Christian Aid, Sawit Watch, and Via Campesina document and publicize these violations, amplifying the voices of poor and marginalized communities that are being violently displaced in Paraguay, Indonesia, Brazil, Uganda, and around the world.

Few studies exist that document how many people worldwide are being forced off their land to feed the agrofuel craze. The United Nations estimates that in the province of West Kalimantan, Indonesia, alone, up to 5 million Indigenous people are likely to be displaced by palm oil expansion. "Indigenous people are being pushed off their land to make way for the expansion of biofuel crops around the world, threatening to destroy their cultures," says Victoria Tauli-Corpuz, chair of the U.N. Permanent Forum on Indigenous Issues.

One villager in West Kalimantan lost his farm in 2006. "I went to my land one morning and found it had been cleared. All my rubber trees, my plants, had been destroyed," he told a BBC reporter. "Now I have to work as a builder in Malaysia, so I can feed my three children."

Runoff Pollution at Home

It's like something you'd watch on television on a lazy Saturday afternoon: the *Dead Zone*. Here's what's happening. As ethanol booms here in the United States, corn prices are increasing, leading more farmers to plant more corn more frequently. Most farmers used to rotate soybeans and corn crops annually to maintain soil quality and reduce the need for fertilizers and pesticides. Now, however, many are extending the time between rotations, often planting corn for several straight seasons.

As a result, many farmers are increasing their use of chemical fertilizers, causing increased soil runoff and water contamination. Corn production consumes 40 percent of all commercial fertilizers used in the United States, including nitrogen and phosphate. These nutrients flow straight into our waterways, causing algae blooms, which in turn deplete the water of oxygen. No oxygen means no fish. One of the largest "dead zones" can be found in the Gulf of Mexico, where the Mississippi River dumps fertilizer runoff from the Midwest. The Gulf's dead zone has doubled since the 1980s and is expected in 2010 to grow as large as eighty-five hundred square miles and hug the Gulf Coast from Alabama to Texas.

Pass It On

The dead zone in the Gulf of Mexico has more than doubled since the 1980s, growing to about eighty-five hundred square miles—larger than Massachusetts—in part due to fertilizer runoff from increased corn production.

The Ecological Society of America calls it "the most widespread water quality problem in the United States and many other nations," and a 2008 National Research Council report warned of a "considerable" increase in damage to the Gulf if ethanol production rises. It may be painfully obvious that the 2010 oil spill disaster in the Gulf will only build on the existing problem, as bacteria that help consume the oil also eat up more oxygen.

If these nutrients are damaging aquatic ecosystems and killing fish, you can imagine that they are threatening human health as well. Fertilizers wash off farms and contaminate underground water supplies. High levels of nitrates in drinking water cause a wide range of health effects, from spontaneous miscarriages and birth defects to ovarian, uterine, and bladder cancers.

More Hot Air?

Another controversy is whether agrofuels actually save energy—in other words, does it take more fossil fuels to produce them than they can put in the gas tank? This "net energy balance" is calculated by subtracting the energy required to grow and harvest the fuels (fertilizers, tractor diesel, transport, etc.) from the stored energy those fuels contain.

Until recently, many studies showed that corn-based ethanol had a negative net energy balance. The calculation is complicated by the fact that ethanol contains 33 percent less energy than gasoline, meaning that you need more fuel to go the same distance. The industry has become more efficient in recent years, however, leading some (though not all) researchers to believe that corn-based ethanol has achieved a positive energy balance. Other agrofuel sources require much lower inputs of fuel. Biodiesel from soy, for example, produces five times as much fuel as it consumes, while ethanol from sugarcane produces eight times as much.

Unfortunately for most agrofuels, that's the easy part. The next challenge is to determine whether the fuel will decrease greenhouse gas emissions. To calculate this, we must remember the role that forests and soils play in mitigating climate change, because carbon is stored in trees, plants, and soil. The Intergovernmental Panel on Climate Change estimates that, on average, 20 percent of annual greenhouse gas emissions come from agriculture, deforestation, and other "land use changes." The worst of these is the clearing of tropical rainforests, which, because of their ability to absorb carbon, are critical to moderating the effects of climate change.

Most agrofuels do not pass the test of lowering greenhouse gas emissions. In February 2008, two articles in the prestigious journal *Science* examined the life-cycle impacts of many agrofuel sources. They found that almost all agrofuels actually caused *more* greenhouse gas emissions than conventional fuels, in large part due to the conversion of wild lands—whether rainforests or grasslands—to plantations. Other factors, including which crops were grown, how they were cultivated, and how much fossil fuel was used to fertilize them and process the fuel, caused further increases in emissions, to varying degrees. Only ethanol from sugar in Brazil was believed to reduce greenhouse gas emissions.

Without strict controls, the agrofuels industry could create a climate disaster. Nowhere is this problem worse than in Indonesia. A study by Wetlands International reveals that the draining and burning of peat forests to produce palm oil in Indonesia results in the release of up to thirty-three tons of carbon dioxide for each ton of palm oil produced, or as much as ten times the emissions that come from petroleum! It's crazy, but true: when we clear tropical forests to grow agrofuels, we're destroying one of the best tools that we have to protect our climate in an ill-fated attempt to . . . protect our climate.

Fueling Responsibly

Biofuels may have an important role to play in replacing some oil use—provided that at least five conditions are met. They must reduce greenhouse gas emissions substantially; not displace food crops and threaten food security for the world's poor; uphold the integrity of critical ecosystems, particularly in tropical forests; and strengthen the human rights of community farmers and Indigenous people. Most important, biofuels should be developed only as part of a broader strategy to reduce fuel consumption and redesign mobility. If these standards can be enacted and strictly enforced, then biofuels can be one element in a sustainable transportation system.

Fortunately, there is a small but growing movement of individuals and organizations showing how it can be done. Organic Valley Family of Farms is one example. It's North America's largest organic-farming cooperative, with more than eleven hundred farmers in twenty-nine states and one Canadian province, and more than $334 million in sales in 2006. "We were formed by just seven farmers in 1988," says Cecil Wright, its director of local operations. "Our aim is to provide safe and healthy organic food to American families, and to sustain family farms and rural communities while doing so."

Organic Valley recently decided to provide locally grown, 100 percent biodiesel fuel for its distribution fleet. Local Organic Valley farmers will alternate between fuel and food crops. They'll use fuel crops that have short growing seasons, such as camelina (another flowering plant in the same family as rapeseed), so that they can grow their own fuel without limiting food production or increasing prices. Since most organic farms must maintain buffer areas of twenty-five to fifty feet around conventional farms (to stay clear of pesticide spraying), Organic Valley farmers can also grow fuel crops in those areas, where organic food can't be grown. "We're just experimenting now," says Wright. "But our farmers know that there's a way to reduce oil dependence, help the climate, and support family farms at the same time. We're determined to make this work."

One form of biofuels with a passionate following is biodiesel made from recycled oil, grease, and animal fat. This waste oil can be collected from restaurants, hotels, and other places where food is prepared, and converted into a fuel. While it's an excellent alternative, waste oil is available in limited quantities, currently providing less than 5 percent of all agrofuel production in an industry that provides less than 5 percent of the nation's gasoline.

An early waste-oil pioneer is a former diesel mechanic, Robert King. Back in the mid-1990s, workers at a Maui landfill were concerned that restaurant grease brought to the site was not only creating a fire hazard but also could contaminate local groundwater. King did a little homework, discovered that the waste oil could be made into a fuel, and set up his new company, Pacific Biodiesel, Inc., within months. Four years later, his company had built a small biodiesel plant in Honolulu, with a capacity of fifteen hundred gallons per day, and today operates similar plants in Oregon, California, Texas, Nevada, and Nagano, Japan.

Who Makes the Rules?

Between exacerbating world hunger, degrading endangered ecosystems, violating human rights, and increasing greenhouse gas emissions, there are too many ways in which agrofuels can create more problems than they may solve. The rapid growth of the industry only increases these risks further. But the absence of any strong, binding national or international standards for responsible production is what makes the growth of the agrofuels industry a recipe for disaster. It would be wise to put a global moratorium on the expansion of the industry until we can get it right, seeking input from the stakeholders that would be most affected by agrofuels development.

In the meantime, there are some nascent efforts to develop voluntary standards. For the small but growing U.S. biodiesel market, a strict code of ethics is being developed by the Sustainable Biodiesel Alliance (SBA). This group represents biodiesel producers, farmers, distributors, consumers, and even a few celebrity biodiesel enthusiasts such as Willie Nelson and Daryl Hannah. The SBA requires that biofuels not degrade or damage soils nor contaminate or deplete water supplies, and that they produce significantly lower greenhouse gas emissions than fossil fuels over their life cycle.

Internationally, several voluntary initiatives are under way. The Roundtable on Sustainable Biofuels (RSB) has brought together corporations, nonprofits, farmers, scientists, governments, and intergovernmental agencies to develop guidelines for improved production. Utilizing a "bioenergy wiki" (based on the online user-generated encyclopedia Wikipedia), participants share their perspectives on sustainable biofuels. There's also the Roundtable on Sustainable Palm Oil in Southeast Asia and the Roundtable on Responsible Soy in South America—both of which seek to bring together diverse stakeholders. On the one hand, it's good that these discussions are taking place. But the processes have no enforcement mechanisms and little accountability, and certainly are not yet pushing the agribusiness giants to reform their practices.

The European Union may offer the first sign of real hope. In March 2007, the EU made its commitment to produce 10 percent of its vehicles' fuels from biofuels by 2020. Almost immediately, there was an outcry from European citizens about the dangers of unregulated agrofuels. The EU quickly pledged to develop sustainability standards. It is establishing guidelines that would prohibit imports of agrofuels that do not meet minimum standards for greenhouse gas reduction and endangered ecosystem protection. As of this writing, those standards were still being developed.

As for the United States, the only policy seems to be to increase agrofuels production as fast as possible. So far, agribusiness and its supporters have resisted developing any social or environmental standards. But pressure is mounting, and the U.S. ethanol industry is nearing a key deadline. The industry's primary subsidy mechanism, the Volumetric Ethanol Excise Tax Credit (VEETC), is due to expire at the end of 2010. In 2007, federal subsidies for ethanol and other biofuels were more than eighteen times larger than federal investments in solar power, and in 2009 ethanol subsidies were worth roughly $5 billion. Any extension of these subsidies should be limited to research for advanced fuels that don't accelerate climate change, use large amounts of water, or degrade important ecosystems.

The Way Forward

Let's remember, above all, that biofuels can make only a small dent in fuel consumption. Even though the yield per acre for different crops varies, there's not enough arable land in the United States to replace all—or even most—of the gasoline we use. Biofuels will need to be combined with other solutions.

The first three steps to promote sustainable transport don't involve biofuels at all. They are: (1) prioritize mass transit so that more people can drive less, (2) switch to plug-in hybrid or electric vehicles as quickly as possible, and (3) "green the grid" by producing electricity with renewable energy. When we get serious about fighting climate change and reducing oil consumption, those steps come first.

Let's call biofuels step 4. "Simply replacing one fuel with another won't work," says Heidi Quante, former director of the Sustainable Biodiesel Alliance. "In the end, it's not about volume; it's about finding a sustainable way to produce energy. Focusing on a single cheap and abundant source is what got us into trouble the last time. Biofuel is a solution, but it's only one part."

On the horizon are the development of cellulosic ethanol and the use of algae to produce biodiesel. At present this sector is mainly a parking lot for excess cash from billionaire investors: Richard Branson is a believer. So are Microsoft founder Bill Gates and Sun Microsystems cofounder and venture capitalist Vinod Khosla. These moguls, along with the U.S. Department of Energy and others, are investing millions in a race to convert native plants into low-cost fuels. What they're counting on is the ability of scientists—often using genetic engineering—to find an efficient and cost-effective way to break down the cellulose in fast-growing plants and grasses that have very high yields but comparatively low energy requirements.

Don't bet the farm on it, though. Production costs for these greener bio-fuels are still prohibitively high. The Department of Energy estimates that cellulosic ethanol costs twice as much as corn-based ethanol, which itself is one of the more costly and heavily subsidized agrofuels on the planet. The biggest technical hurdle is that the cellular bonds in the tissues of these plants are much more "recalcitrant," as the experts say, to being broken down into simple sugars.

Khosla isn't worried. "Today there are companies willing to invest around $60 million to $70 million of their own money [to commercialize cellulosic ethanol]. That is serious private money," observes Khosla (who stands to profit handsomely if this prediction comes true): "So, my guess is, if we're lucky, we'll have commercial-scale plants in three years. If we're very unlucky, it will be six."

I have to admit that it all sounds a little too much like boosterism to me. Khosla made his prediction in 2006; but as of 2010 those commercial-scale operations still don't exist, and it's not clear when they will. Perhaps there may be some breakthrough that doesn't cause unintended negative consequences, but in the meantime, let's push ahead with the sustainable transportation solutions that are available right now.

And let's set some simple rules, for cellulosic ethanol and all agrofuels. The true "fuels for the future" shouldn't poison our bodies or our waterways. They shouldn't degrade priceless ecosystems or kick people off their land. They certainly shouldn't cause people to go hungry.

If allowing our country to get hooked on oil and coal was America's biggest energy mistake in its recent past, then fostering dependence on ethanol and other agrofuels might be the worst blunder we could make in the near future. We'd be solving one set of problems by creating new ones. If we see ethanol, palm oil, and other agrofuels as a silver bullet, we'll be more likely to use that bullet to shoot ourselves in the foot.

Take Action

Take it personally

1. There are plenty of ways you can help promote sustainable fuel use. Do you drive a diesel car? Go veggie, but only if the fuel is from recycled waste oil or from local sources that don't degrade ecosystems and displace food crops. Visit the Sustainable Biodiesel Alliance at www.sustainablebiodieselalliance.org for a list of distributors in your region.

2. If you don't drive a diesel, hold off on buying your next new car until automakers provide "tribrids": plug-in hybrid, flexible-fuel vehicles. This choice lets you plug in and use electrical power for most trips, and then switch to biofuels (if they're sustainable) and some gasoline for longer trips.

Express yourself

1. You can start to encourage responsible fuel production by holding corporations accountable. Archer Daniels Midland (ADM) is the largest promoter of agrofuels in the United States. Write to ADM CEO Patricia Woertz (or her replacement). Let her know that you don't support agrofuel production that violates human rights, degrades pristine ecosystems, and threatens our climate. Write to the CEOs of Bunge and Cargill, too.

2. Contact your congressional representatives and urge them to put a moratorium on agrofuel expansion by cutting all agrofuel subsidies to ADM and other companies. Remind them that America can't grow its way out of our oil addiction, and pressure them to support legislation ensuring that all biofuels meet standards as strong as those established by the Sustainable Biodiesel Alliance.

3. Besides cutting subsidies, we must have strong standards to ensure that agrofuel production does not add to global-warming problems, nor contribute to hunger, deforestation, poverty, and human rights abuses. Please join one of many organizations, listed under this topic in the Resources section of this book, that can help your city, state, or the federal government put a moratorium on agrofuel consumption until those standards can be developed.

Stay engaged

Join Rainforest Action Network, Indonesia-based Sawit Watch, and Birute Galdikas's Orangutan Foundation International's campaign to protect rainforests in Indonesia and throughout Southeast Asia from the expanding biofuels industry, a long-term effort. Be part of an international movement that challenges the agribusiness practice of establishing giant food and fuel factory plantations that push communities off their lands and destroy ecosystems. Organizations listed in the resources section can help you make a positive difference.

CHAPTER 8

Greening the Grid
How Sun and Wind Can Generate Power and Prosperity

The best time to have taken action on energy
issues would have been thirty years ago.
The second best time is right now.

— Republican governor Tim Pawlenty
of Minnesota, May 2007

Price. It all comes down to price. Renewable energy may sound exciting, and it will probably grow a little over the next twenty years or so, but it just won't be able to replace coal, oil, nuclear power, or natural gas in any real way. There might be some room for the occasional rooftop solar system here, or even the odd wind farm there, but both solar and wind will be playing on the margins for at least the next several decades.

"Why? Because coal is cheap, and America has lots of it. Designing and installing a photovoltaic (PV) solar system on a rooftop, building a wind farm, or even siting a utility-scale solar array in the desert is far more expensive than power from coal or even natural gas, in almost every location around the country. We owe it to ratepayers to get our energy as cheaply as we can.

"But let's say for argument's sake that somehow prices drop and renewable energy becomes competitive. There's still no way that renewable power can produce electricity on the scale America needs. And what do you do when the wind doesn't blow or the sun doesn't shine? Face it, solar and wind just can't be relied on to do the job. Renewable energy will remain only a bit player for the foreseeable future."

That sales pitch, my friends, is exactly what the coal, oil, nuclear, and natural-gas industries want you to believe. These interests (which energy expert Harvey Wasserman collectively dubs King CONG) will work to convince you that America's energy needs are too great to rely upon solar, wind, or any other renewable form of energy. They want you to believe that electricity demand is growing so quickly that we'll risk widespread blackouts if we try to change course. Most of all, they say that coal is abundant, and cheap, cheap, cheap.

And if you believe all this, those industries would like to keep on selling you new coal-fired plants, new deepwater drilling projects, and new pipelines. But not only are the costs of dirty energy much higher than King CONG would have us believe, the advantages of switching to renewable power are much greater. Embracing clean energy is not an obligation, it is an opportunity. Coming clean has never felt so good.

For the past three chapters we've been talking about transportation, where oil still rules. Now we move into a different realm of energy use: the electricity that powers other sectors of our economy. Here, coal is king, generating about 47 percent of the electricity in the United States. Coal's dominance produces a common misunderstanding about our future energy choices: that we don't have many options, and that utilities must continue to build coal plants or risk pulling the plug on the American economy.

Fortunately, neither is true. Since it's not possible to eliminate all coal use completely and immediately, the transition from coal to renewables will occur in two stages. Our first challenge is to avoid locking in our coal addiction for decades to come. We've managed to defeat 131 proposed new coal plants as of the middle of 2010, but as mentioned in chapter 2, others are still on the drawing board. Over the next few years, policymakers must choose between building those plants and finding a better solution. If business-as-usual sentiments prevail and the proposed plants are built, hundreds of billions of public and private investment dollars will be sunk into expanding coal industry infrastructure, and we'll be stuck with a new generation of inefficient plants, each belching millions of tons of greenhouse gases, plus heavy metals and other pollutants, into the air year after year.

But there are increasing signs that policymakers are embracing a cleaner energy pathway. Over the next several years, utilities will be forced to install pollution controls on our country's oldest and dirtiest coal-fired power plants.

The combination of strong federal rule making and community organizing has led analysts to estimate that more than 20 percent of the existing fleet of coal plants could be retired by 2015. And as proposed new plants are rejected one by one, we can begin to set our sights on the second stage of the clean-energy transition: identifying the most polluting plants, shutting them down, and filling that market share with clean power. The Sierra Club's Beyond Coal campaign has set a goal to almost completely eliminate coal-fired plants from the energy sector by 2030.

Detailed energy analyses by a wide range of research groups show how the U.S. economy can be carbon-free and nuclear-free within the next thirty to fifty years. Many claim that a full transition to clean power sources will require a massive public investment on the scale of fighting World War II, or at least comparable to the Apollo Project, which put a man on the moon in the 1960s. In some ways, this is accurate, but it's also misleading. We'll be making vast investments in our future energy supply anyway. The question is whether we devote billions of dollars to the same fossil-fuel sources we've exploited since the Industrial Revolution, or whether we can break from our past.

Green-Collar Jobs

Persuading America to buy into a future of power without pollution will take pragmatism as well as idealism. Yes, it's a good thing that moving to renewables will lower our greenhouse gas emissions, thus preventing seas from rising and storms from intensifying. And of course, limiting the likelihood of oil spills and coal-mining catastrophes is a smart thing to do. But a rapid transition to renewable energy—solar, wind, geothermal, biomass, tidal energy, and some hydro projects—will help our economy as much as the planet. We'll focus on solar and wind in this book because they have the potential to grow most quickly and provide "energy security" for farmers and families. They'll also serve as an economic stimulant, creating new, well-paying jobs and saving taxpayer dollars.

Through the first half of 2010, 4.6 percent of the United States' electricity was generated by renewables, nearly twice the amount as when this book first appeared. The Union of Concerned Scientists estimates that increasing renewable energy's contribution to our power supply to 25 percent by 2025 will create 297,000 new jobs and save consumers a total of more than $60 billion in lower electricity and natural gas bills. The Apollo Alliance, a coalition of unions, churches, elected officials, and environmental, farm, and business groups, in 2004 conducted a broader analysis of the impact of a major clean-energy initiative that would include transportation, electricity, and energy efficiency. Its report, "New Energy for America," showed that a $300 billion, ten-year investment in clean energy would create 3.3 million new jobs, add $1.4 trillion to the U.S. gross domestic product, and save $284 billion in energy costs over that period.

The prospect for new jobs from a major commitment to renewables is especially strong. While fossil-fuel development is capital intensive (a typical coal plant costs at least $1 billion to build), renewable energy is more labor intensive. University of California researchers found that wind power could produce nearly three times as many jobs per unit of power produced as coal. Rooftop solar could generate seven to ten times as many jobs. According to a 2010 report released by the American Wind Energy Association, the BlueGreen Alliance, and the

> **Pass It On**
>
> Clean energy equals good jobs. An analysis of thirteen independent reports studying the effects of clean energy on employment found that wind power could produce up to nearly three times as many jobs as coal per unit of power produced. Solar photovoltaics were found to generate seven to ten times as many jobs.

United Steelworkers, "While the growth in wind energy manufacturing has been steady—growing from 2,500 workers in 2004 to 18,500 in 2009—tens of thousands of additional jobs manufacturing wind turbines and components, such as towers, gearboxes, and bearings, could be created with policies that establish a long-term, stable market and support the manufacturing sector's transition to the wind industry."

Whether it's installing solar panels on rooftops; manufacturing, repairing, or maintaining utility-scale solar and wind farms; or weatherizing and improving the efficiency of millions of homes, there's plenty of work to be had in a postcarbon economy. On the 2008 campaign trail, Senators Edwards, Obama, and Clinton all announced proposals for increased funding for green-jobs training. The eventual Democratic candidate and forty-fourth president later said, "As we recover from this recession, the transition to clean energy has the potential to grow our economy and create millions of jobs—but only if we accelerate that transition. Only if we seize the moment. And only if we rally together and act as one nation—workers and entrepreneurs; scientists and citizens; the public and private sectors."

Such jobs may also offer economic self-sufficiency for those who need it most. Green-collar jobs "can do more than just save the planet or help avoid oil wars in the future," explains Van Jones, cofounder of Green for All, a project to secure $1 billion in government funding for job training in green businesses. Jones, who served in 2009 as senior advisor in the White House on clean-energy jobs and later became a fellow at the Center for American Progress, adds, "For the tens of thousands of Americans who are falling behind in the global job market, these work opportunities can also create green pathways out of poverty." One woman making a direct and positive impact in her community is Michelle McGeoy. A successful computer entrepreneur in the 1980s and 1990s, she grew increasingly concerned about the growing digital divide and gave up her lucrative career to form a nonprofit social enterprise to teach disadvantaged youth computer skills, from data entry to creating Web pages to running their own Web development businesses.

Also a passionate environmentalist, McGeoy a decade later started a new career as a solar-design technician, climbing up on rooftops to determine where best to install solar panels and assisting customers with installations. But she soon noticed that the solar industry lacked diversity and wasn't fulfilling its potential to lift low-income workers out of poverty. McGeoy saw an opportunity to improve the economy of her hometown of Richmond, California—which has some of the state's highest homicide rates—reduce violence, and protect the environment all at once. "Solar power is a great antidote to pollution, but jobs are also a wonderful antidote to violence," she says.

McGeoy founded Solar Richmond, a nonprofit designed to train residents in the new-energy economy. Operating in the shadow of the city's giant, toxic Chevron refinery, Solar Richmond in August 2007 began a jobs program that teaches community members to install solar panels, places trainees into jobs with local installers, and advocates with municipalities to enhance economic development with smart-energy policies. It's working. McGeoy recalls the day when one of her early trainees came back to announce that he had just got a job installing solar. "I did everything I could not to break down in tears in front of everyone," she says.

It's an exciting opportunity. If the first Industrial Revolution established the modern economy, bringing great convenience to many and great wealth to a few, the clean-energy revolution can restore a balance between economy and ecology and bring jobs to a broad spectrum of Americans. But is renewable power ready for prime time? Can we foresee the day when solar and wind and other clean-energy sources begin to displace "King CONG"? Judge for yourself.

Watt's That?

For background, let's look at how the United States produces and consumes electricity today. Our power is measured in watts: a thousand watts is a kilowatt, a million watts is a megawatt. We also measure power use over periods of time. So if your lamp has a 100-watt bulb and you read this book for ten hours in bed this week (glad you're enjoying it!), you'll use 100 watts times ten hours, or 1 kilowatt-hour of electricity. The average American home uses 920 kilowatt-hours on a monthly basis. About two-thirds of that is for appliances (8 percent for refrigerators, 15 percent for lighting, 6 percent for clothes dryers).

A great many of these kilowatt-hours used to come from burning oil, but oil is no longer a major player. In the autumn of 1973, before the Arab oil embargo, the United States derived nearly 25 percent of its electricity from burning oil. The subsequent oil shock raised prices, cooled the economy, and motivated many Americans both to buy more fuel-efficient vehicles and to lobby their legislators for policies aimed at reducing dependence on foreign oil. Fifteen years later, oil produced only 10 percent of the nation's electricity, and in 2008 the figure was less than 2 percent. America's success at eliminating oil as a source of electricity demonstrates that smart public policies joined to individual action can make a big difference.

Coal remains the largest source of electricity, providing nearly 47 percent of U.S. power as of the first half of 2010. In the same period, natural gas generated 20.9 percent and nuclear 20.3 percent. The rest is split between hydroelectric

(6.4 percent), renewable and miscellaneous power sources (4.6 percent), and oil (.9 percent). Nationwide demand has been increasing by about 1 to 2 percent per year. To meet it, natural-gas usage has grown at an average annual rate of 4.6 percent in the last decade, while coal has declined slightly. Renewable energy enjoyed a surge in 2009, led by wind, which increased its generating capacity by 39 percent in one year alone, installing a record 10,000 megawatts.

A typical coal-fired power plant is often described in terms of the maximum number of megawatts it can generate at any one time: a "400 megawatt plant" or a "750 megawatt plant." In contrast, the numbers for renewable power are typically much smaller. A typical photovoltaic (PV) solar installation on a rooftop produces 3 kilowatts of electricity. Utility-scale solar farms (which I'll discuss later in this chapter) can be much larger, generating 100 to more than 700 megawatts per site. An individual modern onshore wind turbine is often 1.5 megawatts or more. Wind farms can generate 50 to 3,000 megawatts of power.

To track progress in reducing our dependence on coal, here's the number to remember: the total generating capacity of U.S. coal plants is about 313,000 megawatts. And with the goal in mind of breaking with our dirty-energy past to create a clean-energy future, here's another number: there are just under six hundred power plants in this country using coal as a predominant fuel source. That many and no more. With enough vision, innovation, and commitment, we can start rolling that number back, as more and more megawatts are saved through efficiency and others are generated by solar and wind.

Every Rooftop Matters

It was my fault that the meeting got off track.

We were in the studio office attached to the sunny Palo Alto, California, home of Herman Gyr and Lisa Friedman. They are consultants who have worked with an impressive list of Fortune 500 CEOs and management teams, and were eager to help Rainforest Action Network (RAN) catalyze a shift toward sustainability in corporate America. Just as we sat down after a short break, I happened to ask Gyr about the solar panels on the roof of their home.

His face brightened. "Do you want to see them?" he asked. "You bet." Everyone jumped out of their chairs and followed Gyr as he gave us a tour.

The remarkable thing about solar-powered homes is how thrillingly unremarkable they are. The lights work, the refrigerator hums, everything is normal. Throw a few dozen photovoltaic (PV) cells on your roof and you can achieve energy independence. "I care deeply about climate change, but I also want to support sustainable business," Gyr explained. "By putting solar panels on my home, I can do both."

"Here's the best part," Gyr said, leading us to the side of the house to look at the electricity meter. In a typical home powered by coal, nuclear, or gas, the meter spins day and night, counting the watts used by each DVD player, clock, light, radio, and other appliance. But as we gathered in the sunshine in Gyr's yard and bent to look at the meter, we could see that it was spinning backward. The solar panels were producing not only enough electricity to power the home and office, but also excess power that could be sold back to the utility for another home or business to use.

"Most solar homes are connected to the grid these days," Gyr explained. "Imagine if there were a million of these homes in California. Or five million. We could start shutting down polluting power plants one by one."

What's not to like about solar power? The fuel source doesn't have to be mined, refined, gasified, or blown out of a mountain. The power doesn't have to be shipped long distances, and it doesn't pollute our water, bake the planet, or give our kids asthma. Solar energy bypasses the long fossil-fuel supply chain. Whereas a single coal plant is fed daily by a train of coal cars up to a mile long, solar power can be delivered straight to the user, every day, for free.

Solar power began to ascend in response to the first oil crisis and rising energy prices in the mid- to late 1970s. That's when solar houses started to be built, and PV panels were installed on the roof of the White House. Then Reagan was elected president, the panels were torn down, oil prices tanked, and the dream of solar power was put on hold. Those dreams were delayed again in the 1990s when natural-gas prices collapsed, leading to a national stampede to add gas-fired power plant capacity. But now solar (and wind) are growing much faster than dirty-energy sources and are the target of a major boom in clean-energy investment.

In 1997, global solar PV production totaled 126 megawatts. By 2010, installations worldwide reached 7,300 megawatts. Installation of PV cells and modules around the world has been growing at an average annual rate of greater than 35 percent since 1998. "This level of growth is more akin to the PC, wireless, and Web industries during their heyday than the usually staid and slow-moving energy sector," notes Clean Edge, a market research firm.

As part of its commitment to photovoltaics, California in October 2006 passed SB1, the "Million Solar Roofs" legislation, setting aside $3.2 billion in rebates over a ten-year period for homeowners who install solar panels on their roofs. "Every rooftop matters," says Danny Kennedy, cofounder and president of Sungevity, a California-based solar provider. "Our goal is to make clean energy available to everyone. Every time we install a new solar rooftop system, we're cutting away at the market for coal and nukes."

Commercial use of solar is also growing quickly. In June 2007, Google completed a 1.6 megawatt PV system (enough to power a thousand homes), installed by union workers at its corporate headquarters. At the time it was announced, the solar installation was the largest by any corporation in the United States. Wal-Mart announced in early 2007 that it would install 20 megawatts of solar power at twenty-two stores in California and Hawaii, and the company has set a goal of ultimately sourcing 100 percent of its power from renewable energy.

Other firms, such as Staples, Whole Foods, and Walgreens, have installed solar arrays on dozens of their stores across the country. "The solar revolution does not require new breakthroughs in technology," says Travis Bradford, author of *Solar Revolution: The Economic Transformation of the Global Energy Industry*. "You could do it with the technology we have, scaling it up and learning how to do it incrementally better every year—which is what naturally happens with scale."

Achieving large-scale installation of rooftop solar systems would have a profound impact on the U.S. energy landscape. For starters, individual home-owners and business owners could achieve energy security, controlling their own energy supply right where they live or work. In a time of volatile energy prices and climate destabilization, the value of a reliable and consistent supply of energy should not be underestimated.

Furthermore, rather than predominantly produce electricity at central coal, nuclear, or natural-gas plants, our future energy grid would feature power that has been generated from literally millions of rooftops, wind farms, and other locations. This decentralized, consumer-oriented power network is similar to the revamped media and telecommunications industries, which have undergone sweeping changes in how they distribute information. Gone are the days when three broadcast networks controlled most television news and entertainment programming. Today, consumers not only customize how they want to receive information but generate and distribute it to others. In a similar way, distributed energy generation can empower individuals and communities.

But if you're like me, you still have that number—313,000 megawatts of coal-fired power capacity—branded in your head. You're probably feeling a little skeptical right now, realizing that if we had just over 400 megawatts of solar PV installed in 2009, then we have a long way to go to replace coal. We do. Then you might add a few dozen megawatts for Wal-Mart here and some more from Starbucks there, and think . . . we still have a long way to go.

Here's the good news. The solar industry grew over sevenfold globally in the years from 2004 to 2009, according to a report by Clean Edge. State policies will accelerate this growth further. For example, California's SB1 went into effect on January 1, 2007. By the end of September that same year, new solar installations nearly matched the total amount of solar the state had installed in the previous twenty-six years.

That's just the beginning. "Renewable portfolio standards" have been enacted in twenty-nine states and the District of Columbia. Arizona has committed to generate 15 percent of its energy from renewable resources by 2025. Montana pledged to reach the same goal ten years earlier. New Hampshire and Montana have both committed to use renewable power for 25 percent of their electricity by 2025. Meanwhile, California mandated a 20 percent renewables standard by 2010 and is beginning to set rules to ensure that at least 33 percent of its energy will come from renewables by 2020.

Pass It On

Twenty-nine states and the District of Columbia have made commitments to increase their purchases of renewable power.

The potential for solar energy to meet America's electricity needs is enormous. Enough energy from the sun hits the earth's surface in forty minutes to meet the world's total energy consumption for an entire year. A 1999 report in *Science* magazine showed that the United States could meet its entire electricity needs with a single hundred-square-mile solar array in the Nevada desert. Taking notice are investors and utilities in California and throughout the Southwest, who are beginning to build some of the largest solar power plants on the planet.

The Promise of Big Solar

In ten to twenty years, the U.S. energy mix is likely to include large amounts of power from solar rooftop systems. To accelerate the transition away from coal, however, we need to install massive quantities of clean power as quickly as possible. Enter Big Solar. Industrial-strength solar facilities are being constructed in the sun-drenched deserts of California and other parts of the West. These facilities are orders of magnitude larger than the PV arrays on residential and commercial rooftops and thus produce much larger volumes of solar energy at a greatly reduced cost. One by one, these solar farms will soon cut into the market for coal-fired power.

There are several different technologies, including "parabolic troughs" and other technologies that focus the sun's rays, as well as solar-dish engines, thin-film solar panels, and concentrating photovoltaics. The first large solar facility in the United States was built in the Mojave Desert in the 1980s and early 1990s. The Solar Energy Generating Systems, or SEGS, is a solar thermal power plant that uses parabolic troughs, or curved mirrors, that track the sun and concentrate its rays to heat a liquid and make steam. The steam moves a turbine, producing electricity. SEGS was built in 30- and 50-megawatt installments over a period of seven years and is a good indication of how costs decline with scale and experience. The first 50 megawatts of power cost 28 cents per kilowatt-hour. The last installment of 50 megawatts cost less than 16 cents.

Pass It On

Every forty minutes, enough sun hits the earth's surface to meet the entire world's energy needs for a year.

SEGS has a capacity of 354 megawatts and has been reliably producing solar power from the strong desert sun for more than twenty years. The promise of rapid growth in the concentrating solar power industry was thwarted in the 1990s, as natural-gas prices plummeted, flooding the market with cheap fossil fuels. SEGS was the largest solar plant in the world when it was completed, and it's still the largest facility today. But that will soon change. Solar thermal technology has improved, and concerns about climate change are driving demand for clean energy. Three new concentrating solar power projects came online in 2009, and by the end of 2010 there will likely be three more, bringing the U.S. total to 500 megawatts.

Solel Energy Systems signed a contract in July 2007 to produce 550 mega-watts of solar power (about as much as a coal-fired power plant) for Pacific Gas and Electric (PG&E). Another company, Ausra, Inc., which is using similar solar thermal technology but with less expensive, nearly flat mirrors, has an agreement with PG&E to produce 177 megawatts of solar power. Both facilities are expected to be online by 2011 or 2012. "What I find attractive about Ausra is that it's taking approaches used in the past and driving the price down, making it cheap," says PG&E CEO Peter A. Darbee. "It's lower risk and environmentally friendly. I'm very enthusiastic about the technology."

Another way to concentrate solar power is the solar-dish engine, popular-ized by Stirling Energy Systems of Phoenix, Arizona. Whereas the parabolic troughs use steam to drive a turbine, dish engines use steam to move pistons. Although this technology has not yet produced electricity at large scale, some believe a breakthrough can be achieved. Stirling Energy has signed contracts to deliver 900 and 850 megawatts of solar energy to San Diego Gas and Electric and Southern California Edison. Other technologies also hold promise. At Nellis Air Force Base in Nevada, construction was completed in December 2007 on a field of seventy thousand photovoltaic cells—the largest PV solar array in North America.

Meanwhile, New Mexico utility Public Service of New Mexico (PNM), in partnership with Sandia National Laboratories and others, is seeking bids for concentrated solar power. In September 2007, PG&E announced that it would double the amount of solar thermal power it would purchase, pledging to add a thousand megawatts of solar power within five years. It's boom times for the solar industry, and with every 100-, 250-, or 500-megawatt solar installation, we move closer to being able to shut dirty-coal plants down.

But taking coal plants offline isn't as simple as replacing one 500-megawatt coal plant with a single 500-megawatt concentrating solar plant and calling it even—or even with a few thousand rooftop solar arrays generating an equivalent amount of power. A coal plant, unless it's down for maintenance or has a supply disruption, can generate 500 megawatts of electricity twenty-four hours a day. Solar power, of course, can be generated only during the daytime. One way to extend the reach of solar power into nighttime hours is through energy storage, which I'll discuss later. But solar power can also be complemented by other clean-energy solutions, including biomass, geothermal, tidal energy, and, most important for now, wind.

Wind at Our Backs

I still remember the first time I saw a wind farm. It was 1985, I was thirteen years old, and my family was about to complete a great adventure through California and the desert Southwest. Growing up on the New Jersey shore, I had never been west of the Appalachians before and had experienced a near-religious introduction to the Grand Canyon two weeks earlier. On this day, we were driving from Yosemite National Park to San Francisco. I had dozed off with my legs stretched across my younger brother's lap, much to his dismay.

I woke up just as we were winding through the golden hills of Altamont Pass near Livermore, California. I rubbed my eyes and saw hundreds of turbines on the hilltops, turning gracefully in the wind. I thought they were beautiful. My father told us that the former governor, Jerry Brown, had pushed to have them installed, and that this wind farm alone produced enough power to light up most of San Francisco. As a teenager, I had seen how California skateboards and, earlier, surfboards had swept across the country, and I wondered how long it would take before these wind farms would do the same.

Wind power hasn't taken over the country yet, but much has happened in the last twenty years. Total installed wind power exceeded 35,000 megawatts in 2009, enough for 9.7 million homes. Moreover, wind power has been one of the fastest-growing sources of energy in the past five years, second only to natural gas. In 2009, wind accounted for 39 percent of all new installed power plants, as its costs have dropped dramatically. Many of today's larger wind farms can compete on a price basis with coal, even if coal's water- and air-pollution costs are not included in its price.

The cost of wind power has dropped as knowledge in the field has grown. Bob Dylan famously sang, "You don't need a weatherman to know which way the wind blows," but if you're designing a wind farm, a slight variance in wind speed makes all the difference. The energy the wind contains is a calculation of the cube of the speed of the wind. This means that a site with an average wind speed of sixteen miles per hour can create nearly 50 percent more wind energy than a wind farm with an average speed of just fourteen miles an hour, and costs about half as much. Choosing the best sites for wind farms is critical to optimizing their power output.

Pass It On

The wind energy available in twelve midwestern and Rocky Mountain states is equal to two and a half times the total electricity consumption in the United States today.

Also, bigger is better. A modern wind turbine with fifty-meter blades can generate up to fifty-five times more electricity annually than a typical model installed in the early 1980s, which had blades just ten meters long. The new turbines take advantage of an increase in the swept area and a substantial increase in wind speeds at greater heights. There are also significant advantages of scale for an entire wind farm. The American Wind Energy Association estimates that a 51-megawatt wind project delivers electricity 40 percent more cheaply than does a 3-megawatt project, mostly because the administrative costs to finance, operate, and maintain larger farms can be spread out over more kilowatt-hours.

As advancements in wind-energy technology have lowered the price, it's becoming more profitable to expand the size and generating capacity of wind farms. And the potential for wind power to meet a substantial portion of U.S. electricity needs is real. The amount of wind energy available in twelve midwestern and Rocky Mountain states is about two and a half times the electricity production of the entire country. Six of those states—North Dakota, Texas, Kansas, South Dakota, Montana, and Nebraska—could each supply more than 20 percent of America's electricity needs. Put another way, just three of those states could create more power than all of the country's coal plants combined.

Wind power has its detractors, however. Some environmentalists and bird enthusiasts have raised concerns about the threats that the rotating blades pose to birds and bats, as well as their risk of electrocution from power lines. One study estimated that an average of two to five birds is killed per wind turbine, per year. However, bird mortality can be significantly reduced through proper location of wind farms and other best-management practices. The American Bird Conservatory recommends conducting detailed studies on the potential impact of a wind farm on local birds and bats before the wind farm is constructed. Kansas, Washington, and the U.S. Fish and Wildlife Service have all adopted standards for siting and operating wind farms to minimize bird mortalities. Wind-power providers would be wise to adopt these guidelines.

Then there's the question of aesthetics. Although some find wind turbines to be sleek and attractive, others (and not just coal executives, mind you) find them ugly and intrusive. A bitter fight erupted over a proposed 420-megawatt wind farm to be built in Nantucket Sound off the Massachusetts coast. The farm would produce up to three-quarters of the electricity needs of residents of Cape Cod, Nantucket, and Martha's Vineyard but has provoked fierce opposition from some residents of the Cape and islands. But as Greenpeace's Kert Davies told the *New York Times,* "As environmental advocates, [we] have to be consistent. . . . It's not fair to stump about how scary global warming is one week, then oppose this the next. It's not fair, in terms of environmental justice, for communities with cash to demand that projects they don't want be built somewhere else." Cape Wind was approved by Interior secretary Salazar in May 2010.

Aside from the occasional local skirmish, producing energy from wind enjoys broad-based support. The advantages of the technology are obvious. Even a small, 750-kilowatt turbine will prevent twelve hundred tons of carbon dioxide from being released into the atmosphere annually. That same turbine will prevent 6.9 tons of sulfur dioxide and more than 4 tons of nitrogen oxide from being emitted each year, in addition to other pollutants. Moreover, wind farms can help rural communities diversify their income sources and keep their homes and farms intact, through a process called community-based energy development. Leading the way is Dan Juhl in Minnesota.

Rescuing Rural Economies

Fortune Small Business magazine says, "When the history of wind power is written, Dan Juhl will rate a chapter." A Vietnam vet, Juhl has more than thirty years' experience in the wind-power industry. He installed windmills up in Fairbanks, Alaska, then came home to Minnesota and plowed his life's savings into setting up his own wind farm in the southwestern part of the state, signing a contract to sell the power to Xcel Energy. Juhl also worked for Aerostar, a Danish wind turbine manufacturer, creating wind farms in India and China.

"When we started, we were so committed to renewable energy, but the technology for wind was barely ready," says Juhl. "We've spent years refining the technology, getting everything to work right, and it's like night and day compared to the beginning. Now everybody's jumping on the bandwagon because we can compete with coal, even though so many of the costs of coal are hidden." Juhl soon turned a profit and began consulting on the side, helping farmers in the region install wind turbines on their land.

Besides operating his own wind farm, Juhl works to promote community-based energy development, or C-BED, in Minnesota and elsewhere. C-BED promotes local ownership of wind energy and other clean-power sources, which helps rural people diversify and stabilize their income and ensures that the financial benefits of renewable energy stay within the community. A September 2004 General Accounting Office study showed that local ownership of wind generates 2.3 times more jobs and has 3.1 times the economic impact in a region when compared with out-of-town ownership. In May 2005, a Department of Energy study for Arizona, Colorado, and Michigan showed that wind energy would bring the "highest direct economic benefit to the state," compared with coal and natural gas. Minnesota passed C-BED legislation later that year. Nebraska followed in May 2007 with similar legislation that exempts C-BED projects from sales and other taxes.

"C-BED is so good for so many people, it's hard to beat down," says Juhl. He estimates that a farmer who owns his own wind turbines can generate $25,000 to $30,000 in profits for the first ten years, and then $100,000 annually after the capital costs are fully paid. "I started doing this work because I cared about the environment," says Juhl. "Learning about climate change made it even more important. But the social aspect is the most important to me now. C-BED can give a life-changing economic boost to so many farmers. That's why this is so important."

From Here to There

If you've purchased this book and read this far, you're probably not opposed to renewable power. You might like solar because of the energy security it can give your family or business. You may be a fan of renewables in general because of the jobs they'll create, or the greenhouse gases, air pollution, and smog they'll prevent. Perhaps you're just a sucker for new technology and think that mining and burning coal to keep the lights on is so . . . nineteenth century. If so, you'll undoubtedly want clean energy to be the dominant source of power as soon as possible. The question is how we get from here to there—from an economy that's mostly powered by coal, oil, nuclear, and gas to one that is smart, secure, and sustainable.

One common concern is "intermittency"—the term used to describe the unsteady supply of renewable power. Although wind speed is variable, and the sun doesn't always shine, the intermittent capabilities of these and other clean-power sources, such as geothermal energy, can offset each other. Advances in energy storage will increase renewables' potential even more. In late February 2008, Arizona Public Service, the state's largest utility, announced plans to build a 280-megawatt solar array in the desert seventy miles southwest of Phoenix. Notably, the plant will produce power for up to six hours after sunset, using molten salt to store solar energy. "When the suns sets, this plant keeps on ticking," says Arizona Public Service president Don Brandt. "We'll have solar energy in the dark."

Making a full transition to a clean-energy economy will take determination and commitment at all levels of society. We'll need individual homeowners, farmers, and businesses to become distributed suppliers of solar and wind as they are able. We'll need city, state, and regional policies to strengthen the market for clean energy and solidify long-term demand. And we'll need all levels of government to end all subsidies of dirty power.

But to complete the transition to clean power, we'll need strategic public policies that support large-scale investments in clean energy. Here are several ways in which local, state, and federal policies can give us the clean electricity that we deserve.

Encourage Long-Term Investments

Germany receives as much sunshine annually as Nome, Alaska, yet it's become the world's top producer of solar energy. Germany collects a small fee from electricity users, about $1.80 per month per household, and then reinvests that money to provide solar tax and investment incentives and, most important, a "feed-in tariff." Feed-in tariffs, sometimes called advanced renewable tariffs in the United States, are a price support system that commits utilities to buy renewable power at a price that will ensure profitability for clean-power providers. When Oregon offered this incentive to businesses in 2010, enrollment in the program filled up in most parts of the state in less than fifteen minutes. In California, a smaller but similar charge of about $0.50 per month per household has put the state far above any other in solar-power generation.

Such public policies can assure investors and entrepreneurs alike that clean energy is a long-term priority, which in turn stimulates more renewable energy development. In the United States, rather than provide tax breaks to oil and coal companies, we should provide them to the purveyors and purchasers of renewable power.

Another innovative approach was recently launched by Berkeley, California, which approved a policy in November 2007 enabling homeowners to install rooftop solar with no money down. The city pays for installation and is repaid through an assessment added to property taxes over twenty years. There's very little risk for homeowners or the city: the monthly payment for property owners is set at a level equal to or less than the savings on each month's electricity bill.

Create Significant Demand Incentives

Twenty-five states have already issued standards to increase the percentage of clean power that is produced. On top of that, more than five hundred local organizations in more than fifty states and Canadian provinces have undertaken the "Campus Climate Challenge" to help inspire colleges and universities to reduce greenhouse gas emissions and increase their utilization of renewable energy. Meanwhile, the Sierra Club's "Cool Cities" program has signed up more than a thousand towns and cities to join the clean-energy revolution. Evanston, Illinois, committed to add wind farms to its electrical grid; Seattle, Boulder, Salt Lake City, and many others have climate-action plans.

A major reason the solar and wind industries are growing so rapidly is that grassroots activists have been building consumer demand for clean power. As more schools, cities, and states join this effort—and as the renewable-power standards increase over time—the industry will continue to grow. Is your campus pushing utilities to provide more green power? How about your city or state? Or your church?

Share Power Fairly

When the sun is shining, many homes or businesses with rooftop solar panels generate more electricity than they need. And when the wind is blowing, the same may be true for small wind-farm owners. In many states, regulations allow homeowners or businesses to sell the excess power to the grid and then buy it back at night or on calm or rainy days. These so-called net-metering laws allow small renewable energy providers to pay for the "net" charge on their electricity meter by subtracting the amount of power produced by solar or wind from the total amount of electricity consumed in the home or business.

It sounds simple, but although forty states have net-metering laws, many of those laws are rigged to favor large corporate utilities. For instance, some regulations force homeowners to sell clean power to the utility at wholesale prices, then compel them to buy power back at a higher retail charge. Other rules limit the size of solar installations that are eligible for net-metering provisions. For example, New York limits the maximum size to which net-metering laws apply to just 10 kilowatts, which limits the profitability of large commercial systems. New Jersey has the best standard, giving net-metering rights to all systems up to 2 megawatts in size. By copying the best elements of policies in each state, we can help more homeowners and businesses to provide their own clean power on site.

Build a Clean Energy Infrastructure

For the past hundred years, our country has created and expanded a fossil-fuel infrastructure, including the sites where coal is mined and oil is extracted, railroad lines and pipelines to ship materials, power plants, and then lines to transmit power over long distances. We'll need to modernize parts of this infrastructure to transmit clean power across the country. For instance, in many regions, wind resources are underutilized or neglected entirely due to the lack of high-voltage transmission lines. Similarly, large areas of the desert Southwest are unsuitable sites for utility-scale solar because there's no way to deliver the electricity to towns and cities that will use it.

At each point in the clean-energy infrastructure, we'll want to avoid the mistakes of the past. Wind farms and solar stations will need to be sited in an environmentally responsible way. Transmission lines, if they're established, must also be built with minimal impact on communities, wildlife, and wilderness values. And distributed power will play an important role in the electricity grid of the future, by reducing the number of miles our energy must travel.

Fill the Leadership Gap

While just 4 percent of our electricity is derived from renewable sources, we can reach 20–30 percent within a decade and create an economy that is carbon-free by midcentury. What we need most is strong leadership. "The greatest obstacle to implementing a renewable U.S. energy system is not technology or money," observe Ken Zweibel, James Mason, and Vasilis Fthenakis in a *Scientific American* article entitled "A Grand Solar Plan." "It is the lack of public awareness that solar power is a practical alternative."

The researchers show how the United States would be able to derive 69 percent of its electricity from solar alone by 2050—including enough power for 350 million plug-in hybrid electric vehicles. The price tag? A public investment of $10 billion per year from 2011 to 2050. Compare that to annual U.S. fossil-fuel subsidies of about $49 billion, as discussed in chapter 3.

Shifting public investments toward clean energy will hasten the phase-out of dirty coal. With each passing year the price of renewable power drops and the economics of clean energy versus coal become more favorable. To illustrate, in May 2008 the California Energy Commission evaluated the cost of generating new capacity from different sources. Wind was cheapest, at $8.91 per kilowatt-hour. Pulverized coal with unregulated greenhouse gas emissions came in at $10.55 and concentrated solar power at $12.65. However, solar was far less expensive than "clean coal." When attempts to store emissions are factored in, power from coal would cost $17.32 per kilowatt-hour.

Future trends don't look good for Big Coal, either. Coal prices, like those of oil, have increased significantly in recent years as demand from China and India strains the industry's capacity. And as coal prices climb, so too do the costs of building new power plants. Cambridge Energy Research Associates released a report in February 2008 showing that the cost of building U.S. coal-fired power plants has increased 130 percent since 2000 and 27 percent from October 2006 to October 2007 alone. And let's not forget that the cost of financing risky coal plants will also increase as banks become more cautious of accepting the carbon risk associated with coal plants.

With strategic public policies and corporate pressure, we can make coal more obsolete with each passing year. As investor Vinod Khosla puts it, we can reverse the common question "How soon will solar be competitive?" and instead ask, "How long will coal be competitive?"

Take Action

Take it personally

1. Every rooftop matters. Installing solar on the roof of your home, school, church, or office will save money, help create well-paying jobs, and reduce our country's reliance on dirty coal. Financing is sometimes available with which homeowners can get solar with no money down. Other packages are structured so that each month's payment for the system is less than the savings you'll enjoy in your electricity bill. More information is available in the resources section to help get you started.

2. If you live in a rural area, consider wind power and community-based energy development to put money in your pocket and keep coal in the ground.

Express yourself

1. *Local.* Organize in your community to make clean energy a priority. Does your employer have solar panels installed? How about municipal buildings? Your school or church? Not only can your town or city utilize clean power for its own buildings, but it also can provide financial incentives and tax credits to help area businesses and homeowners to do the same.

2. *State.* Help make your state a leader in clean energy. Urge state leaders to enact strong net-metering laws, establish a renewable portfolio standard and/or feed-in tariffs to rapidly advance wind and solar, and give tax and other financial incentives to encourage homeowners and businesses to switch to clean power.

3. *Federal.* For starters, let's get solar panels on the White House and all government buildings. Let Congress and the White House know that they should provide stable, long-term investment and production tax credits that reward investments in clean energy. Support a carbon tax or other means of putting a price on greenhouse gas emissions, which would begin to make the price of coal reflect its cost to society.

Stay engaged

In every household, city, and state across the country, there are ways to accelerate the development of renewable power. If you're passionate about climate change and clean-energy issues, join the Vote Solar Initiative and visit the Web sites of some of the other organizations listed in the resources section. Attend meetings of your local and state public utility commission meetings, and urge them to adopt strong policies on the issues discussed in this chapter. Your voice matters, so please use it.

CHAPTER 9

Less Is More

Fighting Climate Change While Living the Good Life

That's not a free lunch—it's a lunch you're paid to eat.

— AMORY LOVINS, SPEAKING OF
ENERGY-EFFICIENT DESIGN

As far as I know, no universities or concert halls are named after Amory Lovins. Nor are there any bridges, parks, or city centers named after Ed Mazria or Art Rosenfeld. In truth, most Americans probably don't know who these men are or what they've accomplished. Yet they are leaders of a movement that is reshaping how Americans live, work, and play. Their ethos—doing more with less—offers some of the best ideas for fighting climate change and breaking our addiction to dirty energy.

A hundred years ago, leading industrialists like John D. Rockefeller, Andrew Carnegie, and J. P. Morgan were lauded for creating vast empires in the oil, steel, railroad, and banking industries. Called "captains of industry" by some and "robber barons" by others, these men built much of the industrial foundation of this country and were usually regarded as heroes in their day.

As America faces the challenges of climate change and fossil-fuel dependence early in the twenty-first century, it's time to pick some new heroes—the visionaries who show how proper planning, design, and construction can reduce energy use and greenhouse gas emissions and improve the quality of our lives at the same time. Another innovator, Michael Corbett, helped design a Davis, California, development that set a standard for residential efficiency in the late 1970s. He says, "You know you're on the right track when you notice that your solution for one problem accidentally solves several other problems."

A refreshing optimism permeates the pronouncements of many leaders in the efficiency field. In a 2005 *Scientific American* article, "More Profit with Less Carbon," Lovins wrote: "A basic misunderstanding skews the entire climate debate. Experts on both sides claim that protecting Earth's climate will force a trade-off between the environment and the economy. According to these experts, burning less fossil fuel to slow or prevent global warming will increase the cost of meeting society's needs for energy services. . . . Yet both sides are wrong. If properly done, climate protection would actually reduce costs, not raise them. Using energy more efficiently offers an economic bonanza—not because of the benefits of stopping global warming but because saving fossil fuel is a lot cheaper than buying it."

Aggressive investments in efficiency offer immediate opportunities for businesses and municipalities alike. McKinsey and Company estimates that 85 percent of the projected growth in electricity demand through 2030 can be met through better efficiency in our buildings, appliances, and factories alone. Implementing these technologies will bring some up-front costs, but they would pay back those costs and more over time.

Gone are the days when utility companies handed out free hair dryers to encourage more energy consumption. Nobody wants to increase waste. Yet many regulators, lawmakers, and corporate executives still find it easier to call for more power plants than to figure out the best ways to use energy more effectively. With a few rule changes and some tough love for these decision makers, however, we can put efficiency at the top of the list of energy choices. And watch the leaders of the new energy economy continue to shine.

Cold Beer, Hot Ideas

Using energy efficiently is different from conserving energy. Conservation can be described as making do with less—shutting off lights and turning down the heat for the good of the planet. Energy efficiency, on the other hand, entails finding clever ways to use energy more effectively while enjoying the same level of comfort. Conservation can involve sacrifice, while efficiency does not; the latter is so sensible and appealing that it should be a no-brainer.

Here's how the Center of the American West and the Southwest Energy

Efficiency project describe what it would be like to take "energy efficiency" out on a date: "On your first outing, you will need to remember to bring your wallet. Energy efficiency is not a cheap date; you will have to make an investment to get this relationship off the ground. But, in short order, after you have paid for the first dinner or two, and maybe for theatre or concert tickets, the terms will shift and energy efficiency will begin treating you. Each time you reach for your wallet, energy efficiency will snatch the check and say, 'No, really, this one's on me!' In no time at all, energy efficiency will pay you back—and more!—for the investment you made at the start of your relationship."

Indeed, there are some barriers to entry in the field of efficiency. Some money must be invested: perhaps by a family stocking up on compact fluorescent lightbulbs that cost more at the register but pay back over time, or a business seeking to install more efficient motors and pumps in its factories. Planning and research are also required. There are as many ways to be wise with energy consumption as there are ways to consume energy. Keeping up with the latest technologies and techniques can be a tall order.

But opportunities abound. In consumer electronics or home appliances, a little research will turn up energy-efficient options for everything from televisions to dishwashers to floor lamps, often at a comparable cost. For home, office, and commercial buildings, advanced materials and good design principles can cut energy use in half, then in half again. Nearly everywhere energy is being used, consumption can be reduced.

Even so, the rules are stacked against energy efficiency in most states. Guidelines force regulators to add generating capacity to match increases in population, regardless of whether energy demands can be met another way. Meanwhile, regulators allow utility companies to earn a far greater profit by selling power than by saving it, in most cases. As a result, the energy policy for much of the United States has been consistent: if you build them (more power plants), demand will come.

But we can't continue to build our way out of this problem. The biggest remaining energy source won't be found in a deep coal seam in the northern Rockies, nor in a newly discovered oil field in the Amazon. The largest "new" source is the energy we can save in our lights, homes, appliances, computers, and office buildings. Dozens of examples show that investing in energy-efficient systems is cheaper than extracting, processing, transporting, and burning fossil fuels. And it will create far more well-paying and safe jobs than we'll find in a coal mine or oil field.

Using energy efficiently is a winner on every front; it creates sustainable jobs, cleans the air, protects the climate, and saves money for consumers, businesses, and governments alike. Setting high efficiency standards will not only prevent new power plants from being built, it will help shut the dirtiest ones down. Best of all, our lifestyles will improve. We can indeed have cold beer, hot water, loud music, bright lights—and use far less energy. To show how this can be done, we need look no further than California—and not just the state's recent leadership on energy but a decades-old history of innovation.

California Dreaming

On a Friday night in late November 1973, physicist Art Rosenfeld was still at work at Lawrence Berkeley National Laboratory. He had received his bachelor of science degree at the young age of eighteen, joined the navy toward the end of World War II, and then, in 1954, earned his PhD under the acclaimed physicist Enrico Fermi at the University of Chicago. In the late 1960s, Rosenfeld led a team of researchers that helped UC Berkeley professor Luis Alvarez win the Nobel Prize for Physics. By 1973, Rosenfeld was in the midst of a stellar career. But, though he didn't know it at the time, he was about to begin an entirely different one.

The country was experiencing its first oil shock. In October, Arab nations had announced an oil embargo against the United States and other Western countries in retaliation for their support of Israel in the Yom Kippur War. Within a year, the price of oil in the United States soared by a factor of four. Inflation increased, and the economy dipped into recession. Gas was rationed; vehicles with license plates ending in an odd number could buy gas on odd-numbered dates, the others on even-numbered dates. Hour-long lines at gas stations were common.

As Rosenfeld was preparing to leave work that Friday evening, he thought of the long gas line awaiting him the next day. He looked around the building and noted that nearly every office had been vacated with the lights still blazing.

Rosenfeld quickly calculated that his twenty-floor building would consume energy equivalent to a hundred gallons of gas between Friday night and Monday morning. Never a fan of waste, Rosenfeld spent the next half-hour turning off the lights and vowing to get UC Berkeley and its laboratories to do something about conservation.

Rosenfeld suspected, as did many of his colleagues, that the United States wasted far more energy each year than it imported from OPEC countries. A crisis soon became an opportunity: by identifying and implementing ways to use energy more efficiently, the country could shrug off the oil embargo and save money at the same time. In the summer of 1974, with Robert Socolow at Princeton University (who with Stephen Pacala in 2005 developed the famous "wedge" theory of fighting climate change), Rosenfeld organized a month-long strategy session with the country's top scientists, engineers, and policy experts. As he recounted in his autobiography, "By the end of the first week, we realized that we were discovering (or had blundered into) a huge oil and gas field buried in our buildings, factories, and cars, which could be 'extracted' at pennies per gallon of gas equivalent. . . . Many of us became aware that our new knowledge would soon change our lives."

Rosenfeld gave up his career in particle physics and devoted himself to the new field of energy efficiency, cofounding the Energy Efficient Buildings program, which later became the Center for Building Science at Lawrence Berkeley Lab. The center has played a vital role in helping the state develop efficiency standards for appliances, buildings, and lighting systems.

Other efficiency programs took root across the country, focusing primarily, though not exclusively, on reducing oil consumption. The results were impressive. From 1977 to 1985, total oil consumption dropped by 17 percent, even as the economy grew by 27 percent. In that same period, American dependence on oil from the Persian Gulf declined by 87 percent.

Beginning under the leadership of former governor Jerry Brown (who as of 2010 was again running for the office), California initiated a multitude of programs to increase efficiency in lights, appliances, buildings, and more. Many of these programs save a kilowatt of power more cheaply than coal can generate it, and the standards are continually updated as technology improves. From 1977 to 2005, California produced savings of more than 40,000 gigawatt-hours of electricity each year, eliminating the need to build twenty-four coal- or gas-fired power plants. There's good news in all directions: consumers and businesses have saved billions of dollars, greenhouse gas emissions have been reduced by millions of tons, and the competitive position of the state's businesses has been strengthened.

Recently, more ambitious targets have been established. Rather than continue to build more power plants to meet ever-increasing demand, California's "Energy Action Plan" mandates that energy efficiency must be the top priority in all energy investment and policy decisions. This means that electric utilities in the state must maximize gains in efficiency before they can consider adding any new generating capacity. After efficiency measures, expanding renewable power comes next, according to the California plan. Fossil-fuel plants can be built in the state only after investments in efficiency and renewable power are made. Even then, the only power plants permitted are those at least as efficient as a modern natural-gas plant, effectively banning new coal-fired plants in the state.

Pass It On

From 1977 to 2005, California's energy-efficiency program saved 40,000 gigawatt-hours of electricity, avoiding the need to build twenty-four large coal plants. The state's per capita energy use has remained constant since the late 1970s, while demand in the rest of the country has risen by more than 50 percent.

From 2006 to 2008, California invested at least $2 billion in efficiency projects and educational programs run by the state's investor-owned utilities—Pacific Gas and Electric, Southern California Edison, San Diego Gas and Electric, and Southern California Gas. "This is the most important thing we can do for long-term energy reliability in the state," said Susan P. Kennedy, a former California public utilities commissioner and a longtime leader on energy-use reduction in the state. "What this plan does is help us meet our growing needs, first and foremost, with the cleanest, most cost-effective energy of all—greater efficiency."

Funded by ratepayers through a charge of about 1 percent of a typical electricity bill, the efficiency program was expected to produce savings of more than 1,500 megawatts over three years, enough to avoid the construction of another three large power plants. After paying back the initial investment costs, California's efficiency program will produce net ratepayer savings of $2.7 billion and prevent 3.4 million tons of greenhouse gas emissions, equivalent to taking 650,000 cars off the road.

Since the mid-1970s, California's per capita electricity consumption has remained constant, whereas per capita consumption for the rest of the United States has surged by more than 50 percent. It's an impressive feat. The state boasts the largest economy among the fifty and the seventh-largest economy in the world. Culturally, California can hardly be called a place of restraint and self-denial. Yet with foresight and wise long-term investments in efficiency, California gets far more in savings than it spends, year after year.

Obstacles and Opportunities

There's a disconnect here. If California is making such substantial gains, why wouldn't businesses and governments everywhere sink all the resources they could into increasing efficiency, so long as they could do so cost-effectively? In fact, many states, cities, and businesses are making at least small investments in efficiency. But few of them pursue efficiency opportunities with much tenacity, instead wasting energy and leaving money on the table. How can this be?

One explanation is that inertia is difficult to overcome. Not everyone acts in his or her own best interest, at least not right away. Think about it from your own perspective. You've probably read about the benefits to wallet and planet of buying compact fluorescent lightbulbs, but be honest: have you changed the bulbs in your home and office yet? If so, how long did it take you to act on this? If it takes time and initiative to be energy efficient at home, imagine the difficulty of doing the same for an entire school or building or factory.

Another reason is the widespread misconception that saving energy in significant amounts demands austerity, discomfort, a rejection of the good life—essentially, a lifestyle of "less with less." Yet another obstacle is the difficulty of keeping up with new technologies and practices to conserve energy. Energy is used in thousands of ways, and just as many techniques can be employed to save it. Even the most dutiful energy planners and efficiency experts update their guidelines only every two to three years, so their policies become dated only months after being finalized.

But perhaps the biggest challenge is a lack of clarity regarding the economic benefits of using energy more wisely. Without conducting an energy audit and devoting resources to the issue, most companies and public officials remain in the dark about efficiency's potential. "Everyone knows that there's money out there (in energy efficiency)," explains Matt Arnold, former codirector of Sustainable Finance, Ltd., a consultancy that helps Fortune 500 companies manage sustainability issues. "The difficulty is finding out just how much. Are there $100 bills lying on the floor, or just piles of dimes and quarters here and there?"

One metric used to determine whether substantial investments make sense is to evaluate the cost to save energy. If the cost of saving energy is less than the cost of generating it, then it's a good deal for governments and businesses alike. One reason California is making such robust investments in energy efficiency is that its cost of saving energy to date is less than half what the state otherwise spends to produce it. Many other municipalities and companies are capitalizing on similar opportunities.

Vermont adds a small charge to ratepayers' utility bills each month to fund the nation's first energy-efficiency utility—one that doesn't create new power but is devoted solely to reducing demand. Efficiency Vermont is operated by a nonprofit corporation that works directly with state households and businesses to help reduce energy costs. The program offers free technical advice for residents seeking to make their home or business more efficient, gives rebates on purchases of efficient lamps and bulbs, and provides free or subsidized home-weatherization services to low-income homeowners. These programs have cut residents' energy bills by $31 million from 2000 to 2006. In 2006 alone, Efficiency Vermont helped 38,655 residents—more than 10 percent of state residents—make energy investments that will produce annual savings of 56 million kilowatt-hours.

Connecticut has a similar system of rebates and incentives. The state subsidizes the cost of making new homes more efficient by reimbursing new homeowners for the average incremental costs incurred with energy-efficiency investments. Connecticut offers free energy audits to many businesses, as well as rebates for purchases of efficient lighting, heating, cooling, and other equipment. The American Council for an Energy-Efficient Economy ranked

California, Vermont, and Connecticut tied for first in its annual state-efficiency scorecard in 2007.

In the private sector, some leading businesses are lowering emissions and expenses in tandem. Bayer cut its overall greenhouse gas emissions 60 percent from 1990 levels by 2004, even though production increased 16 percent in that period. DuPont increased its production by 35 percent while reducing greenhouse gas emissions by 67 percent between 1990 and 2005, saving more than $2 billion in the process. At Johnson & Johnson sales have increased 372 percent since 1990, but greenhouse gas emissions dropped 16.8 percent from 1990 to 2006. The company's investments in greenhouse gas reductions create positive cash flows and "internal public relations benefits," meaning that employees like it. When this book first appeared, Johnson & Johnson was the second-largest nonutility user of solar cells in the country.

Creating a Climate for Efficiency

Amory Lovins calls it a "negawatt revolution," estimating that electricity consumption can be cut by radically increasing standards in appliances such as refrigerators, dryers, and consumer electronics; installing more efficient industrial pumps and motors; and investing in advanced lighting fixtures and efficient bulbs. William McDonough—a pioneer of the sustainable-design movement whose imaginative designs for factories, office buildings, and homes have earned him a bevy of honors, including three U.S. presidential awards and a "Hero of the Planet" recognition by *Time*—prefers the term "abundance by design," believing that we cannot just minimize waste but can eliminate it altogether. Both emphasize that growth can be achieved by using less resources, not more—addition through subtraction. Joining them in making this vision real are hundreds of other designers, planners, builders, and a growing list of companies and municipalities.

Smart public policies that accelerate energy-efficiency efforts can have a profound effect on the American energy landscape. They could allow us to retire the country's dirtiest coal plants, replace those plants with efficiently utilized renewable energy, and rejuvenate our economy in the process. Here's how we can cover ground quickly.

Getting Priorities Straight

All fifty states could adopt a "loading order" for energy, similar to California's, mandating that energy efficiency is the first choice for energy development in the state. In practical terms this means that energy planners must endeavor to match incremental growth in energy consumption by saving energy elsewhere. In a December 2007 report suggesting greenhouse gas abatement strategies, the international consulting firm McKinsey and Company identified energy efficiency as a significant "negative cost option," meaning that investments in energy efficiency would pay off. The report's authors warn that time is running short: "Many of the most economically attractive abatement options we analyzed are 'time perishable': every year we delay producing energy-efficient commercial buildings, houses, motor vehicles, and so forth, the more negative cost-options we lose. The cost of building energy efficiency into an asset when it is created is typically a fraction of the cost of retrofitting it later, or retiring an asset before its useful life is over. In addition, an aggressive energy-efficiency program would reduce the demand for fossil fuels and the need for new power plants."

A loading order that puts efficiency and renewable energy at the front of the line for policymakers would give us our best chance to create an energy U-turn: stopping the expansion of fossil-fuel consumption, and advancing efficiency and renewables rapidly enough that they can begin to replace the dirtiest power plants as quickly as possible.

Decoupling Profits from Sales

In many parts of the country, utilities can still make more money by producing power than by saving it. This creates a powerful incentive for waste.

One solution is "decoupling," in which regulators offer utilities a chance to increase profits by being more efficient. "Decoupling breaks the link between a utility's financial health and their gas or electricity sales," says Ralph Cavanagh, senior attorney for the National Resources Defense Council. "Until you do that, it's very hard to get a utility to make significant efficiency investments."

Here's how it works. First, regulators determine how much revenue a utility needs to cover its costs and bring a return to shareholders. They then establish electricity rates based on demand forecasts so that utilities can meet their revenue targets. If utilities collect too much from ratepayers—or too little—adjustments are made in the next period's rate structure. All of this provides different profit incentives for utilities, including rewards if they achieve certain efficiency goals. When those goals are met, everyone wins: customers save money, the utility earns a higher rate of return, and greenhouse gas emissions and other pollutants are reduced. "The most environmentally benign . . . power plant I can build is the one I don't build," says Duke Energy CEO Jim Rogers.

Pass It On

Decoupling legislation creates efficiency incentives by allowing utilities to make money by selling less power. As this book was written, only five states had adopted decoupling legislation.

The California Public Utilities Commission (CPUC) first enacted decoupling legislation for gas in 1978 and for electricity in 1982. These moves were an integral part of the state's efficiency success story. As of August 2009, however, only eight states—California, Connecticut, Idaho, Maryland, New York, Oregon, Vermont, and Wisconsin—had enacted decoupling legislation for electricity. Ten others were considering it. Twenty-three states either had adopted or were considering decoupling legislation for gas.

Pulling the Plug on Incandescents

This has to be the simplest and most cost-effective way to save energy: switch to more-modern lightbulbs. Producing light from a typical incandescent lightbulb lit up by a coal-fired power plant is only 3 percent efficient, according to the Rocky Mountain Institute. The efficiency of lightbulbs is typically measured in lumens per watt, which is a function of how much brightness is produced (lumens), relative to how much power (watts) is consumed. An average incandescent lightbulb emits twelve to fifteen lumens per watt, whereas compact fluorescent lightbulbs (CFLs) produce around sixty lumens per watt (and last up to ten times longer). Some CFLs were criticized for producing a cold, harsh light when they were introduced, but new designs offer a much softer light, comparable to most other lighting available on the market, and a variety of hues.

With one policy shift, an entire nation's energy consumption can be painlessly reduced. Australia was the first, adopting legislation in February 2007 to ban incandescent bulbs by 2010, which will save an estimated 4 million tons of CO_2 by 2012. "If the whole world switches to these (compact fluorescent) bulbs today, we would reduce our consumption of electricity by an amount equal to five times Australia's annual consumption of electricity," said Malcom Turnbull, Australian environment minister. Canada followed one month later with a similar ban.

Some U.S. lawmakers are trying a different approach, choosing not to ban a particular technology (like incandescent bulbs), but to set higher efficiency standards and allow any technology to compete to meet that standard. This seems fair enough. The only danger is that the standards will be set too low. Here's what I mean: In June 2007, Nevada became the first state to adopt higher lighting efficiency guidelines. The Nevada law prohibits the sale of any bulbs that produce less than twenty-five lumens per watt by 2012. By all accounts, this is genuine progress. The bill is expected to save consumers $1.3 billion by 2020 and about 300 megawatts of peak power, the equivalent of about 40 percent of one of Nevada's proposed new coal-fired power plants. The trouble is that a compact fluorescent bulb is already more than twice as efficient as what Nevada will require in 2012. In December 2007, as part of the energy bill, President Bush signed into law a similar measure, requiring that all bulbs use 25 to 30 percent less energy by 2014. It was progress, but not much to get excited about when bulbs available today could reduce consumption by a factor of four or more.

Developing technologies of so-called solid-state lighting, such as light-emitting diodes (LEDs), are even more efficient. Some LED lamps in the marketplace are already producing up to ninety lumens per watt, and industry experts believe greater gains and cost savings will be realized in the next few years as the market expands and prices drop. "The efficiencies of LEDs keep increasing, and there's no reason to think that they won't continue to do so," says Robert Steele of Strategies Unlimited, a market research firm.

In October 2007, Ann Arbor, Michigan, became the first U.S. city to commit to converting 100 percent of its downtown streetlights to LED technology. These streetlights will last five times as long as the bulbs they'll replace, using half the energy. The switch will save the city at least $100,000 annually. In November 2006, Wal-Mart announced that it would install LED lighting in refrigerated display cases in five hundred stores. "You're saving energy, and in the case of Wal-Mart, reducing the heat," says Steele. "In a commercial setting, those benefits are quantifiable." The company estimates that it will save $2.6 million annually.

In 2007 Congresswoman Jane Harman (D-CA) introduced a bill in the U.S. House of Representatives that would require all bulbs to produce 60 lumens per watt by 2012, 90 lumens per watt by 2016, and 120 lumens per watt by 2020. This is the current gold standard for lawmakers at the local and national levels. The Harman provision was included in the 2007 energy bill and is now law.

Slaying the Vampires

Have you noticed that more and more cell phones, printers, and even computers don't have an "off" switch? Take a walk around your home at night, after all the lights are turned off. You'll notice that the clocks on the microwave and coffee maker continue to keep time, the iPod and cell phone are charging, and the computer, television, cable box, and DVD player are all plugged in.

You have "vampires" in your house. That's the term energy experts use to describe consumer electronics that suck electricity from the grid even when they're turned off. A microwave might draw 3 watts per hour, a DVD player 6 watts. Computers can draw 50 watts an hour or more while in standby mode. It adds up. The Department of Energy estimates that 5 percent of U.S. electricity used is for electronics in the "off" or "standby" mode, the output of about twenty-four midsize coal plants, wasting $5 billion every year. Globally, the International Energy Agency estimates that electronics in standby mode waste 200 to 400 terawatt-hours (1 trillion megawatt-hours) annually. How much is that? About as much as the entire country of Italy uses in a year.

There are two ways to deal with this. One is for a couple hundred million Americans to unplug their chargers, computers, DVD players, and other devices each night—or, to make it easier, consolidate many of these onto power strips (without blowing a fuse!) so they can be all turned off with one switch. That will help, but there's a surer way: set government standards for manufacturers so that products use a minimum—or zero—electricity when not in use. Dell voluntarily introduced a computer in 2004 that used 1.4 watts per hour (compared to 50 watts) while on standby and just 1 watt when turned off. Why not make that the standard and set similar guidelines for all products?

Establishing New Building Efficiency Standards

Ed Mazria is a partner in Mazria Odems Dzurec, a design firm based in Santa Fe, New Mexico. Mazria authored *The Passive Solar Energy Book,* a guide to fully utilizing the sun's energy to heat and cool homes. Reading about his work, Mazria seems like a nice enough guy, but he may not be too popular at industry get-togethers. That's because he goes around saying that architects are responsible for nearly 50 percent of all greenhouse gas emissions.

We tend to think in terms of big SUVs or polluting power plants when considering how to limit climate change, Mazria notes. But as of 2009, 76 percent of all coal-fired electricity was consumed by residential, commercial, and industrial buildings, which are responsible for 44 percent of all greenhouse gas emissions. "Over the next twenty years, we'll add 22 million homes and other buildings in this country," Mazria says. "When did you ever hear someone say, 'Hey, we're going to put in 22 million little power plants . . . in the next twenty years'?" he asks.

It is a design axiom that all the really important design errors are made on the first day, when the purpose of a project is defined. Architects determine what a building looks like, how it functions, what materials will be used, and how efficiently energy will be utilized—decisions that will affect a building's energy performance for the next fifty to a hundred years. So they must be encouraged and trained to make smart energy choices.

In 2005, Mazria founded an organization called Architecture 2030 to help lead his profession in the fight against climate change. One objective is to train new designers and planners for a clean-energy economy by requiring students to design buildings that consume little or no fossil fuel. Another priority is the Architecture 2030 Challenge, whose goal is to make all new buildings—and a substantial number of existing buildings—carbon-neutral by 2030. The challenge urges all architects and builders to pledge to design buildings using 50 percent less fossil fuel than the regional average for the particular building type. Structures built in 2010 would use 60 percent less energy; in 2015, 70 percent; and so on.

The goals are ambitious, but the project is gaining momentum. The U.S. Conference of Mayors has signed the Architecture 2030 pledge. So have the U.S. Green Building Council, the American Institute for Architects, the World Business Council on Sustainable Development, the cities of Santa Fe, Albuquerque, Plano (Texas), and many others. Up next is to make these goals not voluntary but mandatory. Architecture 2030 advocates national building codes that would require 50 percent reductions in fossil-fuel use immediately. As Winston Churchill once said, "We shape our buildings, and afterwards our buildings shape our lives."

The Home Star Act of 2010, a two-year federal program that would provide direct consumer incentives for residential efficiency retrofits, was included in the Clean Energy Jobs and Oil Company Accountability Act of 2010, pending as of this book's second edition. Home Star will drive home efficiency rebates while creating clean-energy jobs. The program will produce energy savings equivalent to taking 615,000 cars off the road and begin to build an energy-efficiency industry in this country that can effectively attack the 21 percent of national carbon dioxide emissions that come from the residential sector.

• • •

This is only a sampling of public policies that can foster investments in efficiency, from standards for bulbs and buildings to state decoupling legislation or loading orders. Federal policymakers can also accelerate efficiency investments by enacting legislation to put a price on carbon, but individuals and companies alike can pursue their enlightened self-interest and cut costs and carbon at the same time. Over the next few decades, fighting climate change will present some tough challenges. Saving energy through efficiency isn't one of them. Let's not squander any easy victories.

Take Action

Take it personally

1. Do you know how much energy you consume in your home or apartment each month? How much does your office consume? Your school or church? Look closely at your energy bill and keep track of your progress. If you like gadgets, consider buying a home energy monitor; for advice on choosing one, see http://planetgreen. discovery.com/tech-transport/.

2. Want to know how much of your electricity comes from coal, nuclear, gas, or renewable power? Try using the U.S. Environmental Protection Agency's Power Profiler at www.epa.gov/cleanenergy/energy-and-you/how-clean.html.

3. Reduce your own consumption. Visit www.greenmadesimple.com and enter your zip code to find out the rebates, incentives, and financing programs available for energy efficiency and renewable power in your area. Consult the organizations in the resources section to learn how to cut your energy bills and greenhouse gas emissions.

Express yourself

1. Write to your governor, utility commission, and state representatives urging that your state pass decoupling legislation and prioritize efficiency and clean power.

2. Another bright idea: write to your state and congressional representatives to press for policies that either ban inefficient incandescent bulbs outright or set a standard of sixty lumens per watt or more. Encourage your city's leaders to follow Ann Arbor's example and install energy and budget-saving LED lights for municipal lighting.

3. Slay vampires—call on your state and congressional representatives to enact electronic "vampire" legislation that minimizes or eliminates the amount of electricity appliances use when turned off.

4. If you're an architect, designer, or planner, take the Architecture 2030 challenge to begin designing buildings to use at least 50 percent less energy. The rest of us can lobby officials to change building codes so that this efficiency level becomes the norm.

Stay engaged

Efficiency is not a one-time effort. As Earth's population increases and new technology develops, there will be constant pressure to use even more energy, not less. Organizations such as Natural Resources Defense Council, Rocky Mountain Institute, and the Union of Concerned Scientists publish extensive information online on how to cut energy bills. Finally, many important decisions affecting our energy systems are made at state and local public utilities commissions. Learn more about your local PUC, and get involved.

CHAPTER 10

Power Shift

Shaping a Clean-Energy Society

*The difference between what we do and what we
are capable of doing would suffice to solve most
of the world's problems.*

—Mahatma Gandhi

Someday soon, our kids will say to us, "So let me get this straight. You guys used to blow up entire mountains and dump the rubble in rivers and streams just to get coal. Then you'd 'wash' it and contaminate billions of gallons of water that made people sick and gave them cancer. After that you'd ship the coal by rail for hundreds or thousands of miles, and when you finally burned it, you made enough pollution to kill twenty-four thousand people every year—*and* generated more solid waste than all of the municipal garbage in the country. Oh, and by burning that coal, you created the biggest source of greenhouse gas emissions in the world. All to make electricity. Wow! Now tell me, why did it take so long before you realized there was a better way?"

As a parent, I'd rather not be on the receiving end of that question. By now you know that the story of how we arrived at this moment in our energy history is long and complex. But the ending hasn't been written. We can alter our course. We may have a long way to go, but we can still change the question from "Why did it take so long?" to "How did you move so quickly?"

For perhaps the first time since the Industrial Revolution, Americans have a legitimate choice about how power is produced in this country. We can choose to mine our factories, commercial buildings, and homes for inefficiency and waste, and then make a rapid transition to clean energy with renewable power. An aggressive, national program with these goals not only would create hundreds of thousands of well-paying, "green-collar" jobs, but would also remind Americans that we can meet our toughest challenges.

When we do, life gets better. Twenty years ago, it was perfectly legal to dump highly radioactive nuclear waste directly into the ocean, but citizens rallied globally and now the practice is banned. People of all colors couldn't drink from the same water fountain or sit at the same lunch counter, until Americans of good conscience taught the rest of the country to try to live as brothers and sisters. Until recently, a planeload of passengers would be trapped for hours breathing unhealthy air anytime a fellow traveler decided to light up and smoke—but health advocates enabled us all to breathe more easily in flight.

Bullies in the Schoolyard

But it won't be easy. Too many of our corporate and political leaders are play-acting when they talk of energy independence. If we're to believe the petroleum industry, there simply aren't any practical alternatives to oil on which we can depend in the near future, and forget about those pesky electric cars and plug-in hybrids. Most politicians are clever enough to introduce or at least vote for patriotic-sounding legislation that claims to help achieve American energy independence. If you look closely at the fine print, however, those bills barely make a dent in the problem; typically they're an excuse for more corporate welfare for clean coal, corn-based ethanol, or other misguided adventures. Coal companies, for their part, don't see much of a problem: coal can be "clean," climate change is a hoax, mining is safe, and pigs can fly.

What's missing from this whole debate is an honest conversation about power—but not the electric kind. There's one predominant reason we're hooked on dirty energy. It isn't because Americans are gluttonous and wasteful, although acknowledging our personal responsibility is important. It isn't because of a lack of solutions. It isn't even because of fears about high energy costs. We're addicted to oil and coal because most politicians and their power-wielding appointees lack the courage, determination, and grit to take these industries on. It's also because the business and banking communities traditionally have been in bed with the extraction industries, or lack the incentive to take risks on cleaner innovations.

We're taught on the playground in grade school to stand up for ourselves and not be pushed around by bullies. As children we learn about fairness, respect, and how to be kind to each other. But as adults, we find ourselves in a world where too many businesses are exempt from rules of fairness and decency and are able to pollute our environment and threaten our rights with impunity. Just like in the schoolyard, we have to stand our ground.

To be successful, we'll need to turn the might and power of these corporations to our own advantage. It will always be useful to confront oil and coal companies directly and expose their mistakes and untruths, but it will be even more important to dry up their government subsidies, cut off their corporate financing from Wall Street, challenge them in the courtroom, refuse their products in the marketplace, and put every ounce of consumer, political, and financial power behind clean and beneficial energy solutions.

They'll resist. Oil and coal companies will do whatever they can to distract attention from their misdeeds and deflect any criticisms. They'll distort the political and scientific debate by fomenting doubt about factual matters. And when the situation gets dire, they'll depress prices in order to defend their turf. Like all bullies, they may fight mean, but they also have their weaknesses. Rather than adjust to a changing world, many of these companies cling to outdated technologies and assume that politicians will always maintain the status quo. They've misjudged the values of Americans who don't believe we should have to sacrifice our health, climate, or freedoms to keep the lights on and the economy healthy. We can learn to fight back, and because we have a better vision, we'll prevail.

Brilliant Distractions

Here's one trick that some corporations are turning into an art form: green-washing. It's a popular trend in corporate PR. If you're a big polluter and find yourself battling with regulators, citizens groups, and angry customers, don't accept the role of villain. Reinvent yourself as a sensitive, helpful, multinational corporation that cares. Here's one example. The world's largest tobacco company, Philip Morris, has fought legal, regulatory, and public relations battles for years because its products kill people. In an attempt to put a positive spin on this inconvenient fact, Philip Morris in 2000 commissioned a report in the Czech Republic extolling some unexpected "positive effects" of smoking deaths on the country's finances: smokers' early mortality would save the country money by reducing pension and housing costs for the elderly. That didn't go over so well, as you might imagine.

In 2003, the company changed its name to Altria and began a vigorous new ad campaign touting the company's human-centered values. Altria's Web site warned people of the dangers of smoking the company's products, hoping to buy time and curry favor with lawmakers negotiating a settlement with the tobacco industry. Health advocates weren't fooled, and the industry remains on the defensive.

British Petroleum gave corporate reinvention a try in 2000, when it bought Solarex Corporation for $45 million and rebranded itself as BP—Beyond Petroleum. BP's new ads adopted a concerned but friendly tone. One asserted, "It's time to think outside the barrel," and discussed the dangers of, and alternatives to, oil dependency. That's ironic, since the company continues to invest far more money in new oil exploration than in renewable energy. And the stark truths behind the greenwashing became all too clear after BP's Deepwater Horizon rig exploded, flooding the Gulf of Mexico with oil: BP had been cutting corners on safety, ignoring contingency planning, and accumulating a record of safety violations in Texas, Alaska, the Great Lakes region, and elsewhere—pushing the limits on ocean-floor digging for many years before the disaster.

Chevron launched a new Web site and ad campaign in the summer of 2005. Chevron urges visitors to the site to "join the discussion" with this rhetoric: "We can wait until a crisis forces us to do something. Or we can commit to working together and start by asking the tough questions: How do we meet the energy needs of the developing world and those of industrialized nations? What role will renewables and alternative energies play? What is the best way to protect our environment? How do we accelerate our conservation efforts? Whatever actions we take, we must look not just to next year, but to the next 50 years."

One Chevron ad says, "A 5 percent reduction in global energy use would power Australia, Mexico, and the entire U.K. So what are we waiting for?" Another billboard proclaims, "Over half the world's oil lies in five countries. So where do you live?"

"Chevron's ads are brilliant distractions," notes Peter Walbridge, creative director for Big Think Studios. "They're provocative because they appeal to the reader or viewer's better self. They attempt to remove the consumer's guilt in buying their gasoline, and throw into question what is really happening in regard to Chevron's environmental record. Like a good card trick, the goal is to distract. And in Chevron's case to make it seem as though the company itself bears no responsibility."

When you notice companies or politicians lying about their records on human rights or the environment, don't despair. Rejoice: it's another opportunity to tell the truth.

Paralysis by Analysis

Here's another trick that's even more common: the independent review. Let's say that there's a U.S. president under intense criticism for—oh, I don't know, a costly and seemingly endless war. (Sadly, just as true when this book's second edition was prepared as when I first wrote it.) Pressure is mounting, voters are impatient. Politicians from the president's party are starting to worry about the upcoming election. Presto! Faster than you can say "task force," "pilot program," or "blue-ribbon panel," a bipartisan group of unassailable experts is appointed to study the issue. Everything is on hold until that study is released. It's a double victory for cowardly decision makers: they avoid taking responsibility and undermine their critics at the same time.

In some cases, a pilot project or in-depth analysis may be appropriate. More often it's just a smokescreen. During a campaign to protect British Columbia's Great Bear Rainforest, we used to call this tactic "talk and log." Logging companies would readily agree to extensive negotiations with environmentalists. They'd hire facilitators, rent conference rooms, sit on conference calls to develop detailed agendas, and schedule check-ins before and after the negotiations. In the meantime, clear-cut logging continued.

The best way to combat this tactic is to keep the pressure on. Rarely do task forces and committee meetings save forests, stop unjust wars, or protect the climate. Vigilant opponents should contest the legitimacy of these panels, projects, and studies when they're announced, and keep the heat on. It wasn't until profits were threatened by a boycott of the wood and paper coming from British Columbia that the industry agreed to halt all logging in pristine forests while negotiations took place.

Skeptics for Hire

The fossil-fuel industry has one quality in spades: tenacity. You won't often find its executives, lobbyists, and PR officials relaxing after a victory; rather they are racing to secure their position. In the spring of 1998, fossil-fuel companies were riding high. Most of the world's nations had recently passed the Kyoto Protocol, but the oil, coal, and utility industries had so thoroughly intimidated federal lawmakers that the U.S. Senate voted 95–0 to withhold support.

Within just a few weeks of the vote, the industries pushed even harder by forming a "Global Climate Science Communications Team" designed to sow confusion about climate change. This team has since been disbanded, but it's instructive to see how early efforts were coordinated. The project's goal was to create conditions in which a "majority of the American public, including industry leadership, recognizes that significant uncertainties exist in climate science, and therefore raises questions among those (e.g., Congress) who chart the future U.S. course on global climate change." Among those developing the plan were executives from coal-burning utility Southern Company, Exxon, and Chevron; the Frontiers of Freedom, an extreme right-wing group that among other things has fought tobacco regulation, endangered species protection, and forest conservation; and Steven Milloy of the so-called Advancement of Sound Science Coalition. In his former career Milloy was a tobacco lobbyist. Today he is a regular commentator on Fox News. Meetings were held at the American Petroleum Institute headquarters. Victory would be achieved when, among other things, "media 'understands' (recognizes) uncertainties in climate science."

Though the Global Climate Science Communications Team didn't last long, it achieved its goals up to a point. Strong climate legislation has escaped

Congress in the decade or so since the Kyoto Protocol was first rejected. Studies have shown that elements of the mainstream media continue to profess doubt about climate change being human-caused. And in seizing on anything that has a whiff of controversy—such as the revelations that some British climate scientists had behaved less than honorably out of concern that their data might be misrepresented—fossil-fuel industry lobbyists have given fodder to the skeptics and manufactured doubt in the public's mind.

Exxon in particular has long been the sugar daddy for climate skeptics. In a report for *Mother Jones,* journalist Chris Mooney details how Exxon has funded more than forty organizations dedicated to creating confusion and uncertainty about the science of climate change. The oil giant has given at least $155,000 to the Acton Institute for the Study of Religious Liberty, which calls CO_2 limits "a misguided attempt to solve a problem that may not even exist." Exxon has made grants of more than $960,000 to the American Enterprise Institute, which counts Dick Cheney as a former senior fellow and has fought climate change legislation at the state and federal levels for more than a decade.

Industry-funded public relations and lobbying campaigns also abound globally, many with deceptive names. You might see ads in major newspapers paid for by these groups "proving" that climate change is natural, or that it really isn't so bad. There's the New Zealand Climate Science Coalition and the Scientific Alliance in the United Kingdom. Up in Canada, the Friends of Science was formed not too far from Alberta's tar sands. The Friends are "active and retired earth and atmospheric scientists, engineers, and other professionals" who believe that "the current obsession with global warming is misguided in that climate fluctuations are a natural phenomena." The group won't reveal where it gets its funding, but reporters at the *Toronto Globe and Mail* tracked down one significant source: Canada's oil companies. Are you shocked?

Climate skeptics are playing a losing game, and they know it. Their objective isn't actually to win a scientific debate, but simply to make it seem like there is a debate. In an infamous memo to Republicans in 2003, strategist Frank Luntz advised candidates, "Voters believe that there is no consensus about global warming within the scientific community. Should the public come to believe the scientific issues are settled, their views about global warming will change accordingly. Therefore, *you need to continue to make the lack of scientific certainty a primary issue in the debate.*" (The italics are Luntz's.)

Coal and oil companies are entitled to their own set of opinions and values, but not their own set of facts. The truth is there is no scientific uncertainty: climate change is real and human activities are the cause. We will also be the solution.

Twenty Years to a Clean-Energy Society

It's clear that the dinosaurs of dirty energy aren't dying out fast enough, and we can't wait for a planetary catastrophe to hasten their extinction. But we won't have to. Thanks to the work of entrepreneurs, innovative public servants, forward-thinking investors, and people like us demanding a better way, a vision of a clean-energy society has begun to emerge. And as that vision becomes manifest—in the form of high-speed rail, community-based energy development, a million-strong workforce in energy efficiency and renewable power, and more—the fossil-fuel industry will decline. When people experience the benefits of living with clean energy, we won't want to go back.

Whether deciding on a new home or car, where to work, or where to live, Americans increasingly will enjoy practical options that depart from a fossil-fuel-based economy. Gaining energy security with a solar rooftop will make the health and environmental costs of coal-fired power seem prohibitive in comparison. Zero-emission electric vehicles will render gas-guzzling cars and trucks obsolete and unpatriotic. The contrasts between old and new technologies and dirty- versus clean-energy choices will become ever more stark as public policy and consumer demand fuel further innovation.

In this and other ways, the clean-energy revolution will be self-reinforcing. Take the electricity market. Congress undoubtedly will soon pass climate legislation that will increase the price of carbon-intensive fuels, affecting coal-fired power plants the most. Meanwhile, growing demand for renewable power will continue to drive down the costs of clean energy. Solar and wind will become less expensive relative to fossil fuels, which in turn will further stimulate the demand for clean power, reducing costs even more. Similar dynamics will be at play in other industries.

Coming clean will impact every facet of our lives—our homes and offices, jobs, health, how we get around, what we eat, and even how America views itself. In some ways a clean-energy society will be very similar to the one in which we live today: we'll still enjoy much the same services and conveniences that we tend to take for granted. But in other ways, breaking the hold that fossil fuels have on our world will change almost everything. Within twenty years or so, here's what we could expect to see:

In Our Cars and Trucks

Perhaps the most dramatic evidence of the move to clean energy will be the vehicles we drive. By 2030, every new vehicle manufactured in the United States should be an electric vehicle, or at least a plug-in hybrid electric vehicle. It will take years after that to get all the older gas-powered cars and trucks off the road, but twenty years from now we should only be manufacturing the cleanest cars possible. Transportation can be fully electrified, connected to an increasingly clean grid. Cars will conveniently recharge at home, work, or public parking facilities; parking lots shaded with PV solar panels will be common.

This is eminently achievable, but it will take Congress, state legislatures, and automakers themselves to set industry standards as though the climate really mattered. Pilot projects and solitary showcase models just won't do. As discussed in chapter 6, all of the necessary technology is available today. Electric vehicles are already on the road in small quantities. Plug-in hybrids will be produced in the tens of thousands within a couple years. As the technology becomes more widespread, most plug-in owners will be able to go weeks on end without using a drop of gas. With advances in battery technology, electric-vehicle owners will travel several hundred miles or more on a single charge. By 2030, vehicle-to-grid technology will be widespread; millions of vehicles will offer extra storage capacity for clean power to help meet peak energy demand.

In Our Towns and Cities

In the next few decades, achieving energy self-sufficiency is likely to be a top priority for local communities. Volatile energy prices and the growing impacts of climate change will lead many public officials to secure access to reliable, inexpensive, and carbon-free energy resources. Communities and municipalities that take early action will be best positioned in a clean-energy economy.

The choices our towns and cities make will transform the transportation sector. Changing the cars we drive will determine how much gas we consume, but changing how our towns and cities are zoned and redeveloped will determine to what extent cars are needed in the first place. Integrating carbon-conscious urban planning with a rededication to mass transit will make our communities more walkable and our transit systems more coordinated. By 2030, urban residents—representing more than 80 percent of the U.S. population—will be able to reject the automobile as their primary way to get around. Housing, shopping, and office space will be close together. Transportation will become multimodal, as residents will be able to choose from an array of convenient options, whether bike, bus, streetcar, light rail, or a good pair of shoes. Eventually the car will become unnecessary for most trips, and people will enjoy less time in gridlock, less pollution, and less income being diverted to the gas tank.

Communities large and small will directly determine the degree to which they become self-sufficient producers of clean power. Smart public policies will help local homeowners secure reliable access to renewable energy. State laws in California, Rhode Island, Ohio, and other states already allow communities to act as purchasing collectives, with the ability to buy clean energy and bypass utilities dependent on fossil fuels. One by one, as families, businesses, and municipalities choose renewable power, cities can break ties with dirty-power producers, so the most polluting plants can be retired and replaced.

Getting out of our cars and producing clean power also will make our towns and cities much cleaner places to live. When my wife and I lived in San Francisco, each week we'd have to wipe away a layer of city smudge that accumulated on a white table on our small deck. Residents of coastal areas worry about fouled beaches; people in Appalachia are being poisoned by runoff from MTR mining; people in the rural Midwest and other areas are concerned about nearby pipelines and hydraulic fracturing affecting their water supplies. The clean-energy revolution will stop this pollution at its source.

In Our Homes and Offices

The impacts of climate change will become clearer with each passing year, bringing greater urgency to eliminate dirty power as quickly as possible. Energy retrofits to both residential and commercial buildings will become more common as conspicuous consumption is replaced by creative conservation. Strong national efficiency standards will be consistently updated for all appliances and consumer electronics. Strategic efficiency guidelines plus continued growth in renewable power will help every new building to be carbon-neutral by 2030.

Over the years to come, millions of buildings will become sources of clean power, accelerating the process by which our electricity grid becomes decentralized and diversified. Office towers, such as the recent Condé Nast building in New York's Times Square, will use solar panels not just on roofs but integrated into the facade.

In Our Economy

Making the transition to clean energy offers an unprecedented opportunity to pioneer new development pathways for an economy that grows in wise directions. Rather than plunder endangered ecosystems such as the Gulf of Mexico for their natural resources, we'll create and expand entire new industries to produce sustainable energy and to use it efficiently. At the local level, achieving energy self-sufficiency will mitigate against fluctuating energy prices and will offer regional economies a buffer against recessions as well. Weatherizing homes, installing solar panels, maintaining wind turbines: many jobs in a clean-energy economy can't be outsourced and will benefit local communities.

Developing clean energy will help rejuvenate rural economies in particular. Community-based energy development will provide steady and diversified income to struggling farmers and ranchers. As the wind industry grows, more jobs will be created for wind technicians in rural areas throughout the Midwest and other regions. In Texas, the country's largest supplier of wind energy, the rapid growth of wind farms has brought much-needed new revenue to towns that once suffered the collapse of the local oil industry. "Wind has invigorated our business like you wouldn't believe," says Marty Foust, the owner of a clothing store in Sweetwater. "When you watch the news you can get depressed about the economy, but we don't get depressed. We're now in our own bubble."

Reinventing a postcarbon economy will be an engine for job growth: in the automotive sector, producing a new generation of zero-emission vehicles; in energy generation, installing and maintaining large-scale solar facilities; and in scrapping old coal plants.

In How America Views Itself

When we break our addiction to oil and coal, our country can get its mojo back. Rather than just talk about climate change, America can face it head-on and catch up to China and other countries that are investing more in clean energy than we are. Rather than exploit other countries' dirty-energy sources—or use their failures as an excuse for inaction—we can win the race to create a clean-energy economy, exporting energy-efficient technologies, wind turbines, solar collectors, and effective public policy solutions.

In the process, Americans will take part in literally hundreds of individual victories: to stop the construction of coal plants, resist an oil-drilling proposal, pass an efficiency standard, install a wind farm, and train or retrain tens of thousands of new workers. Each victory will build momentum for the next. As Cesar Chavez said, "Once social change begins, it cannot be reversed. You cannot uneducate the person who has learned to read. You cannot humiliate the person who feels pride. You cannot oppress the people who are not afraid anymore. We have seen the future, and the future is ours."

Join Us: It's Fun Over Here

The hardest part of standing up for your rights is to stand up the first time. In her book *Love Canal: My Story,* Lois Gibbs writes of being so nervous the first time she went to talk to neighbors about pollution in Love Canal, New York, that she went home after knocking on one door. The next day, she summoned the confidence to begin anew. Years later, Gibbs not only forced the polluters to pay for the cleanup and relocation of residents but helped inspire legislation that forced hundreds of companies elsewhere to do the same.

We don't all have to be national heroes like Gibbs. But every time one of us takes a stand for what we believe is right, it contributes to a collective impact. One letter to Home Depot didn't convince the company to change. After more than a hundred thousand letters, actions by consumers and shareholders, and public advertisements, the company overhauled its environmental policy and is now a leader in green purchasing.

We deserve to be able to drink water from a stream just as our grandparents did or to eat fish from a river as people have done for thousands of years. We should be free to swim at any beach without fear of getting a nasty rash or disease. And when Americans work together to reinvent our industrial way of life, we can have more of what we want, not less.

Health care costs will decrease as our air quality improves. Fewer children and adults will experience the gripping panic of an asthma attack. Less dioxin, sulfur dioxide, nitrogen oxides, and other pollutants in our bodies will result in more pregnancies carried to term, healthier babies, and reduced cancer rates. Diminished particulate matter will decrease the likelihood of heart attacks, and reduced soot and smog will produce cleaner cities and clearer skies from the Grand Canyon to the Great Smokies.

Getting serious about clean energy will also be an economic bonanza, as Amory Lovins says. Using less energy in our homes and businesses will save money for families and corporations alike, while allowing factories to increase productivity. Cutting off all government subsidies for oil and coal and related industries will save even more taxpayer money and permit reinvestment in new energy projects that offer broad social benefits.

America has the resources. When this book first appeared, our country was spending an estimated $4 billion each week on a war in Iraq; as of this second edition, the president had requested an additional $20 million for the Afghanistan war for fiscal year 2011. Imagine how that money could be better spent in mobilizing for energy independence—helping our automobile industry produce a fleet of zero-emission vehicles and resurrecting our manufacturing base in the process. We could weatherize millions of low-income homes, put solar panels on the rooftops of millions of homes and businesses, and so much more. Rather than rely on centralized power plants, our power grid would become diversified and distributed, more resistant to a terrorist attack or systemwide blackouts due to malfunctions.

When we achieve energy independence, America no longer will be sending billions of dollars in oil money overseas, but will be able to reinvest its energy dollars here at home. Our trade deficit will disappear. Our balance of payments with other countries will be restored. Our national debt and annual national deficits will also decrease as energy is conserved. As Paul Hawken points out in Leonardo DiCaprio's film *The 11th Hour,* "The great thing about the dilemma we're in is that we get to reimagine every single thing we do." We can see this as a burden, he observes, but I share his preferred view: that it's an incredibly exciting time to be alive.

Described in this book are dozens of different ways to make a difference. Dozens more can't fit between these pages. We can challenge airlines to recycle their aging fleets and utilize newer planes that burn less gas, so they become "Jet Green." Push United Airlines to stop using oil from the Alberta tar sands as a source of jet fuel. Urge plastic manufacturers to replace petroleum-based plastics with sustainably grown, plant-based alternatives. Eat less meat and buy organic food (many pesticides are oil-based)—or better yet, eat local (it takes a lot of oil to ship those blueberries from New Zealand). We can gather friends, our church group, family members, or fellow students for a conference call to a CEO; mobilize thousands on Facebook and Twitter; visit a member of Congress; hold a house party; join a press conference; or donate to a favorite nonprofit. In the United States, we have the right to remain silent. But we also have a responsibility to speak out and to stand up for what is right. America isn't getting the action we need from Wall Street or Washington, so we citizens need to inspire, persuade, embarrass, support, direct, and demand greater accountability. It's up to us to break our national addiction to dirty energy.

And we will. If you think it's a disgrace that we're fighting terrorists on one hand and funding them with the other, then take action. If you believe that we can meet the challenge of climate change and create a safer, healthier, and more peaceful world, then please raise your voice. If you're already involved, bless you. Don't give up.

Beyond the Gulf Oil Disaster

T he first thing I noticed was how beautiful the Gulf of Mexico is. With a bevy of reporters, I took off from Belle Chasse, Louisiana, and flew over some of the outer islands, marveling at the pristine, white-sand beaches, sparkling waters, and sprawling green marshes of the coastline. Those wetlands nurture one of the richest and most productive fisheries in the world, and I saw shrimp trawlers and oyster boats making what might be their last runs in years.

Then I saw the oil. It wasn't in one contiguous blob but in long, thin bands of orange-brown crud. At this time, two weeks after BP's Deepwater Horizon blowout, perhaps 25 to 30 million gallons had been released into the Gulf—a small fraction of what would eventually become the largest oil spill in our country's history. Yet we flew for miles and miles and saw no break in the pollution. As one reporter put it, the oil was heading straight for the coast like an approaching storm.

I began this book with a story about the depredations of the oil industry in far-off Amazonia. I wanted readers to know about how oil extraction was hurting communities in places they might not know about. Two years later, I was witnessing an oil disaster right here at home, only a month after stepping into my new job as executive director of the Sierra Club. The days that followed were full of surprises—horrifying and heartwarming, dispiriting and energizing. I learned a lot about the strengths of my new organization and the limitations of the nation's new president. I got an instant, real-world feel for how stubborn the oil addiction described in this book really is and a refined notion of what it might take for the nation to come clean.

When I returned to the Gulf a month later, oil had begun covering the shoreline. Touring some islands in a small boat, I found myself gliding through a sea of oil. It had been effectively "dispersed" (with toxic chemicals), but this only meant that, instead of a homogeneous pool, hundreds of thousands of fist-sized clumps were floating on the water, washing in with the currents. Many of the booms deployed to contain the oil were having little effect. In choppy seas, the oil went over or under them—or the sea ripped the booms from their moorings and washed them up on shore with the oil.

Witnessing firsthand the mayhem among wildlife was heart-wrenching. The brown pelican, only recently taken off the endangered species list, came to symbolize the disaster. Our boat passed by one of the big-billed birds smothered with oil, struggling again and again to take off from the water. Other pelicans would approach and then move away. We also saw oil-drenched flamingos drifting out to sea, immobilized. Dolphins swam listlessly, surfacing through an oily sheen.

On the horizon were a couple of oil-skimming boats trying to clean up the mess, but they were far outnumbered by all the oil rigs, platforms, and process-ing facilities. Even now, more than four thousand rigs operate in the Gulf.

But it was on a hot day in early July that I saw a glimpse of the Gulf's future: a decades-long, tedious process of sopping up as much oil as possible in an uphill battle to help a region and its people survive. On this third trip, I traveled with a delegation of religious leaders who had come to bear witness. A week of heavy storms had shut down the containment rig at the Deepwater Horizon site. On the Gulf itself, waves pushed the oil deep into the marshlands, a tangle of veg-etation that protects the coast from the brunt of hurricanes and, by nurturing invertebrates and small fish, provides the foundation of the Gulf's commercial fishery. After looking around, Episcopal priest Sally Bingham told a reporter that the blowout was "an insult to God and a sin against creation."

We didn't see any skimmers that day. They seem to have been replaced by airboats, the kind you commonly see in the Everglades or on *CSI: Miami,* crisscrossing the salt marshes. Each boat had two cleanup workers on it, many of them recently unemployed fishermen hired by BP to mop up the surface oil.

One worker would lean over one side of the boat. The other worker would lean over the other side. They were blotting up the oil with twenty-four-inch-square absorbent cloths, much the same way that you'd clean up spilled milk on your kitchen counter—but by this point somewhere between 150 and 200 million gallons of oil had gushed into the Gulf. All day long in the hot sun, the workers would reach down, fill up a cloth with oil, straighten up, throw the cloth in a black plastic bag, and repeat. And repeat. And repeat.

So much for "advanced cleanup technology." BP is one of the richest companies in the richest industry in the history of the world. It has created the biggest environmental disaster in our country's history. And how does the company respond? With heavy-duty trash bags and absorbent cloths. By setting the ocean on fire. By dumping more than a million gallons of poisonous, bio-accumulative dispersants into the water. By injecting golf balls and shredded tires into a damaged well site. Is this the best we can do?

The Good, the Bad, and the Backlash

Only weeks before the blowout, President Obama had proposed expanding oil development in the Gulf and opening up new areas to exploration along the Atlantic and Alaska coasts starting in 2012. A few weeks after the tragedy, he came to his senses: in May, his Interior Department placed a six-month moratorium on new deepwater drilling and canceled some new lease sales and exploration already in the works. The change of heart seemed a tacit acknowledgment that the administration was wrong to accept oil industry assurances that the risks of expanding offshore drilling are minimal.

For a time, it seemed that the BP disaster was accelerating federal action on several clean-energy fronts. In late April, Obama approved our country's first offshore wind farm. In May, the EPA began the process of improving the already much-improved vehicle-fuel standards it had put in place in April. (As I pointed out in chapter 6, more efficient cars and trucks can significantly reduce the nation's overall oil consumption.) In a televised address from the Oval Office in June, Obama declared, "The tragedy unfolding on our coast is the most painful and powerful reminder yet that the time to embrace a clean energy future is now. Now is the moment for this generation to embark on a national mission to unleash America's innovation and seize control of our own destiny."

Those words were worthy of a Sierra Club speech. But even as Obama embraced the idea of clean energy, he knew that a backlash was building. Unwilling to take on the oil industry and its allies in Congress, the president didn't set clear goals or timetables for Congress to help us break our addiction to oil and other fossil fuels. He didn't tell Americans how they could join the effort. Rather, he mentioned a few low-controversy reforms and said he'd be "happy to look at other ideas and approaches from either party."

Then there was that May 2010 drilling moratorium, which was greeted with relief by many Americans who daily or nightly watched the oil spewing on their TV and computer screens. At the same time, some Gulf-state residents were howling about it even before the BP gusher had been contained. It may seem odd for people to protest a measure designed to protect their home environment from harm. But I've watched more or less the same thing happen in the coalfields of Appalachia and the forests of the Pacific Northwest. People who make a living extracting natural resources (and the politicians who represent them) may criticize the corporations they work for, but they want the extraction to continue because it puts food on their tables. The only way to approach these folks with integrity is to offer them a prosperous alternative. If you support a drilling moratorium—which the Sierra Club emphatically does—you also have to support a massive shift toward green jobs.

A federal judge in New Orleans, Martin Feldman, struck down Obama's moratorium in late June, asserting in his ruling that the Obama administration failed to provide adequate reasoning to impose it. The ruling was immediately repealed, and by early July, the Interior Department had rewritten and reinstated it to address the concerns of the court. With oil still gushing, the president was doing what he could to staunch the flow and prevent similar accidents. But—incredibly, given what we were experiencing—federal legislation to move the country toward clean, green energy had stalled. In a June 24 radio interview Republican senator Lindsey Graham of South Carolina said, "I will work with the President, the Democrats, and the Republicans to come up with an energy policy, but I'm not going to do it in the middle of an oil spill, when the political environment doesn't favor what I want." Apparently, it was better to consider solutions after we'd forgotten the problem.

The oil industry was doing its best to fuel this backlash, of course. The industry had pumped $169 million into lobbying in 2009 and was investing far greater amounts in 2010. People familiar with Big Oil's dirty deeds in Santa Barbara in 1969, Prince William Sound in 1989, or Ecuador in the past twenty years said that BP's actions were straight out of the industry playbook: minimize damages, lie if you must, put a clean face on your operations, and change the story.

At first, other oil companies kept quiet about BP's role in the spill. But in a contentious July 2010 congressional hearing, some broke ranks. Top executives from four major oil firms claimed that the blowout would never have happened if they'd been in charge. *They* had advanced technology and fail-safe plans. The Gulf disaster was an isolated incident, they claimed, made possible only by the extreme negligence of BP.

Democratic representative Edward Markey of Massachusetts countered that *all* of the companies were poorly prepared for a big spill. Their response plans came from the same "cookie-cutter" document, he said, noting that three of those plans listed the phone number of the same long-dead wildlife expert. BP's plan even cited walruses as one of the animals that could be affected by a spill. Walruses, in the Gulf? "The only technology you seem to be relying on is a Xerox machine," Markey said.

In one sense, though, BP-style blowouts *are* isolated . . . to a certain segment of the energy industry. Wind farms don't cause pollution disasters. Solar roof-panel installations don't displace workers or wreck people's occupations. Oil companies do. Just eight months before the Gulf incident, a deepwater rig owned by a Thai company had a massive blowout off Australia in the Timor Sea. Just three months after the Gulf incident, a pipeline burst in China, pouring crude oil into the Yellow Sea. A few weeks later, a rupture near Lake Michigan spilled nearly a million gallons into the Kalamazoo River. In the Gulf of Mexico alone, offshore oil development has caused 858 fires, 69 deaths, and 1,349 injuries in the last ten years. The public may not be paying much attention, but oil crises happen all the time.

Time to Come Clean

In early June 2010, BP offered to donate profits from oil recovered from the Deepwater disaster "to create a new wildlife fund to create, restore, improve and protect wildlife habitat along the coastline of Louisiana, Mississippi, Alabama, and Florida." That's not only inadequate—it's insulting. If BP genuinely cared about wildlife in the Gulf, it would have allowed inspectors to measure exactly how much oil was gushing into the Gulf's waters and put money into a trust to finance independent scientific studies on the impact of the toxic dispersants it has used. The company would pay the full cost of all the wildlife rescue and habitat restoration. It would also pay for the devastation the disaster has wrought upon the economy of the Gulf Coast.

If BP truly wanted to make amends to U.S. taxpayers, not only would it pick up the full cost of this recovery, it would refuse any further government subsidies. If it wanted to regain the confidence of American citizens and demonstrate that it was not seeking to benefit from a continued cozy relationship with regulators, it would make no further political contributions to candidates. (As outlined in chapter 3 of this book, we need to separate oil and state.) Finally, we'd see an end to many oil companies' practice of registering rigs overseas to avoid paying their fair share of taxes.

Government regulators and their watchdogs will need to keep their eyes on the cleanup for a long time. Long after reporters and camera crews leave the Gulf—even after investigations into BP's apparent negligence and perhaps criminal malfeasance come to a close—the effects of BP's spill will be felt. The *Exxon Valdez* ran aground in 1989, releasing nearly 11 million gallons of oil into Alaska waters. But the killing did not stop after cleanup efforts ceased. "Buried oil is still contaminating wildlife and Prince William Sound has not returned to pre-spill conditions," says Alaska-based marine biologist Riki Ott. "The remnant population of once-plentiful herring no longer supports commercial fisheries and barely sustains the ecosystem."

For the families of the eleven workers who died on the Deepwater Horizon rig on April 20, there will be no "cleanup" or recovery. Nor can BP ever fully account for the economic damage felt by workers who have been displaced and by the communities in which they live. We know it will take decades for the delicate ecosystems damaged throughout the Gulf to approach their former vitality. But shame on us—all of us—if we can't wrest something good out of this terrible tragedy. This should be one of those rare events that rivets attention, bolsters resolve, and encourages pivotal change. If ever there was a time to come clean, it is now.

But in truth, that time was yesterday. Or last year. Or somewhere in 2003 when we invaded Iraq. Or in 1991 when we invaded the first time. Or perhaps in 1989 during the *Exxon Valdez* spill, or in the 1970s during the twin oil crises, or at any time over the past several decades when it was clear that the cost of oil included polluted air, poisoned land, fouled water, a twisted foreign policy, and an economy always at risk of another oil shock.

In fact, one of the biggest obstacles to breaking our oil addiction is that we've been *talking about it* for so long. Countless officials have railed against Big Oil, vowed to cut oil consumption, and then utterly failed to adopt the policies to get the job done. Each time they failed, Americans grew a bit more cynical about what we can accomplish as a nation. Lack of confidence has become our biggest problem.

In the weeks after the Deepwater Horizon blowout, I did countless interviews with TV, radio, and newspaper reporters. Inevitably, the question would come up: how do we prevent these disasters? Invariably, I'd say that we need to reform the Minerals Management Service (now called the Bureau of Ocean Energy Management, Regulation, and Enforcement), which was supposed to oversee BP's offshore drilling operations, and to stop the expansion of offshore drilling while improving the safety standards for existing rigs. I'd then say that as we worked to hold BP accountable to bring some justice to the Gulf we also needed to develop an aggressive but achievable plan to move beyond oil. At that point in the interview, most reporters would say something like, "Sure. Almost everybody agrees with that, but how do we actually get it done? Why do you believe we can get off oil now, when we haven't succeeded in the past?"

Whether the aftermath of the BP blowout finally convinces the president and congressional and corporate policymakers to move beyond rhetoric remains to be seen. But several factors influencing the current debate should give Americans hope. There's technology available today—plug-in hybrids and electric cars, clean energy that's cost-competitive, advancements in an efficient electricity grid—that we didn't have ten or twenty years ago. Thanks to BP, there's a heightened public understanding of the hollowness of "Drill, baby, drill." And we have an unusually sympathetic and well-informed president, who has promised to lead us to a clean, green economy—and now must follow through on that commitment. For him, too, the BP disaster has made the price of delay painfully real.

President Obama's job now is to inspire and challenge both parties in Congress to move beyond oil and other fossil fuels. Perhaps he could emulate another man who sat behind the same desk in the Oval Office almost a half century ago: "We choose to do these things not because they're easy, but because they are hard, because that goal will serve to organize and measure the best of our energies and skills, because that challenge is one that we are willing to accept, one we are unwilling to postpone, and one which we intend to win." That 1962 speech by President John F. Kennedy didn't say, "We've been trying to go to the moon for years, and it's important that we do it someday." He set a specific, time-bound goal, rallied the federal bureaucracy and the rest of the country, and set in motion a focused project to meet the challenge that the country embraced. It took just seven years to transform his vision into reality.

Transforming how our entire economy is powered might take a little longer, but there's no question that it's doable. Our biggest asset is not Obama, or a Democratic Congress, or a high-profile celebrity or two, but the millions of Americans who would be ready to pitch in if their leaders showed some political courage. At heart, most people want to do what's right for their country and for the planet. Ending our dependence on oil is vital on both counts.

My e-mailbox is full of stories of amazing people making the world a better place. Take eleven-year-old Olivia Bouler. A New Yorker whose family vacations along the Gulf, Olivia decided to raise money for the pelicans and other birds affected by the BP oil disaster by sending her own bird artwork to people who donated to wildlife recovery efforts. She's raised thousands of dollars, has a Facebook page with more than twenty-five thousand fans, and had a $25,000 donation made in her honor by AOL to the Audubon Society.

Olivia started with little more than a simple but pure sense of justice—she was deeply concerned about the Gulf birds that she knew would suffer. But then she followed up with creativity and a focused sense of purpose. When her first idea didn't work out (selling drawings through Audubon to raise money), she adapted and came up with a new strategy. Last but not least, she worked hard, making hundreds of drawings for supporters.

That's a basic recipe for success in any grassroots campaign. As the Sierra Club's executive director, I'm thrilled by the challenge of finding a way to scale the kind of passion, focus, and energy that you find in people like Olivia Bouler and in countless Sierra Club volunteers to a national organization with more than a million members and supporters. The Sierra Club has a chapter in every state and a group in almost every major city, as well as strong partnerships with other environmental organizations, labor unions, people of faith, environmental justice groups, and athletes and entertainers. Over the years, we've helped build the nation's solid framework of environmental laws, expand its national park system, and protect wilderness areas from Florida to Alaska.

More recently and resoundingly, the Sierra Club achieved what a July 15, 2010, article in *The Nation* called "a de facto national moratorium" on the construction of coal-fired power plants. "Uniting environmentalists, local public officials, health professionals, youth groups (especially at colleges and universities), and others," author Christine MacDonald wrote, "the Beyond Coal campaign used lobbying, demonstrations, legal challenges and other activist tools to block 129 of some 200 planned coal plants around the country."

So we've significantly slowed down King Coal, a feat that would have been considered impossible a few years ago. Now we're in a head-on confrontation with Big Oil. The goal of Sierra Club's Beyond Oil campaign is to end U.S. oil addiction in twenty years. Why twenty years? For one thing, it's doable: if we put our minds to it, we're fully capable of freeing our country from the grip of oil in two decades. But let me say it another way. Given irreversible effects from climate change that are just around the corner, twenty years is all the time we have.

Momentum for the Beyond Oil campaign began building even before the BP gusher was capped. On June 26, 2010, the Sierra Club, Surfrider Foundation, Audubon, Greenpeace, and other groups teamed up with Florida restaurateur and surfer Dave Rauschkolb to draw a line in the sand. Thousands of people in fifty states and thirty countries lined up on their favorite beaches, holding hands in solidarity against Big Oil.

A week later, the Sierra Club coordinated another demonstration of the American public's resolve to move beyond oil—this time in Washington, D.C. At an open, grassy spot on the National Mall, we flew ten thousand American flags representing the tens of thousands of Americans who want to make sure something like the BP disaster never happens again.

In his speech that day, Iraq veteran and former army captain Jon Powers made it clear why the flags were there. "It's a shame that we will let another Fourth of July pass us by without ending our unnecessary dependence on oil," he said, "a dependence that is funding the bullets that our enemies fire at our troops in Iraq and Afghanistan. It is for that reason, and many more, that the fight for energy independence is being fought here at home—a struggle we hope more Americans will join in support of those who are fighting abroad."

My own remarks that day focused on jobs. The oil industry had been saying that deepwater oil drilling in the Gulf shouldn't be halted—even temporarily—because too many people would lose their jobs. To me, that was like declaring the region an economic "dead zone" in which only oil companies could participate. Right around the time I called for leadership in creating green jobs, Obama flew over in a helicopter, on his way to a town hall meeting on the economy in Racine, Wisconsin. I'd like to think he got a good view of our flags, which spelled out "Freedom from Oil."

First Steps

Fortunately, fixing our energy problems won't require the combination of complex engineering and sheer luck that BP needed to get a grip on the Gulf spill. Unlike the engineers sweating it out at the Deepwater Horizon gusher that summer, we know exactly what will work. It's outlined between the covers of this book—and in countless other books and reports. We need our leaders to deliver a plan to get us off oil by promoting clean-energy solutions that already exist. But prevailing against the oil and coal industries will take focused and determined organizing at the local, state, and federal levels.

We can start by investing in a future-oriented transportation system that provides real choices, including public transit, rail, biking, and walking—as outlined in chapter 5. Right now, the U.S. transportation sector is almost entirely dependent on oil—sucking down more than 14 of the nearly 20 million barrels we use every day. Because cars, minivans, pickups, and sport-utility vehicles consume almost 9 million barrels daily, we must set stringent standards for fuel economy and greenhouse gas emissions and move more quickly to bring electric vehicles to market and onto our roads. (You'll find details in chapter 6.) Investing in rail will make it possible to move both goods and passengers cleanly and efficiently, as outlined in chapter 5. And when we must use trucks for freight, let's switch them from diesel to electric power and (if it can be safely drilled) natural gas. But why stop there? If we move away from using oil for residential hot-water heaters and for generating electricity, as outlined in chapter 8, we'll help eliminate the need for any risky drilling plans, from Alaska to the Amazon.

Of course, given our experience in the Gulf, we need to stop the expansion of offshore drilling, immediately. We need to eliminate subsidies and giveaways to companies like BP, which made more than $5.5 billion in profits in the first quarter of 2010 alone. According to Sima J. Gandhi of the Center for American Progress, "We're giving tax breaks to highly profitable companies to do what they would be doing anyway. That's not an incentive; that's a giveaway."

Simply maintaining our current fossil-fuel-based energy infrastructure will be enormously expensive over the next several decades. More than a trillion dollars of public and private investment will be required, regardless of whether energy development is clean or dirty. What's at issue is how we spend that money—some of which is ours. Like all investors, we have many choices: more offshore drilling, nuclear plants, solar parks, wind farms, geothermal plants, wave-energy installations, big coal facilities, and so on.

To be smart investors, we need to establish criteria to evaluate those choices. Before deciding our energy future, we should be asking ourselves which energy sources score highest in four areas: Which is safest? Which is cleanest? Which can come online the quickest? And which is cheapest (especially with the costs of pollution factored in)? Offshore oil, foreign oil, nukes, and coal plants all come up short by those standards.

Hard as it is, we have to take the long view as we make these choices. The oil platforms off the coast of Santa Barbara have been there my whole life. The next generation of power plants we build will last at least forty to fifty years. In

2060, what will people think about the choices we make today? What will our children think? Somehow, I wouldn't expect to be congratulated for squeezing every last barrel of oil out of the Amazon and off our coastlines.

When we talk about our future energy policy, there's a lot of fear and anger in the country right now, along with an absence of both accountability and clear guiding principles. The fear is understandable, especially if you're out of work and unsure about your future. And the anger is justified, as corporations continue to put profits over common sense and then act surprised by the consequences.

But fear and anger can't get us where we need to go—by themselves, they'll only hold us back. We need to roll up our sleeves, sharpen our pencils, and get to work solving this challenge. The anger must become action. Sure, we must hold BP accountable, and the successor to the Minerals Management Service, and the rest of the Obama administration, and Congress. But let's also hold ourselves accountable. Have you called up your senator or congressional representative yet to demand a plan to get us off oil?

Have you taken action at home or at work or at your kids' school to advance a specific clean-energy solution? At the office, have you lobbied your boss to put bike lockers in the basement and install controls to turn off lights when they're not needed? If you work for a big company, how about starting a conversation to make the next fleet of company vehicles plug-in hybrids? Still using incandescent lightbulbs at home or at the office? Really?! How about putting solar panels on your house? Companies like Sungevity will now install them with no money down.

Change doesn't come easily, whether it's in your personal life or our country's. And we lead such busy lives that taking time away to volunteer is hard. But it works. We can reject cynicism, power through inertia, and overcome any one of a dozen obstacles to reenergize our country. And as for the fear: when people discover that clean energy also means good jobs, national security, and a safe environment, a funny thing happens to the fear. It becomes hope.

Resources

You're not alone. Polls show that most Americans support a future in which our energy is safe, secure, and sustainable. And history has shown that there is great power in collective action.

In this section, I've listed some of the most active organizations promoting a clean government, zero-emission vehicles, renewable energy, and other issues addressed in this book. Please give them a hand. The list begins with organizations that tackle climate change and our dependence on dirty energy with multiple initiatives. You'll also find suggestions for further reading or other sources of information on particular issues, and listings of visionary companies where you can get information about retrofitting your home with renewables, learn about incentive programs, and so on.

Multiple Issues

SUPPORT THESE ORGANIZATIONS AND PROGRAMS

Earthjustice
www.earthjustice.org
> Earthjustice is a nonprofit public interest law firm dedicated to protecting the magnificent places, natural resources, and wildlife of this earth and to defending the right of all people to a healthy environment.

Natural Resources Defense Council
www.nrdc.org
> One of the nation's largest environmental groups is a strong voice in the campaign to stop expansion in Canada's tar sands. Join NRDC in its effort to seek "friendlier skies" by urging major U.S. and Canadian airlines, including United, American, and others, to swear off jet fuel from unconventional oil sources. NRDC is also a leader in promoting energy efficiency and clean, renewable power.

Rainforest Action Network

www.ran.org

Do you think it's outrageous that your money is being used to fund coal plants and build oil pipelines? Or that American companies such as Archer Daniels Midland and Cargill destroy rainforests in the name of biofuels? RAN thinks so too. Join its Global Finance, Rainforest Agribusiness, or Freedom from Oil campaigns and get involved with a group the *Wall Street Journal* calls "some of the savviest environmental agitators in the business."

Sierra Club

www.sierraclub.org

In a saner world, we wouldn't have to fight to keep the oil industry from trampling our best parks and last wilderness areas. Nor would we have to challenge automakers and utilities to do what's right. Through its Beyond Coal and Beyond Oil campaigns, Public Lands and Resilient Habitat programs, lobbying of Congress and automakers to increase fuel efficiency, and more, the Sierra Club has been doing heroic work for decades to defend the environment.

Union of Concerned Scientists

www.ucsusa.org

UCS's team of experts produces credible, timely information to help consumers and policy-makers alike improve performance and reduce emissions in American cars and trucks. UCS has also been a leading voice promoting clean-energy solutions, exposing utilities and the coal industry's impact on human health and the environment, protecting the Arctic National Wildlife Refuge, and more.

LEARN MORE

Books, films, and other sources of information:

Carbon Monitoring for Action (CARMA)

http://carma.org

CARMA is a massive database containing information on the carbon emissions of more than fifty thousand power plants and four thousand power companies worldwide.

DeSmogBlog

http://desmogblog.com

Highlights the most creative actions and solutions to fight climate change, while "clearing the PR pollution that clouds the science on climate change."

Global Community Monitor

www.gcmonitor.org

Led by Denny Larson, GCM provides hands-on tools for affected communities to monitor the environmental health of oil refineries and other pollution sources in their own neighbor-hoods.

Grist

www.grist.org

Compiles the best in environmental journalism, delivering a daily dose of "gloom and doom with a sense of humor."

It's Getting Hot in Here

http://itsgettinghotinhere.org

This blog, which collects the writings of a hundred voices from the youth movement to stop climate change, is one of the best sites to visit to take action on clean energy.

Solving Climate

http://solveclimate.com

This blog assumes that the country knows what is needed to meet our climate challenge and can afford to implement climate solutions—and aims to show how it can be done.

WiserEarth

www.wiserearth.org

This community directory and networking forum connects more than one hundred thousand environmental and social justice organizations around the world, enabling individuals, organizations, philanthropists, media, and others to find each other, build alliances, and share strategies and resources.

Big Oil

SUPPORT THESE ORGANIZATIONS AND PROGRAMS

Amazon Watch

www.amazonwatch.org

Tracks the operations of oil companies throughout the Amazon basin and exposes them in the boardroom and the court of public opinion. Has led the campaign to hold Chevron accountable for toxic oil spills in Ecuador, which could help establish a global precedent for the overseas operations of the world's largest energy corporations.

Communities for a Better Environment

www.cbecal.org

Works to amplify the voice of communities of color and working-class communities to promote environmental health and justice. Fights toxic oil refineries throughout California.

EarthRights International

www.earthrights.org

Led by Ka Hsaw Wa, a 1999 Goldman Environmental Prize recipient, and Katie Redford, a 2006 Ashoka fellow—both honored for their courageous work to defend environmental and human rights in Burma—EarthRights uses the power of law and of grassroots organizing to support communities affected by fossil-fuel extraction in Burma, the Amazon, and beyond.

ForestEthics

www.forestethics.org

A small but highly effective grassroots environmental organization, ForestEthics made its name helping to protect the majestic Great Bear Rainforest in British Columbia and has since added its muscle to the fight to stop Canada's tar sands expansion.

Indigenous Environmental Network

www.ienearth.org

A network of Indigenous peoples "demanding environmental justice and maintaining the Sacred Fire of our traditions." Its Native Energy campaign has helped lead the fight to protect the Arctic National Wildlife Refuge and stop Canada's tar sands expansion, among other projects.

Keepers of the Waters

www.keepersofthewaters.org

An alliance of Indigenous organizations working to resist tar sands development and to protect the Arctic Ocean drainage basin.

Oil Change International

www.priceofoil.org/thepriceofoil

In addition to running sophisticated campaigns aimed at restraining Big Oil, this group has a Web site that examines the high social and environmental costs of our oil dependency.

Pachamama Alliance

www.pachamama.org

Collaborates closely with the Achuar and other native communities in Ecuador to preserve the region's tropical rainforests through public education, advocacy, and lobbying. Pachamama has been a vital, long-term ally to the Kichwa and other communities resisting the incursion of oil companies into pristine forests.

LEARN MORE

Beyond Oil: The View from Hubbert's Peak

Kenneth Deffeyes's book unpacks the science and challenges of peak oil.

Blood and Oil: The Dangers and Consequences of America's Growing Dependency on Imported Petroleum

Michael T. Klare's book offers a perceptive analysis of the human costs of our oil addiction.

Crude

There are two worthwhile films with this name: the 2009 American documentary directed and produced by Joe Berlinger follows the ongoing class-action lawsuit against the Chevron Corporation in Ecuador; the 2007 documentary by Australian filmmaker Richard Smith explores the links between formation, extraction, and refinement of oil, and interviews peak-oil theorists.

Crude Impact
   An award-winning 2006 documentary film by Chris Vernon of TheOilDrum.com that focuses on peak oil.

Energy Bulletin
http://energybulletin.net
   A clearinghouse for information about peak energy supplies.

Justicia Now
   A documentary film by Martin O'Brien and Robby Proctor about Chevron's legacy of oil spills and toxic waste in the Ecuadorian Amazon.

The Long Emergency
   James Howard Kunstler's book on how the coming oil crunch will put us all in a world of hurt.

The Oil Drum
www.theoildrum.com
   Online community that discusses ideas related to peak oil, sustainable development and growth, and the implications of these ideas on politics, economic communities, and the environment.

Oil: Money, Politics, and Power in the 21st Century
   Tom Bower's gripping and convincing account of the turbulent history of the global oil industry over the past thirty years.

Oil on Ice
   Documentary film by Dale Djerassi about proposed oil drilling in the Arctic Refuge.

Oil Sands Watch
www.oilsandswatch.org
   Provides current information on Canada's tar sands, sponsored by the Pembina Institute.

The Prize: The Epic Quest for Oil, Money, and Power
   Daniel Yergin's Pulitzer Prize–winning book is a comprehensive overview of the oil industry's pursuit of power.

Syriana
   Stephen Gaghan's feature film explores power and corruption in Big Oil and the Middle East.

Winning the Oil Endgame
   Amory Lovins et al. of the Rocky Mountain Institute present an optimistic treatise that advances a set of strategic solutions to our oil crisis.

Coal Industry

Appalachian Voices
www.appvoices.org
> A grassroots environmental organization based in Boone, North Carolina, working to stop mountaintop-removal mining and restore the Appalachian forests.

Black Mesa Water Coalition
www.blackmesawatercoalition.org
> BMWC has been working to end Peabody Coal's wasteful use of scarce and sacred ground-water in the Black Mesa Diné (Navajo) and Hopi lands, calling for a transition to renewable energy practices and sources.

Coal River Mountain Watch
www.crmw.net
> Based in Appalachia; works to stop the destruction of communities and the environment by mountaintop-removal mining and to help rebuild sustainable communities.

Greenpeace International's "Quit Coal" campaign
www.greenpeace.org/international/campaigns/climate-change/coal?page=2
> An international effort by one of the world's largest environmental organizations to stop coal-industry expansion and kick-start a rapid transition to renewables and greater energy efficiency.

iLoveMountains.org
> Action and resource center for the movement opposing mountaintop-removal mining; includes an online tool that enables users to determine whether their power is connected to mountaintop removal.

Little Village Environmental Justice Organization
www.lvejo.org
> A community organization in Chicago working for clean air and environmental justice.

Ohio Valley Environmental Coalition
www.ohvec.org
> Another effective grassroots group fighting in Appalachia to protect the environment and stop mountaintop removal.

Pilsen Environmental Rights and Reform Organization
www.pilsenperro.org
> An ally of Little Village Environmental Justice Organization in Chicago, Pilsen fights for citizens' right to clean air and a healthy environment.

Respiratory Health Association of Metropolitan Chicago
www.lungchicago.org
  Formerly part of the American Lung Association, this Chicago-based organization provides
  support to asthma patients and their families while also advocating for more stringent measures to reduce emissions in the region.

LEARN MORE

Big Coal: The Dirty Secret behind America's Energy Future
  Jeff Goodell's entertaining but unnerving book pays gracious respect to the technical and
  engineering accomplishments that have kept the lights on but looks unflinchingly at the high
  costs of coal's "cheap" price.

Burning the Future
  David Novack's film depicting West Virginia as ground zero in the fight to stop mountaintop
  removal and create a clean-energy future.

Coal: A Human History
  Barbara Freese's book elegantly recounts the story of coal's use from ancient times to today,
  describing how the mineral has helped and hurt human society throughout history.

coalSwarm
www.sourcewatch.org/index.php?title=Portal:Coal_Issues
  A project of SourceWatch and the Center for Media and Democracy, coalSwarm is a wiki that
  allows users to share the latest information about proposed coal plants, sample testimony,
  campaign videos, renewable energy developments, and more.

Environmental Integrity Project
www.environmentalintegrity.org
  Founded by former EPA enforcement attorney Eric Schaeffer, this nonpartisan organization
  helps local communities gain the protection of environmental laws while holding state and
  federal government officials accountable for failing to enforce or comply with those laws.

"Global Boom in Coal Power—and Emissions"
  Mark Clayton's March 22, 2007, article in the Christian Science Monitor about the impact of
  proposed new coal plants on global greenhouse gas emissions.

KilowattOurs
  Jeff Barrie's film provides good background on how to create an energy revolution, one kilowatt at a time.

Who's Got the Power?
  Casey Coates Danson's documentary compares the benefits of energy efficiency and renewable power with the high cost of coal extraction and combustion.

State of the Air

www.stateoftheair.org

> The American Lung Association issues this annual report; an interactive tool on the site allows you to check the air quality for your state and elsewhere.

Clean Government

SUPPORT THESE ORGANIZATIONS AND PROGRAMS

Center for Public Integrity

www.publicintegrity.org

> A nonpartisan organization that provides excellent investigative reports to help promote transparency and good governance.

Center for Responsive Politics

www.opensecrets.org

> Nonpartisan guide to how much oil and coal companies and utilities spend on lobbying and direct corporate contributions.

Friends of the Earth

www.foe.org

> For years, Friends of the Earth's "Green Scissors" program has united conservatives and progressives seeking to end subsidies for polluters. FOE continues as an ally of clean energy and clean government by exposing government subsidies to Big Oil.

Greenpeace USA's Project Hot Seat

www.greenpeaceusa.org

> Will Congress continue to delay taking action on climate change, or will it make a break from the fossil-fuel industry? Greenpeace organizers relentlessly push Congress members to become climate heroes.

MAPLight.org

www.maplight.org

> This group shines a spotlight on the connections between money and politics.

MoveOn.org

www.moveon.org

> A progressive organization of more than 3 million advocating for clean energy, including an effort to promote an "oil-free Congress."

Oil Change International

www.priceofoil.org

> Runs the grassroots campaign "Separate Oil and State," which organizes Americans to persuade lawmakers to refuse Big Oil political donations. Visit this Web site to find out how much your representative is taking from the oil industry.

Crimes against Nature: How George W. Bush and His Corporate Pals Are Plundering the Country and Hijacking Our Democracy
   Robert F. Kennedy, Jr.'s book about how the Bush administration "plundered the country" and how we can't let it happen again.

Earth Track
www.earthtrack.net
   Doug Koplow's project to itemize state, federal, and international energy subsidies.

League of Conservation Voters' Environmental Scorecards
www.lcv.org/scorecard
   Provides clear information for how your representatives voted on the most important environmental bills in Congress and state by state.

"Overcome by Heat and Inertia"
   David Leonhardt's *New York Times* article (July 20, 2010) explains the political realities of passing a climate bill in the U.S. Senate.

"Some Like It Hot"
   Chris Mooney's May/June 2005 article in *Mother Jones* detailing how ExxonMobil has funded groups seeking to undermine scientific consensus on global warming.

Publish What You Pay
www.publishwhatyoupay.org
   A coalition of more than three hundred organizations worldwide that helps citizens of resource-rich countries check the corrupting influence of the oil and other industries by holding their governments accountable for the management of revenues from oil, gas, mining, and other activities.

Banking and Finance

SUPPORT THESE ORGANIZATIONS AND PROGRAMS

As You Sow's Corporate Responsibility Program
www.asyousow.org
   Promotes corporate responsibility by engaging publicly held companies to adopt stronger social and environmental policies. If you're a shareholder of a publicly traded corporation and want to use your voice, As You Sow can help.

Bank Information Center
www.bicusa.org
   Supports communities and nonprofits in developing countries to push the World Bank and other international financial institutions to develop stronger social and environmental safeguards.

BankTrack

www.banktrack.org

An international network of organizations and individuals acting as a watchdog for the global banking industry. Its members have pressured dozens of banks to tighten their environmental and social regulations, and have developed a set of principles for responsible banking known as the Collevecchio Declaration.

End Oil Aid

www.endoilaid.org

A coalition of organizations including Jubilee USA Network, Oil Change International, Friends of the Earth, and others that address the interrelated issues of oil, climate change, and international debt, and seek policy solutions to eliminate all international subsidies for the oil industry.

Green America

greenamericatoday.org

A member-based organization that assists consumers, business owners, investors, and others to take individual and collective action to promote social and environmental justice. Its Climate Action campaign has challenged America's largest banks to show stronger leadership to replace dirty energy with clean-energy sources.

Interfaith Center on Corporate Responsibility

www.iccr.org

This association of 275 faith-based institutional investors has long been a leader in the corporate social responsibility movement. ICCR's Global Warming and Environmental Justice programs compel corporate leaders to accelerate a transition to clean energy while alleviating the burden of pollution borne by low-income communities and communities of color.

International Forum on Globalization

www.ifg.org

A research and educational institution that, among other issues, confronts the "global triple crisis" of climate change, peak oil, and resource depletion and extinction. IFG's *Alternatives to Economic Globalization* is an excellent compendium of development strategies that can create wealth without sacrificing the health of people or planet.

LEARN MORE

"Aiding Oil, Harming the Climate"

http://priceofoil.org/2007/12/06/aiding-oil-harming-the-climate/

An Oil Change International report detailing the impacts of the World Bank's loans and investments in Big Oil.

"Don't Get Burned"

An Interfaith Center on Corporate Responsibility report for investors about the high economic risks of financing coal-fired power plants.

Globalization and Its Discontents
  Nobel Prize–winning economist Joseph Stiglitz's book shows how the World Bank and International Monetary Fund often undermined national sovereignty and environmental and labor standards in service to a discredited economic policy.

Green banking
  For green banking options, visit New Resource Bank at www.newresourcebank.com, ShoreBank Pacific at www.shorebankcorp.com, or www.creditunionsonline.org, as noted in chapter 4.

Oil Aid: Tracking Subsidies to the International Oil Industry
http://oilaid.priceofoil.org/
  The Oil Aid Database is an interactive tool for tracking subsidies to the international oil industry.

"U.S. Sends Mixed Message on Climate"
  August 12, 2007, article by Judy Pasternak in the *Los Angeles Times* revealing hypocrisy in U.S. climate policy.

Public Transportation and Urban Planning

SUPPORT THESE ORGANIZATIONS AND PROGRAMS

Alliance for Biking and Walking
www.peoplepoweredmovement.org
  A national coalition of state and local pedestrian and cycling advocacy organizations working to promote safe cycling and walking in North America.

Bus Riders Union
www.busridersunion.org
  Environmental justice organization that promotes sustainable transportation options for all Los Angeles residents, based on the belief that "affordable, efficient, and environmentally sound mass transit is a human right."

Center for Neighborhood Technology
www.cnt.org
  A Chicago-based research and policy organization—"part think tank, part incubator"—to promote more livable and sustainable communities.

Congress for the New Urbanism
www.cnu.org
  A member-based organization of planners, architects, designers, activists, and others working together to encourage the development, or redevelopment, of walkable, mixed-use neighborhoods as an alternative to sprawl.

League of American Bicyclists

www.bikeleague.org

> Its membership of three hundred thousand affiliated cyclists uses education and advocacy to promote a bicycle-friendly America. Publishes *American Bicyclist* magazine.

Midwest High Speed Rail Association

www.midwesthsr.org

> A membership-based organization promoting fast and frequent rail service connecting the entire Midwest.

National Association of City Transport Officials

www.nacto.org/index.html

> NACTO encourages the exchange of transportation ideas, insights, and practices among large central cities while fostering a cooperative approach to key national transportation issues.

National Association of Railroad Passengers

www.narprail.org

> The nation's largest advocacy organization for train and rail transit passengers. For too many years, NARP has had to fight tenaciously in Congress to maintain even minimum funding levels for passenger rail. Join them to promote a modern, national train network that "provides a travel choice Americans want."

National Center for Safe Routes to School

www.saferoutesinfo.org

> A clearinghouse of information for how to start a Safe Routes to School program in your neighborhood. Runs the annual Walk to School events nationwide, which promote safe walking and cycling routes for students in their hometowns.

Reconnecting America

www.reconnectingamerica.org

> A national organization based in Oakland, California, working to "integrate transportation systems and the communities they serve." Reconnecting America operates the Center for Transit-Oriented Development, which seeks to catalyze greater public and private investment into creating walkable, transit-friendly communities.

Transportation Alternatives

www.transalt.org

> The leading voice for promoting safe and convenient cycling and for reducing car use in New York City.

Urban Habitat

www.urbanhabitat.org

> Based on the belief that an affordable, dependable, efficient transportation system is prerequisite to the economic and social health of a region, Urban Habitat advocates for smart growth and sustainable transportation investments as part of a multifaceted program promoting equitable development and environmental justice.

U.S. Public Interest Research Groups
www.uspirg.org/issues/transportation
　　In almost every state, grassroots organizers affiliated with state PIRGs work to increase the
　　share of public transportation dollars devoted to transit and prioritize a modern, efficient
　　transportation network.

LEARN MORE

Bike 2015 Plan, City of Chicago
www.bike2015plan.org
　　Quite possibly the best bicycle plan in the country.

"Building a Better Bike Lane"
　　May 4, 2007, *Wall Street Journal* article by Nancy Keates reports on how cities in Europe
　　continue to innovate to make cycling more safe and convenient.

The End of Suburbia
　　Documentary film by Gregory Greene that predicts the energy crisis will intensify and sug-
　　gests steps for action.

Online Transportation Demand Management (TDM) Encyclopedia
www.vtpi.org/tdm/tdm12.htm
　　Operated by the Victoria Transport Policy Institute. The most comprehensive resource for
　　sustainable transportation systems.

Race, Poverty, and the Environment
　　A journal of environmental justice, produced by Urban Habitat.

Street Smart: Streetcars and Cities in the 21st Century
　　Beautifully illustrated book by Shelley Poticha and Gloria Ohland, showing how urban plan-
　　ners are creating a renaissance for the American streetcar.

Cars and Trucks

SUPPORT THESE ORGANIZATIONS AND PROGRAMS

CalCars
www.calcars.org
　　A California-based startup nonprofit group of engineers and entrepreneurs that is organizing
　　customer demand and advocating for strong public policy incentives to promote the develop-
　　ment of plug-in hybrid vehicles that can achieve more than 100 mpg.

Electric Auto Association
www.electricauto.org/
　　The EAA is a nonprofit educational organization that promotes the advancement and wide-
　　spread adoption of electric vehicles.

Friends of the Earth's Transportation campaign

http://action.foe.org/content.jsp?content_KEY=2710&t=2007_Smarter-Transportation.dwt

This project of Friends of the Earth works aggressively to uphold California's precedent-setting legislation to reduce auto emissions, while pushing Congress to follow California's lead. Also a leading advocate for plug-in hybrid vehicles.

Global Exchange's Freedom from Oil campaign

www.globalexchange.org

Global Exchange earned its reputation fighting sweatshops and the World Trade Organization. This project challenges automakers at North American locations, such as auto shows, dealerships, and industry conferences, to produce zero-emission vehicles as soon as possible.

Plug In America

www.pluginamerica.org

A collection of electric-vehicle drivers and clean-energy advocates who know a good thing when they see it and drive it. Plug In America is one of the country's most effective advocates for electric vehicles, and is a big reason why plug-in hybrid cars and trucks will be seen on America's roadways in increasing numbers.

Ruckus Society

www.ruckus.org

Ruckus works closely with Global Exchange and Rainforest Action Network's Freedom from Oil campaigns, giving training and strategic advice to individuals and organizations working for human rights and social and environmental justice.

Set America Free Coalition

www.setamericafree.org

One of the country's most diverse coalitions; includes conservative hawks and green energy activists working together to fight climate change and secure energy independence by advancing automotive fuel efficiency.

SmartTransportation.org

www.smarttransportation.org

A leading voice for converting New York City's taxi fleet to hybrid vehicles and encouraging other cities to do the same. Also advocates for congestion pricing and other strategies to reduce congestion and gridlock in New York.

LEARN MORE

American Council for an Energy-Efficient Economy: Greener Cars Guide

www.greenercars.org/

The Web site for ACEEE's Green Book is a consumer resource that rates the environmental friendliness of every vehicle on the market.

"Drilling in Detroit"
www.ucsusa.org/clean_vehicles/fuel_economy/drilling-in-detroit.html
A 2001 report from the Union of Concerned Scientists showing how practical, off-the-shelf technologies can be used by automakers to dramatically increase fuel efficiency.

Environmental Protection Agency: Green Vehicle Guide
www.epa.gov/greenvehicles/
The U.S. EPA's guide provides vehicle ratings based on emissions and fuel economy.

Freedom from Oil: How the Next President Can End the United States' Oil Addiction
David Sandalow's book gives a step-by-step guide for how the next president can help kick our oil habit. Several of Sandalow's steps were suggested in this book.

Pure Green Cars
http://puregreencars.com/
Provides vehicle ratings and showcases the newest breakthroughs in green car and truck technology.

Who Killed the Electric Car?
Chris Paine's critically acclaimed documentary exploring the rise, fall, and potential comeback of the electric car.

Agrofuels

SUPPORT THESE ORGANIZATIONS AND PROGRAMS

Earth Policy Institute
www.earth-policy.org
An organization that has been one of the most influential and powerful voices warning of the dangers of the growing biofuel craze; founded by Lester Brown.

Food First
www.foodfirst.org
Institute for food and development policy. Works to eliminate the injustices that cause hunger, poverty, and environmental degradation globally. An activist think tank, Food First amplifies the voices of communities being affected by transnational agribusinesses and advocates for sustainable food—and fuel—production.

Forest Peoples Programme
www.forestpeoples.org
An expert team based in the United Kingdom that supports forest peoples in securing land rights and sustainably managing their forests and livelihoods.

Grassroots International
www.grassrootsonline.org
> A human rights and international development organization that provides grants to orga-
> nizations and communities in the Global South to support community-led sustainable
> development projects.

Greenpeace International's soy and palm oil campaigns
www.greenpeace.org/international/campaigns/forests
> In Brazil, Greenpeace campaigners helped secure a temporary moratorium on the further
> expansion of the soy industry into the Brazilian Amazon. In Europe, Greenpeace organizers
> are pressuring leading food and consumer products manufacturers to cease using palm oil
> from endangered forests.

Institute for Agriculture and Trade Policy
www.iatp.org
> A longtime advocate for family farmers and responsible U.S. agriculture policy, IATP carefully
> bridges the divide between farmers and agrofuel critics in the United States.

Oakland Institute
www.oaklandinstitute.org
> A policy think tank that specializes in strengthening multicultural social movements. A lead-
> ing voice warning of the dangers of agrofuels.

Sustainable Biodiesel Alliance
www.sustainablebiodieselalliance.org
> An organization of farmers, biodiesel enthusiasts, environmental groups, and others working
> together to try to do it right: developing strong life-cycle standards for sustainable biodiesel
> production and distribution so that consumers can "fuel responsibly."

World Rainforest Movement
www.wrm.org.uy
> One of the earliest critics of how the growth in agrofuel production was increasing deforesta-
> tion and human rights violations, this international network defends the world's rainforests.

LEARN MORE

"The Clean Energy Scam"
> March 27, 2008, report by Michael Grunwald in *Time,* taking a highly critical look at the
> ethanol craze.

"Destination Iowa"
www.sierraclub.org/energy/downloads/IowaBiofuelsReport.pdf
> Report by the Sierra Club and World Watch Institute published in October 2007.

"Green Dreams"
   October 2007 article by Joel K. Bourne, Jr., in *National Geographic* exploring the social and
   environmental impacts of the agrofuel industry.

"How Biofuels Could Starve the World's Poor"
   May/June 2007 article in *Foreign Affairs* by C. Ford Runge and Benjamin Senauer.

"How the Palm Oil Industry Is Cooking the Climate"
www.greenpeace.org/international/news/palm-oil_cooking-the-climate
   Report by Greenpeace in October 2007.

"Palm Oil: The Biofuel of the Future Driving an Ecological Disaster Now"
   April 4, 2007, article by Ian McKinnon in the *Guardian*.

Plan B 3.0: Mobilizing to Save Civilization
   Lester Brown's wide-ranging book highlights many of the dangers of agrofuel production and
   advocates for sustainable alternatives.

Science, February 29, 2008, issue
   Two important articles: "Use of U.S. Croplands for Biofuels Increases Greenhouse Gas Emis-
   sions from Land-Use Change," by Searchinger et al., and "Land Clearing and the Biofuel
   Carbon Debt," by Fargione et al.

Renewable Energy

SUPPORT THESE ORGANIZATIONS AND PROGRAMS

1Sky.org
www.1sky.org
   A diverse coalition of elected officials, students, faith-based institutions, and health and environmental organizations working to promote bold federal action by 2010 on climate change
   and green jobs.

American Council on Renewable Energy
www.acore.org
   A nonprofit organization with members from the wind, solar, biomass, and other clean-power
   sectors; seeks to advance trade and policy tools to promote all forms of renewable energy.

American Wind Energy Association
www.awea.org
   AWEA works to promote wind-power growth through advocacy, communication, and
   education.

Climate Challenge

www.climatechallenge.org

> Students, faculty members, and administrators taking action on climate change at high schools and college campuses across the country. A project of Energy Action and more than six hundred local organizations.

Community-Based Energy Development

www.c-bed.org

> A coalition of farmers, clean-power advocates, business owners, and others working to promote clean energy along with local economic development, so that local ownership of renewable resources will keep the financial benefits in the community.

Environment America

www.environmentamerica.org

> State by state, this collection of grassroots organizations advocates for laws to promote solar and wind power and forces fossil-fuel companies and utilities to cut emissions.

Green for All

www.greenforall.org

> Advocates for local, state, and federal resources to create economic opportunities and job training for green-collar jobs, especially in low-income communities.

Interfaith Power and Light

http://interfaithpowerandlight.org/

> IPL is mobilizing a religious response to global warming in congregations through the promotion of renewable energy, energy efficiency, and conservation.

New Voice of Business

www.newvoiceofbusiness.org

> Seeks to amplify the voices of business people who want to be part of the solution on climate change and other issues.

Vote Solar

www.votesolar.org

> Starting in San Francisco and spreading across the country, one of the country's most effective advocates for strong public policies promoting solar power.

Western Resource Advocates

www.westernresourceadvocates.org

> An environmental law and policy organization working to restore and protect the natural environment of the interior American West. Works to challenge coal-plant proposals and advocate for clean-energy solutions.

LEARN MORE

Carbon-Free and Nuclear-Free: A Roadmap for U.S. Energy Policy
  An excellent book by Arjun Makhijani and the Institute for Energy and Environment
  Research that gives a detailed analysis of America's untapped clean-energy potential.

"Cashing in on Clean Energy"
www.ucsusa.org/clean_energy/clean_energy_policies/cashing-in.html
  A 2007 Union of Concerned Scientists report on the economic benefits of clean energy.

"Clean Energy Trends"
www.cleanedge.com/reports/
  These annual reports by Clean Edge track the rapid growth rates and new developments in
  the renewable energy sector.

Green-Collar Jobs in America's Cities
  Resource guide produced by the Apollo Alliance and Green for All to help policymakers in
  urban areas develop local strategies to create and support green job growth.

"Solar Generation IV"
www.greenpeace.org/international/press/reports/solar-generation-iv
  Report by Greenpeace International in 2007 predicting the creation of 2 million solar jobs by
  2020.

"A Solar Grand Plan"
  January 2008 *Scientific American* article by Ken Zweibel, James Mason, and Vasilis Fthenakis
  proposing how solar technology (the article focuses on solar photovoltaics) can meet a substantial portion of our energy needs.

Solar Revolution: The Economic Transformation of the Global Energy Industry
  Industry analyst Travis Bradford develops a compelling business case for why distributed
  solar power will upend the way power is produced and delivered in the twenty-first century.

"Tackling Climate Change"
www.ases.org/climatechange/
  A comprehensive 2007 report by the American Solar Energy Society showing the potential for
  greenhouse gas reductions through clean energy and efficiency through 2030.

SOLAR PROVIDERS

There will soon be hundreds of solar power installers operating around the country. Most of
them will help you secure local, state, and federal rebates and even help arrange financing. Here
are a few:

SolarCity

www.solarcity.com

A rapidly growing company, awarded the 2008 Aspen Energy and Environment Award for Corporate Energy Generation.

SunEdison

www.sunedison.com

SunEdison works with businesses and municipalities and takes a different approach to providing solar power. It owns the solar panels; will install them on the rooftop of your business, university, or government building; and will sell you clean, secure power at competitive rates.

Sungevity

www.sungevity.com

California-based installers led by some of the country's most experienced environmental advocates.

Energy Efficiency

SUPPORT THESE ORGANIZATIONS AND PROGRAMS

Alliance to Save Energy

www.ase.org

A national coalition of high-profile politicians, business leaders, and others providing research and policy advice to promote the efficient use of clean energy.

American Council for an Energy-Efficient Economy

www.aceee.org

A nonprofit that provides research materials to consumers and policymakers to promote prosperity and sustainability through energy efficiency. Produces the *Consumer Guide to Home Energy Savings* and other resources highlighting businesses and municipalities that are leading innovators in energy efficiency.

Architecture 2030

www.architecture2030.org

Founded by architect Ed Mazria in 2002 to transform the U.S. building sector from a major contributor of climate change to a potential cure. Aims to change the ways in which buildings are planned, designed, and constructed, taking a vocal and determined stance against new coal plant construction.

Climate Group

www.theclimategroup.org

An international organization based in the United Kingdom, United States, and Australia that helps businesses and governments share knowledge of new technologies and techniques to reduce energy consumption and greenhouse gas emissions. Also advocates for clean-energy policies.

Rocky Mountain Institute

www.rmi.org

Colorado-based organization founded by Amory Lovins that has long been an efficiency pioneer, providing advocacy, research, and consultancy services. RMI's mission statement says that its work is "independent, nonadversarial, and transideological, with a strong emphasis on market-based solutions."

LEARN MORE

"More Profit with Less Carbon"

September 2005 *Scientific American* article by Amory Lovins that reshapes the climate debate by showing how reducing greenhouse gas emissions can significantly improve a company's bottom line.

"Reducing Greenhouse Gas Emissions"

www.mckinsey.com/clientservice/ccsi/greenhousegas.asp

December 2007 report by McKinsey and Company showing how efficiency combined with renewable power can significantly reduce greenhouse gas emissions in the short term.

Seven Wonders for a Cool Planet: Everyday Things to Help Solve Global Warming

A collaboration between Sightline Institute of Seattle and writer Eric Sorensen, this little book points to simple lifestyle changes that can make a big difference in our personal carbon footprint.

Notes

Introduction: It's Time to Refuel

Page 14. Victor Hugo epigraph: *History of a Crime,* written in 1852, published in 1877. Quotation taken from English translation by T. H. Joyce and Arthur Locker (New York: Mondial, 2005), p. 409.

Page 14. Sports Illustrated cover story: Alexander Wolff, "Going, Going Green," *Sports Illustrated,* March 2007.

Page 14. "the climate-energy policy debate got disconnected": Thomas L. Freidman, "Want the Good News First?" *New York Times,* July 27, 2010, www.nytimes.com/2010/07/28/opinion/28friedman.html.

Page 15. In 2007, sales of hybrid vehicles increased by 38 percent: HybridCars.com, "December 2007 Dashboard," www.hybridcars.com/market-dashboard/dec07-overview.html. Cars outpacing trucks: Chris Woodward, "Drivers Choose Cars over Trucks as Auto Sales Plunge," *USA Today,* June 3, 2008.

Page 15. Sales and shipments of CFLs: 2001 figures from www.18seconds.org. 2010 projection from www.energystar.gov/ia/products/downloads/CFL_Market_Profile.pdf. Replacing incandescent bulbs with CFLs saved an estimated 16.9 billion pounds of coal: www.18seconds.org.

Page 15. NBC News/Wall Street Journal poll: www.americanprogress.org/issues/2009/12/snapshot122109.html.

Page 15. Ecomagination: Excerpted from General Electric's Web site, the Our Company page, www.ge.com/company/citizenship/ecomagination/index.html.

Page 16. Ford fuel economy below the industry norm: U.S. Environmental Protection Agency (EPA), "Light-Duty Automotive Technology and Fuel Economy Trends: 1975 through 2007," appendix L, "Data Stratified by Vehicle Type and Marketing Group," www.epa.gov/oms/cert/mpg/fetrends/420r07008l.pdf, table L-8, p. 9. The Model T Ford earned between twenty and twenty-five miles per gallon in the early twentieth century (Model T Ford Register of Great Britain Web site, www.modeltregister.co.uk/the-model-t-ford.html). By comparison, over the past twelve years, Ford Motor Company's fleet average has not exceeded twenty miles per gallon.

Page 16. California's vehicle emissions regulations: Details on the Pavley Law from Union of Concerned Scientists (UCS) Web site and "California Regulates Global Warming Emissions from Motor Vehicles," www.ucsusa.org/clean_vehicles/vehicles_health/californias-global-warming-vehicle-law.html.

Page 16. More than fifteen states have adopted California standards: Pew Center on Global Climate Change, "Vehicle Greenhouse Gas Emissions Standards," www.pewclimate.org/what_s_being_done/in_the_states/vehicle_ghg_standard.cfm.

Page 16. Washington Post op-ed: Arnold Schwarzenegger and Jodi Rell, "Lead or Step Aside, EPA: States Can't Wait on Global Warming," *Washington Post,* May 21, 2007.

Page 17. Climate change is already responsible for dwindling snowpacks: United States Global Change Resource Program, "Global Climate Change Impacts in the United States—Key Findings," www.globalchange.gov/publications/reports/scientific-assessments/us-impacts/key-findings.

Page 17. Bush administration rules in favor of the automakers: Juliet Eilperin, "EPA Chief Denies Calif. Limit on Auto Emissions," *Washington Post,* December 20, 2007.

Page 17. Frederick Douglass quote: Frederick Douglass, "The Significance of Emancipation in the West Indies," speech, Canandaigua, New York, August 3, 1857, from the Building Equality Web site, a cooperative project of the Center for Democratic Renewal, Political Research Associates, National Center for Human Rights Education, and the Gustavus Myers Center, www.buildingequality.us/Quotes/Frederick_Douglass.htm.

Page 18. Nearly half of our electricity comes from coal: U.S. Energy Information Administration (EIA), *Electric Power Annual,* EIA Web site, data for 2006 (October 22, 2007), www.eia.doe.gov/cneaf/electricity/epa/epa_sum.html.

Page 18. Oil accounts for 71 percent of transportation: EIA, Independent Statistics & Analysis, "U.S. Primary Energy Consumption by Source and Sector, 2008," diagram in Annual Energy Review, www.eia.doe.gov/aer/pecss_diagram.html.

Page 18. Coal-fired power plants kill an estimated twenty-four thousand Americans each year: American Lung Association, *State of the Air: 2007.* You can view a full copy of the report at www.lungusa2.org/embargo/sota07/ALA_SOTA_07.pdf.

Page 18. Strip mining in Appalachia has leveled more than five hundred mountains: See "End Mountaintop Removal" at the iLoveMountains.org Web site. On the Web site there is a map that shows the locations where mountains have been leveled since 1985, http://ilovemountains.org/resources.

Page 18. Over a hundred thousand Americans died mining coal in the last century: Jeff Goodell, *Big Coal: The Dirty Secret behind America's Energy Future* (Boston: Houghton Mifflin, 2006), p. xx.

Page 18. Toxic coal ash polluting water supplies: Shaila Dewan, "Huge Coal Ash Spills Contaminating U.S. Water," *New York Times,* January 7, 2009, www.nytimes.com/2009/01/07/world/americas/07iht-sludge.4.19164565.html.

Page 19. Records of Saudi Arabia's human rights violations can be found at Human Rights Watch (HRW), "World Report 2007: Saudi Arabia, Events of 2006," HRW Web site, http://hrw.org/englishwr2k7/docs/2007/01/11/saudia14717.htm. Statistics can also be found in Amnesty International USA, "Saudi Arabia: Human Rights Concerns," www.amnestyusa.org/By_Country/Saudi_Arabia/page.do?id=1011230&n1=3&n2=30&n3=980.

Page 19. U.S. Agreement with Saudi Arabia since 1945: PBS series *Frontline,* "A Chronology: House of Saud," February 8, 2005, www.pbs.org/wgbh/pages/frontline/shows/saud/cron.

Page 23. 200 million drivers: U.S. Department of Transportation Federal Highway Administration, Highway Statistics 2008, www.fhwa.dot.gov/policyinformation/statistics/2008/dvlc.cfm.

Page 25. Arundhati Roy quote: "Confronting Empire," talk delivered on January 27, 2003, World Social Forum in Porto Alegre, Brazil.

Chapter 1: Getting Our Fix

Page 26. Al Gore quote: "Al Gore 3.0," *Rolling Stone,* July 13, 2006, www.rollingstone.com/politics/story/ 10688399/al_gore_30/1.

Page 27. More than half of the oil Ecuador produces is shipped to the United States: EIA, "Country Analysis Brief: Ecuador, 'Oil,'" EIA Web site, Energy Information Sheets page (March 2007), www.eia.doe.gov/emeu/cabs/Ecuador/Oil.html/, p. 2.

Pages 27–28. America consumes its oil imports from Ecuador in less than twenty minutes: This is the author's calculation. The United States consumes about 20.5 million barrels per day, more than 850,000 barrels per hour. Ecuador exported 274,000 barrels into the United States each day in 2006.

Page 29. Oil consumption expected to increase: EIA, "International Energy Outlook 2010—Highlights," EIA Web site, Forecasts & Analysis, www.eia.doe.gov/oiaf/ieo/highlights.html. Decrease based on economic downturn.

Page 29. Hubbert's prediction: M. King Hubbert, "Nuclear Energy and Fossil Fuels," *American Petroleum Institute and Production Practice Proceedings* (Spring 1956): 5–75.

Page 30. U.S. oil production topped out at 9.6 million barrels: EIA, "Crude Oil Production," EIA Web site, Energy Information Sheets page (January 2008), www.eia.doe.gov/neic/infosheets/crudeproduction.html/, p. 3.

Page 30. Global oil discoveries peaked in the mid-1960s: Lester Brown, "Is World Oil Production Peaking?" Earth Policy Institute Web site (November 15, 2007), www.earth-policy.org/Updates/2007/Update67.htm.

Page 30. Deffeyes quote: Kenneth S. Deffeyes, *Beyond Oil: The View from Hubbert's Peak* (New York: Hill and Wang, 2005), p. 3.

Page 30. Consuming oil at a far faster rate than it can be replaced: Brown, "Is World Oil Production Peaking?"

Page 30. Oil production has leveled off: Kjell Aleklett, "The Oil Supply Tsunami Alert," Association for the Study of Peak Oil and Gas (April 25, 2005), www.peakoil.net/Oil_tsunami.html.

Page 31. Daniel Yergin quote: Daniel Yergin, "It's Not the End of the Oil Age: Technology and Higher Prices Drive a Supply Buildup," *Washington Post,* op-ed, July 31, 2005.

Page 31. Michael Rodgers quote: Jeffery Ball, "Dire Prophecy: As Prices Soar, Doomsayers Provoke Debate on Oil's Future," *Wall Street Journal,* September 20, 2004.

Pages 31–32. Fatih Birol warned in August 2009: Steve Connor, "Warning: Oil Supplies Are Running Out Fast: Catastrophic Shortfalls Threaten Economic Recovery, Says World's Top Energy Economist," *The Independent* (London), August 3, 2009, www.independent.co.uk/news/science/warning-oil-supplies-are-running-out-fast-1766585.html.

Page 32. No new refineries have been built since 1976: Deffeyes, *Beyond Oil*, p. xiv.

Page 32. Al-Husseini says global oil production reached peak in 2006: David Strahan, interview with Sadad al-Husseini, October 29, 2007. You can listen to the full podcast on the articles page of David Strahan's Web site, www.davidstrahan.com/blog/?p=67.

Page 32. Global oil production has not increased since 2006: According to the EIA, average global average of oil production in thousands of barrels per day was 84,636 in 2006, 84,500 in 2007, 85,429 in 2008, and 84,240 (preliminary figure) in 2009, indicating that in fact oil production has remained fairly stagnant: either increasing at a reduced rate or simply decreasing. From "World Oil Supply, 1970–2009," Table 4.4, www.eia.doe.gov/emeu/ipsr/t44.xls.

Page 32. For every barrel of oil we discover, we now consume three: David Strahan, *The Last Oil Shock: A Survival Guide to the Imminent Extinction of Petroleum Man* (London: John Murray, 2007), www.davidstrahan.com.

Page 32. Global demand for oil is expected to increase: *International Energy Outlook, 2007,* chapter 3, "Petroleum and Other Liquid Fuels," p. 3.

Page 33. Drilling advocates argue that any incursion will impact as little as two thousand acres: Arctic National Wildlife Refuge (ANWR), "Top 10 Reasons to Support Development in ANWR," ANWR Web site, Basics page, www.anwr.org/topten.htm.

Page 33. Oil may be scattered in thirty deposits: U.S. Department of the Interior, "Oil and Gas Potential of the Arctic National Wildlife Refuge 1002 Area, Alaska," *U.S. Geological Survey, 1999,* U.S. Fish and Wildlife Service Web site, Arctic National Wildlife Refuge page, open file report 98-34 (January 17, 2001), http://arctic.fws.gov/issues1.htm. A map of the potential impacts of drilling in the refuge can be found at the National Resources Defense Council Web page, www.nrdc.org/land/wilderness/arcticmap_2000acres.pdf.

Page 33. Exporting oil from ANWR would require infrastructure: U.S. Fish and Wildlife Service (USFWS), Alaska, "Potential Impacts of Proposed Oil and Gas Development on the Arctic Refuge's Coastal Plain: Historical Overview and Issues of Concern," USFWS Web site, Arctic National Wildlife Refuge page (2001), http://arctic.fws.gov/issues1.htm#section4.

Page 34. It would take at least ten years for oil from ANWR to reach American gas tanks: Natural Resource Defense Council (NRDC), "Arctic National Wildlife Refuge: Why Trash an American Treasure for a Tiny Percentage of Our Oil Needs?" NRDC Web site, Water page (November 10, 2005), www.nrdc.org/land/wilderness/arctic.asp.

Page 34. Drilling for much less oil than the United States consumes in a year: U.S. Geological Survey (USGS), "Arctic National Wildlife Refuge, 1002 Area, Petroleum Assessment, 1998, Including Economic Analysis," USGS Web site, http://pubs.usgs.gov/fs/fs-0028-01/fs-0028-01.pdf/, p. 4. The USGS estimates that there is a 95 percent probability of finding 4.3 billion barrels of oil within the Arctic National Wildlife Refuge. U.S. oil consumption in 2006 totaled 7.55 billion barrels. EIA, "Product Supplied," EIA Web site, Consumption/Sales page, www.eig.doe/gov.

Page 34. A federal judge blocked the Chukchi Sea project: Dan Joling for Associated Press, "Judge Puts Chuckchi Sea Leases on Hold for Further Review," *Tacoma News-Tribune,* July 22, 2010, www.thenewstribune.com/2010/07/21/1272181/judge-halts-oil-gas-development.html.

Page 34. Offshore oil moratorium, the 1969 Santa Barbara spill, and Fred Hartley quote: Tom Valtin, "Offshore Drilling Moratorium Threatened," *The Planet* newsletter, May/June 2006, www.sierraclub.org/planet/200603/offshore.asp.

Page 35. Adam quote: Telephone interview, September 16, 2007.

Pages 35–36. O'Conner calls for epidemiological studies: CBC News Canada, "High Illness Rate near Oil Sands Worrisome, Says Alberta Health Official," cbsnews.ca (March 10, 2006), www.cbc.ca/story/canada/national/2006/03/10/oilsands-chipewyan060310.html.

Page 36. Donna Cyprien quote: Ian Austen, "Study Finds Carcinogens in Water Near Alberta Oil Sands Projects," *New York Times,* November 9, 2007.

Page 36. Elsie Fabian quote: Doug Struck, "Canada Pays Environmentally for U.S. Oil Thirst: Huge Mines Rapidly Draining Rivers, Cutting into Forests, Boosting Emissions," *Washington Post,* May 31, 2006.

Page 36. Tar sands landscape excavation: Tom Knudson, "Grubbing for Oil," *Sacramento Bee,* December 10, 2007.

Page 36. Four tons of dirt are dug up for every barrel of oil refined: Dan Woynillowicz, "Oil Sands Fever: The Environmental Implications of Canada's Oil Sands Rush," Pembina Institute Web site, Publications page (November 2005), http://pubs.pembina.org/reports/OilSands72.pdf/, p. 12.

Page 36. Waste from tar sands in two days can fill Yankee Stadium: Justin Bloom, "Where Oil Is Mined, Not Pumped," *Washington Post,* June 15, 2005.

Page 36. Mining of tar sands is energy intensive: Woynillowicz, "Oil Sands Fever," p. 22. Report authors calculate that the average greenhouse gas (GHG) intensity for conventional oil is 28.6 GHG/barrel of oil, versus 85.8 GHG/barrel of oil from the tar sands.

Page 36. Tar sands contribute to growth of climate-change pollution in Canada: Ibid., p. 19.

Page 36. Largest strip mine: Byron W. King, "2006 Boston ASPO: The Canadian Tar Sands" (November 13, 2006), originally published by Whiskey and Gunpowder and by *Energy Bulletin,* www.energybulletin.net/22358.html.

Page 36. Strip mine that will be six miles in diameter: Elizabeth Kolbert, "Unconventional Crude: Canada's Synthetic Fuels Boom," *New Yorker,* November 12, 2007, p. 46.

Page 36. Dozens more strip mines are planned: Woynillowicz, "Oil Sands Fever," p. 5.

Pages 36–37. For every three barrels of oil produced, the energy equivalent of one is consumed: Kolbert, "Unconventional Crude," p. 46.

Page 37. Enough gas will be consumed each year to heat every home in Canada: Woynillowicz, "Oil Sands Fever," p. 15.

Page 37. Reguly quote: Eric Reguly, "Oil Sands Mother Lode Could Doom Gas Reserves," *Globe and Mail* (Toronto), May 28, 2005.

Page 37. In 2007 tar sands produced 1.3 million barrels per day: Knudson, "Grubbing for Oil."

Page 37. Expansion plans would bring production to about 2.2 million barrels: Canadian Association of Petroleum Producers, "Crude Oil Forecast," *Markets & Pipelines* (June 2010), www.capp.ca/getdoc.aspx?DocId=173003, p. 3.

Page 37. Norwegian quote: Tim Reiterman, "A Stand in the Forest," *Los Angeles Times,* July 2, 2006.

Page 37. Tar sands oil production is water intensive: Woynillowicz, "Oil Sands Fever," p. 29.

Page 37. Millions of feet of cubic water is diverted: Ibid., p. 34.

Page 37. Natural systems are not restored: Ibid., p. 38.

Page 38. First Nations Keepers Declaration, "Keepers of the Water Declaration," Kairos: Canadian Ecumenical Justice Initiatives Web site, Ecology page (September 7, 2006), www.kairoscanada.org/e/ecology/water/Declaration_KeepersWater_Sept06.pdf.

Page 38. Output could reach 11 million barrels per day by 2047: Woynillowicz, "Oil Sands Fever," p. 5.

Page 38. Adam quote: Telephone interview, September 16, 2007.

Page 39. Higher sulfur content in tar sands: Gareth R. Crandall, "Prospects for Increased Production—Non-Conventional Oil Market Outlook," presentation to International Energy Agency Conference on Non-Conventional Oil, 2002, http://iea.org/textbase/work/2002/calgary/Crandall.pdf. Higher nitrogen content in tar sands: ADVENT-ENVIRON, addendum to "Case-by-Case Antidegradation Analysis," prepared for BP Whiting, Indiana, submitted to IDEM, November 30, 2006, p. 2, www.in.gov/idem/files/clarification_3.pdf. See also Woynillowicz, "Oil Sands Fever," p. 45; and Minority Staff Special Investigations Division, Committee on Government Reform, *Oil Refineries Fail to Report Millions of Pounds of Harmful Emissions,* prepared for Henry Waxman, U.S. House of Representatives, 1999.

Page 39. Kent Moeckly quote: Kenny Bruno, Bruce Baizel, Susan Casey-Lefkowitz, Elizabeth Shope, and Kate Colarulli, *Tar Sands Invasion: How Dirty and Expensive Oil from Canada Threatens America's New Energy Economy,* a report from Corporate Ethics International, EARTHWORKS, Natural Resources Defense Council, and Sierra Club, May 2010, unpaginated.

Page 39. Ben Gotschall quote: Martin Kaste, "An Oil Pipeline From Canada? Some Say 'No Way'," *The Story,* National Public Radio (July 8, 2010), www.npr.org/templates/story/story.php?storyId=128381963.

Pages 39–40. Investigative report by the Ecological Integrity Project and the Houston Galveston Association for Smog Prevention: "Who's Counting? The Systematic Underreporting of Toxic Air Emissions,", a joint project by the Environmental Integrity Project and Galveston-Houston Association for Smog Prevention, Environmental Integrity Project Web site, Publications page, (June 2004), www.environmentalintegrity.org/pubs/TRIFINALJune_22.pdf.

Page 40. Ortiz quote: Monica Rohr, "Texas Town Has Been Defined by Oil Refineries," Associated Press, October 23, 2007, www.msnbc.msn.com/id/21420793.

Page 41. Larson quote: Telephone interview, January 9, 2008.

Page 41. Rolfes quote: Michelle Nijhuis, "Passing the Bucket: How the Five-Gallon Plastic Bucket Came to the Aid of Grassroots Environmentalists," *Grist: Environmental News and Commentary,* News page (July 23, 2003), www.grist.org/news/maindish/2003/07/23/the.

Page 41. Larson quote: Telephone interview.

Page 41. Christian Aid report: Christian Aid, "Fuelling Poverty: Oil, War, and Corruption," Christian Aid Web site (May 2003), http://212.2.6.41/indepth/0305cawreport/fuellingpoverty.htm/, p. 2.

Page 42. Each fifteen gallons would add three hundred pounds of carbon dioxide to the atmosphere: EPA, "Emission Facts: Greenhouse Gas Emissions from a Typical Passenger Vehicle," EPA Web site, Transportation and Air Quality page (February 2005), www.epa.gov/oms/climate/420f05004.htm.

Chapter 2: Smokescreen

Page 45. Abraham Lincoln epigraph: From a speech delivered in Clinton, Illinois, September, 1858, taken from the Gaia Community Web site, Wisdom page, http://quotes.gaia.com/184/you_can_fool_all_the_people_so/by_abraham_lincoln.

Page 45. Gibson quote: In-person interview, July 14, 2007.

Page 46. Hitt quote: Telephone interview, July 20, 2007.

Page 46. Coal mining accounted for 65 percent of all explosives use in the United States in 2006: Deborah A. Kramer, "Explosives," U.S. Geological Survey, 2006 minerals yearbook (September 2007), http://minerals.usgs.gov/minerals/pubs/commodity/explosives/600495.pdf/, p. 1.

Page 46. Explosives can be set off within three hundred feet of a home: West Virginia Secretary of State, Code of State Rules, Environmental Protection, Series 1 Surface Mining Blasting Rule, sec. 3.6h, p. 7, www.wvsos.com/csr/verify.asp?TitleSeries=199-01.

Pages 46–47. Dennis Davidson story: Carol Morello, "Mining Town Rises in Anger," *Washington Post,* January 6, 2005. Also listen to the story on National Public Radio by Noah Adams, "Virginia Strip-Mining Death Brings Reforms," www.npr.org/templates/story/story.php?storyId=4489461.

Page 47. Mountaintop-removal coal mining described as "strip mining on steroids": This term is commonly used in describing mountaintop removal, and you will find it referred to this way on numerous Web sites. One of the first writers to use the term was Peter Galuszka, "Strip-Mining on Steroids," *Business Week*, November 17, 1997, p. 70.

Page 47. In excess of five hundred mountains have been leveled and twelve hundred miles of rivers and streams completely buried: From "End Mountaintop Removal," at the iLoveMountains.org Web site, where there is a map showing the locations where these mountains have been leveled since 1985, http://ilovemountains.org/resources.

Page 47. U.S. Fish and Wildlife Service report: referenced in Joby Warrick, "Appalachia Is Paying Price for White House Rule Change," *Washington Post,* August 14, 2004.

Page 47. Gibson quote: In-person interview, July 14, 2007.

Page 48. Gunnoe quote: In-person interview, July 16, 2007.

Page 48. Maria Gunnoe is fighting back: Maria Gunnoe, "My Life Is on the Line: A Personal Story." Read the full story on the Stop Mountaintop Removal Web site, the Read Their Stories page, www.stopmountaintopremoval.org/marias-story.html.

Pages 48–49. Gunnoe quote: Personal communication, July 16, 2007.

Page 49. Not a single power plant has ever captured all of its carbon dioxide emissions: While a few power plants have started to experiment with capturing some of their emissions, none has been able to successfully capture all of them or to store those emissions underground.

Page 50. From 1985 to 2008, coal-mine production increased while coal-mining jobs decreased: EIA, Independent Statistics & Analysis, "Coal Production and Number of Mines by State and Mine Type," www.eia.doe.gov/cneaf/coal/page/acr/table1.html; see also http://tonto.eia.doe.gov/FTPROOT/coal/006493.pdf. Meanwhile, according to the National Mining Association, total U.S. coal production increased from 883.6 million tons in 1985 to 1,132 million tons in 2005, an increase of 28 percent. See "Trends in U.S. Coal Mining, 1923–2006," www.nma.org/pdf/c_trends_mining.pdf.

Page 50. More than a hundred thousand miners died in coal mines in the twentieth century: Jeff Goodell, *Big Coal: The Dirty Secret behind America's Energy Future* (New York: Houghton Mifflin, 2006), introduction, p. xiii. The statistic about twelve thousand miners dying from black lung comes from the Sierra Club, "The Dirty Truth about Coal: Why Yesterday's Technology Should Not Be Part of Tomorrow's Energy Future," Moving beyond Coal page, www.sierraclub.org/coal/dirtytruth/coalreport.pdf/, p. 4.

Page 50. Coal is also the dirtiest and most carbon-intensive fossil fuel: Goodell, *Big Coal,* p. xvi.

Page 50. Three tons of carbon dioxide are produced for every ton of coal that is burned: EPA, "Green Power Equivalency Calculator Methodologies," EPA Web site, Tools and Calculators page (2003), www.epa.gov/grnpower/pubs/calcmeth.htm.

Page 50. Coal is the largest and one of the fastest-growing sources of greenhouse gas emissions in the country: Union of Concerned Scientists (UCS), "The Costs of Coal," UCS Web site, Clean Energy page, www.ucsusa.org/clean_energy/fossil_fuels/costs_of_coal.html; and Mark Clayton, "Global Boom in Coal Power—and Emissions," *Christian Science Monitor,* March 22, 2007.

Page 50. Coal plants use far more water than all other forms of electricity besides nuclear power: Union of Concerned Scientists, "Impacts of Coal Power: Water Use," UCS Web site, Clean Energy page (2005), www.ucsusa.org/clean_energy/coalvswind/c02b.html.

Page 50. Coal-fired power plants kill an estimated twenty-four thousand people prematurely each year: American Lung Association (ALA), *State of the Air: 2007,* ALA Web site, www.lungusa2.org/embargo/sota07/ALA_SOTA_07.pdf.

Page 50. In 2008 there were about six hundred U.S. coal plants in operation: EIA, Independent Statistics & Analysis, "Count of Electric Power Industry Power Plants, by Sector, by Predominant Energy Sources within Plant," www.eia.doe.gov/cneaf/electricity/epa/epat5p1.html.

Page 50. More than a billion tons of coal is mined in the United States each year: EIA, *Annual Coal Report,* Executive Summary, EIA Web site (2006), www.eia.doe.gov/cneaf/coal/page/acr/acr_sum.html. Electricity statistic comes from the EIA, "Electricity Power Annual" (2006), www.eia.doe.gov/cneaf/electricity/epa/epa_sum.html.

Page 50. On average, every man, woman, and child in the United States uses about twenty pounds of coal each day: Goodell, *Big Coal,* p. xx.

Page 51. "Clean Coal" PR firms and their activities: See SourceWatch Web site, a project of the Center for Media and Democracy, www.sourcewatch.org/index.php?title=Pac/West_Communications.

Page 51. Americans for Balanced Energy Choices advertisement: These ads were on learnaboutcoal.com, but were pulled in early 2008. Read about the ads at the Center for American Progress Action Fund blog, Think Progress, http://thinkprogress.org/2008/02/14/coal-kids.

Page 52. America's Power Army: Source Watch,"Your Guide to the Names behind the News," www.sourcewatch.org/index.php?title=Americans_for_Balanced_Energy_Choices; see also www.americaspowerarmy.org/.

Page 52. GE Energy ad: Available on YouTube, http://youtube.com/watch?v=J1A146sANdg.

Pages 52–53. An IGCC plant that captured its carbon would increase the cost of power production by 20 to 55 percent: Intergovernmental Panel on Climate Change (IPCC), *IPCC Special Report on Carbon Dioxide Capture and Storage* (Cambridge: Cambridge University Press, 2005), p. 342, sec. 8.2.1, "Capture and Compression," IPCC Web site, http://arch.rivm.nl/env/int/ipcc/pages_media/SRCCS-final/IPCCSpecialReportonCarbondioxide-CaptureandStorage.htm.

Page 53. IGCC plants are more costly to construct: As of this writing, there were only two IGCC plants in operation in the United States, although several more were planned. The Electric Power Research Institute estimated that the capital costs of an IGCC plant were at a 20 percent premium compared to pulverized plants: Electric Power Research Institute (EPRI), *Feasibility Study for an Integrated Gasification Combined Cycle Plant at a Texas Site,* EPRI Web site, Technical Update page (October 2006), www.epriweb.com/public/000000000001014510.pdf/, p. v. See also William G. Rosenberg, Dwight C. Alpern, and Michael R. Walker, "Deploying IGCC in This Decade with 3Party Covenant Financing: Volume I," revised version (May 2005), Belfer Center for Science and International Affairs, Kennedy School of Government, Harvard University, http://belfercenter.ksg.harvard.edu/publication/2100/deploying_igcc_in_this_decade_with_3party_covenant_financing.html/, p. 2.

Page 53. IGCC plants that capture carbon require 14 to 25 percent more power: See *IPCC Special Report on Carbon Dioxide Capture and Storage,* table 8.1, "Summary of New Plant Performance and CO_2 Capture Cost Based on Current Technology," p. 343.

Page 53. A coal plant emits about 3 million tons of carbon dioxide per year: Interdisciplinary study, Massachusetts Institute of Technology, *The Future of Coal: Options for a Carbon Constrained World,* box 1, "Illustrating the Challenge of Scale for Carbon Capture," MIT Web site, Future of Coal page (2007), http://web.mit.edu/coal/, p. ix.

Page 53. Burning coal in the United States caused the release of more than 2 billion tons of CO_2 in 2006: EIA, "U.S. Carbon Dioxide Emissions from Energy Sources, 2006: Flash Estimate," slide 11 (entitled "Carbon Dioxide Emissions by Fossil Fuel Type") of a PowerPoint presentation, EIA Web site (May 2007), www.eia.doe.gov/oiaf/1605/flash/flash.html.

Page 54. A 2007 study from MIT: *The Future of Coal,* p. ix.

Page 54. In Cameroon in 1986, a natural release of poisonous CO_2 at Lake Nyos caused the death of more than seventeen hundred people: Keith Schneider "Cameroon Disaster: A U.S. Team Sifts Causes," *New York Times,* September 14, 1986.

Page 54. Massey Energy violated Clean Water Act more than forty-five hundred times: As reported by the EPA in its 2007 decision to fine Massey for the violations; see http://yosemite.epa.gov/opa/admpress.nsf/dc57b08b5acd42bc852573c90044a9c4/6944ea38b888dd03852573.

Pages 54–55. Massey violated its effluent limits at various operations: Documented in Attorneys for Sierra Club, West Virginia Highland Conservancy, Coal River Mountain Watch, and Ohio Valley Environmental Coalition, 60-Day Notice of Intent to File Citizen Suit Under Clean Water Act Section 505(a)(1) for Violation of Terms and Conditions of 102 West Virginia NPDES Permits and 60-Day Notice of Intent to File Citizen Suit Under the Federal Surface Mining Control and Reclamation Act Section 520(a)(1) for Violations of Federal and State Regulations and Permit Conditions on West Virginia Surface Mining Permits Associated with the 102 West Virginia NPDES Permits, January 7, 2010.

Page 55. Quote from Kidshealth.org: See the Kidshealth.org Web site, Asthma Basics page, www.kidshealth.org/parent/asthma_basics/what/asthma_basics.html.

Page 55. Approximately 20 million Americans suffer from asthma each year: American Academy of Allergy, Asthma, and Immunology (AAAAI), "Tips to Remember: Exercise-Induced Asthma," AAAAI Web site, Patients and Consumers page, www.aaaai.org/patients/publicedmat/tips/exerciseinducedasthma.stm.

Page 55. Asthma leads to 2 million emergency room visits and five thousand deaths each year in the United States: EPA, "Basic Information about Asthma," EPA Web site, Asthma page, www.epa.gov/asthma/about.html.

Page 56. American Lung Association estimates: American Lung Association, *State of the Air: 2007,* p. 53; www.lungusa2.org/embargo/sota07/ALA_SOTA_07.pdf.

Page 56. Damitz quote: Telephone interview, October 25, 2007.

Page 56. Solid waste and hazardous air pollutants from burning coal: Goodell, *Big Coal,* pp. 122–23.

Page 56. Mercury emissions from coal and power plants: See the EPA Web site, Mercury page, www.epa.gov/mercury/about.htm.

Page 56. Air pollution can significantly increase the risk of ischemic strokes: Gregory A. Wellenius et al., "Air Pollution and Hospital Admissions for Ischemic and Hemorrhagic Stroke among Medicare Beneficiaries," *Journal of the American Heart Association* 36, no. 12 (December 2005): 1.

Pages 56–57. Report by Clear the Air: Black Leadership Forum, Clear the Air, Georgia Coalition for the People's Agenda, and Southern Organizing Committee for Economic and Social Justice, "Air of Injustice: African Americans and Power Plant Pollution," Clear the Air Web site, Publications page (October 2002), www.catf.us/publications/reports/Air_of_Injustice.pdf/, p. 3.

Page 57. Harvard University study released in 2001: John Spengler and Jonathan Levy, "Estimated Public Health Impacts of Criteria Pollutant Air Emissions from Nine Fossil-Fueled Power Plants in Illinois," Harvard School of Public Health press release, 2001 Releases page, www.hsph.harvard.edu/news/press-releases/archives/2001-releases/press01032001.html.

Page 57. In 2006, the Crawford and Fisk plants released more than fourteen thousand tons of sulfur dioxide and nearly four thousand tons of nitrogen oxide: EPA, "Clean Air Markets—Data and Maps, 1980–2006 Emissions," facility level emissions quick report, for Fisk and Crawford plants in Illinois, EPA Web site, Clean Air Markets page, www.epa.gov/airmarkets (go to Data and Maps, click on Emissions, then Quick Reports, and do search).

Page 57. The Crawford plant produces more than 3.18 million tons: Bruce Nilles, "Big Cities Want Big Changes in Energy," Sierra Club Climate Crossroads blog, July 15, 2010, http://connect.sierraclub.org/post/ClimateCrossroadsBlog/big_cities_want_big_changes_in_energy.html?cons_id=2213761&ts=1280704458&signature=68f42ea07b068e5ace720bd88b9e5942.

Page 57. Villasenor quote: Telephone interview, October 24, 2007.

Page 57. EPA and the Illinois attorney general filed suit against Midwest Generation: Michael Hawthorne, "Air Pollution Lawsuit: Federal and State Lawyers Sue Midwest Generation over Illinois Power Plant Emissions," *Chicago Tribune,* August 28, 2009, www.chicagotribune.com/health/chi-chicago-pollution-suit-28-aug28,0,2243476.story.

Page 58. Coal consumption tripled in the United States between 1970 and 2000: National Mining Association (NMA), "Fast Facts about Coal," NMA Web site, Statistics page (January 28, 2008), http://nma.org/statistics/pub_fast_facts.asp.

Page 58. Statistics on the 150 proposed new coal-fired power plants: Mark Clayton, "Global Boom in Coal Power—and Emissions," *Christian Science Monitor,* March 22, 2007.

Page 58. Elwood Indeck Energy plant would have released 3.6 million tons of CO_2: CARMA: Carbon Monitoring for Action, "Highest CO_2 Emitting Plants Owned by Indeck Energy Services," http://carma.org/company/detail/9826 and http://carma.org/dig/show/company+9826+plant.

Page 59. The plant had already suffered cost overruns of $2 billion: Michael Hawthorne, "Clean Coal Dream a Costly Nightmare," *Chicago Tribune,* July 12, 2010, http://articles.chicagotribune.com/2010-07-12/news/ct-met-coal-plant-20100710_1_new-coal-fired-power-plant-clean-coal-electricity.

Pages 59–60. Historic and projected rise in temperature of Earth's climate: According to the IPCC's 2007 report, global surface temperature increased 1.33 ± 0.32 °F during the twentieth century. Climate model projections summarized in the report indicate that the global surface temperature is likely to rise a further 2.0 to 11.5 °F during the twenty-first century. From "Summary for Policymakers," *Climate Change 2007: The Physical Science Basis. Contribution of Working Group I to the Fourth Assessment Report of the Intergovernmental Panel on Climate Change,* www.ipcc.ch/pdf/assessment-report/ar4/wg1/ar4-wg1-spm.pdf.

Page 60. Hansen call for a moratorium: James E. Hansen, "How Can We Avert Dangerous Climate Change?" based on testimony to Select Committee on Energy Independence and Global Warming, U.S. House of Representatives (April 26, 2007), Columbia University Web site, Dr. James E. Hansen page, www.columbia.edu/~jeh1/2007/CanWeAvert_20070625.pdf/ (his call for a moratorium is on p. 2).

Page 60. Proposed new coal plants have already been rejected: The following articles refer to the closing of these plants: Oklahoma: American Electric Power (AEP) news release, "OCC Denies Application for Red Rock Power Plant," AEP Web site, Newsroom page (September 10, 2007), www.aep.com/investors/newsreleases/print.asp?ID=1396; Kentucky: *Sierra Club v. Environmental and Public Protection Cabinet,* civ. action no. 06-CI-00640 (Franklin County Circuit Court, August 6, 2007); Florida: Marcia Lane, "Seminole Electric Plans to Appeal Rejection of Coal-Burning Unit," *St. Augustine Record,* August 22, 2007; North Dakota: Dakota Council, "South Heart on Life Support" (August 2007), Dakota Resource Council Web site, Documents page, www.drcinfo.com/documents/DRC%20 newsletterAug07.pdf. Illinois: Alison Carney Brown, "EPA Denies Permit for Coal Plant Near Midewin," *Chicago Wilderness Magazine* (Winter 2007), www.dirtykilowatts.org/ Dirty_Kilowatts.pdf.

Pages 61–62. Coal-plant statistics: Ilan Levin and Eric Schaeffer, "Dirty Kilowatts: America's Most Polluting Power Plants," Environmental Integrity Project (July 2007), www. environmentalintegrity.org/pubs/2007 percent20Dirty percent20Kilowatts.pdf. The greenhouse gas figures are on p. 10, table 2; the sulfur dioxide figures on p. 16, table 4; the mercury figures on p. 25, table 8; the nitrous oxide figures on p. 20, table 6; and the emission rates by pounds of CO_2 on p. 9, table 1.

Chapter 3: Separate Oil and State

Page 65. Supreme Court justice Louis D. Brandeis epigraph: *Other People's Money, and How the Bankers Use It* (1914).

Page 65. A major report from U.K. government concludes: Nicholas Stern, *The Economics of Climate Change: The Stern Review,* (Cambridge, U.K: Cambridge University Press, 2007),"Summary of Conclusions," page 1. Stern, the lead author of the 712-page report, is also former chief economist of the World Bank. You can download a version of the report at the HM Treasury Web site, www.hm-treasury.gov.uk/independent_reviews/ stern_review_economics_climate_change/sternreview_index.cfm.

Page 65. Need to reduce greenhouse gas emissions by 80 percent: Alister Doyle, "World Needs to Axe Greenhouse Gases by 80 Percent," Reuters, April 19, 2007, http://uk.reuters.com/ article/topNews/idUKL194440620070419.

Page 65. U.S. greenhouse gas emissions actually increased: E PA, *2010 U.S. Greenhouse Gas Inventory Report, Inventory of U.S. Greenhouse Gas Emissions and Sinks: 1990–2008,* (April 2010), U.S. EPA # 430-R-10-006, http://epa.gov/climatechange/emissions/usinventoryreport.html. From the Executive Summary: "Overall, total U.S. emissions have risen by approximately 14 percent from 1990 to 2008. Emissions declined from 2007 to 2008, decreasing by 2.9 percent. . . . This decrease is primarily a result of a decrease in demand for transportation fuels associated with the record high costs of these fuels that occurred in 2008."

Page 65. F-Series Ford truck gets less gas mileage than the Model T: The Model T Ford got between twenty and twenty-five miles per gallon in the early parts of the twentieth century: Model T Ford Register of Great Britain, www.modeltregister.co.uk/the-model-t-ford.html. In comparison, the 2007 Ford F-150 gets just 17 mpg, and that's not even for four-wheel-drive vehicles: Ford Motors Web site, F-150 Detailed Comparison page, www.fordvehicles.com/trucks/f150/compare/details/?vehicles=20089|22066|23551|23402.

Page 66. Fuel efficiency standards pushed by the Obama administration: National Highway Traffic Safety Administration (NHTSA), "NHTSA and EPA Establish New National Program to Improve Fuel Economy and Reduce Greenhouse Gas Emissions for Passenger Cares and Light Trucks," NHTSA Web site (April 2010), www.nhtsa.gov/staticfiles/rulemaking/pdf/cafe/CAFE-GHG_Fact_Sheet.pdf.

Page 66. Improve gas mileage in America's cars, trucks, and SUVs by 2016 to reach China's fuel efficiency today: John M. Broder and Micheline Maynard, "Lawmakers Set Deal on Raising Fuel Efficiency," *New York Times,* December 1, 2007.

Page 66. Oil could be saved by using hybrid technology: Sierra Club, "Global Warming and Energy: The Biggest Single Step," Sierra Club, Global Warming and Energy page, www.sierraclub.org/globalwarming/biggest_single_step/intro.asp.

Page 67. Massey Energy violating state and federal regulations: In May 2007, Massey Energy Corporation was accused by federal environmental regulators of thousands of violations of water pollution standards, leading to a proposed $20 million penalty in January 2008. From Ken Ward, Jr., "$20 Million Fine, Improvements Part of Massey Deal: Feds Believe Company Will Now Have to Change," *Charleston Gazette,* January 18, 2008. Also in 2003, Massey CEO Don Blankenship told a *Forbes* reporter, "We don't pay much attention to the violation count." Quote from Bernard Condon, "Not King Coal," Forbes.com (May 26, 2003), www.forbes.com/forbes/2003/0526/080_print.html.

Page 67. Utilities and coal companies spend millions on teams of lawyers: Countless lawsuits and regulatory battles have been wages for decades. Most recently, Massey Energy settled with regulators for $30 million in January 2008. See Clem Guttata, "Massey Energy Settles Clean Water Act Lawsuit for $30 Million," West Virginia Blue Web site (January 17, 2008), www.wvablue.com/showDiary.do?diaryId=1569.

Page 67. Oil companies spent $888.5 million from 1998 through the first half of 2010: "Lobbying Spending Database Oil & Gas, 2009," Center for Responsive Politics Web site (2010), www.opensecrets.org/lobby/indusclient.php?year=2009&lname=E01&id=.

Page 68. Enron and Kenneth Lay donations: CBS News Online, "Bush Edges Away from 'Kenny Boy': Indicted Ex-Enron Boss Ken Lay, and Bush Pal, Made Big GOP Donations," cbsnews.com, Politics page (July 8, 2004), www.cbsnews.com/stories/2004/07/08/politics/main628320.shtml.

Page 68. Lay appoints two out of five members of the Federal Energy Regulatory Commission: Winning Argument Blogspot, "Ken Lay's Influence in the Bush Administration Continues to Undermine America's Energy Policy," Winning Argument Blogspot (July 28, 2004), http://winningargument.blogspot.com/2004/07/ken-lays-influence-in-bush.html.

Page 68. Investigation by Representative Henry Waxman: Scott Lindlaw, "Cheney's Energy Plan Benefited Enron in 17 Ways, Top Democrat Says," Associated Press, January 18, 2002, seattlepi.com, http://seattlepi.nwsource.com/national/54921_energy18.shtml.

Page 68. Kenneth Lay memo: John Nichols, "Enron: What Dick Cheney Knew," *The Nation*, April 15, 2002.

Page 68. Cheney announces that the Bush administration would not support price caps on California's energy prices: Here in Reality, "Enron Photo Album," Enron page, www.here-inreality.com/enron.html.

Page 68. Oil industry gives more than $70 million to politicians: Center for Responsive Politics, "Oil and Gas: Long-Term Contribution Trends," opensecrets.org, Industries page, www.opensecrets.org/industries/indus.asp?Ind=E01.

Pages 68–69. Top twenty recipients of oil industry cash in the 2006 election cycle: Center for Responsive Politics, "Oil and Gas: Top 20 Recipients," Opensecrets.org, Industries page, www.opensecrets.org/industries/recips.asp?Ind=E01&Cycle=2006recipdetail=A&Mem=N&sortorder=U.

Page 69. All recipients sided with oil industry: League of Conservation Voters, "Second Session 109th Congress, National Environmental Scorecard, 2006," www.lcv.org/images/client/pdfs/LCV_2006_Scorecard_final.pdf/. Senate votes listed by state and individual senator on pp. 10–15, House votes on pp. 20–35.

Page 69. Since 2001 mining companies have given more than $180,000 to Kentucky's Republican senator Mitch McConnell: OpenSecrets.org, Center for Responsive Politics, "Mitch McConnell: Campaign Finance/Money—Contributions—Senate 2006," opensecrets.org, Mitch McConnell—Top Industries page, www.opensecrets.org/politicians/indus.asp?CID=N00003389&cycle=2006.

Page 69. Matt Sledge quote: Matt Sledge, "Mitch McConnell Should Return Massey's Dirty Coal Money," HuffingtonPost.com (April 6, 2010), www.huffingtonpost.com/matt-sledge/mitch-mcconnell-should-re_b_527379.html.

Page 69. Boxer had drawn Murray's wrath: Lance Williams, "Fiorina Backed by Coal-Mining Firms," *San Francisco Chronicle*, July 27, 2010, www.sfgate.com/cgi-bin/article.cgi?f=/c/a/2010/07/26/MNUA1EK2FC.DTL.

Page 69. Crandall Canyon Mine in Utah gained notoriety: Kirk Johnson, "Safety Issues Slow Mine Rescue Efforts," *New York Times,* August 8, 2007.

Page 69. Galatia mine in southern Illinois cited more than twenty-seven hundred times in two years: Rachel Sklar, "CNN Delves into Robert Murray's Safety Record—17 Days Later," HuffingtonPost.com (August 23, 2007). Watch the full news report at www.huffington-post.com/2007/08/23/cnn-delves-into-robert-mu_n_61609.html.

Page 69. Ken American Resources: Susan Saulty and Carolyn Marshall, "Mine Owner Has History of Run-ins on Work Issues," *New York Times*, August 24, 2007.

Page 70. Murray quote and information about the transfer of Tim Thompson: "Two for the Money," *Kentucky Herald-Leader* (Lexington), October 20, 2006.

Page 70. Thompson quote: Ibid.

Page 70. Seattle Times report on Oreskes study: Sandi Doughton, "The Truth about Global Warming," *Seattle Times,* October 11, 2005.

Pages 70–71. Analysis of newspaper articles: Jennifer McNulty, "Top U.S. Newspapers' Focus on Balance Skewed Coverage of Global Warming, Analysis Reveals," University of California, UC Newsroom (August 25, 2004), www.universityofcalifornia.edu/news/article/6572.

Page 71. EPA chief Christine Todd Whitman: Cnn.com, "Climate Talks Secure U.S. Support." Whitman assured international leaders that Bush would take climate change seriously: "The president has said global climate change is the greatest environmental challenge that we face and that we must recognise that and take steps to move forward." See Cnn.com, World page (March 5, 2001), http://archives.cnn.com/2001/WORLD/europe/italy/03/04/environment.climate/index.html.

Page 71. Competitive Enterprise Institute and Exxon: Chris Mooney, "Some Like It Hot," *Mother Jones,* May–June 2005.

Page 71. Memo from Myron Ebell to Phil Cooney: A copy of the memo can be read in full on Greenpeace International's Web site, www.greenpeace.org/international/assets/binaries/ceimemo.swf.

Page 71. Internal White House documents leaked: Andrew C. Revkin, "Bush Aide Softened Greenhouse Gas Links to Global Warming," *New York Times,* June 8, 2005.

Page 71. Cooney quote: Robert Lusetich, "Climate Science Was Doctored," *The Australian* (Sydney), March 21, 2007.

Page 72. Jack Gerard quote: Dan Eggen and Kimberly Kindy, "Three of Every Four Oil and Gas Lobbyists Worked for Federal Government," *The Washington Post*, July 22, 2010, www.washingtonpost.com/wp-dyn/content/article/2010/07/21/AR2010072106468_pf.html.

Page 72. Kennedy, Jr., quote: From speech given at Rebekka Chapel in Rock Creek, WV, July 16, 2007.

Page 73. Exxon in 2006 was the most profitable corporation in history: Cnnmoney.com, "20 Most Profitable Companies," 2007 Fortune 500, cnnmoney.com (April 30, 2007), http://money.cnn.com/galleries/2007/fortune/0704/gallery.F500_profitable.fortune/index.html.

Page 73. John Drosdick, Don Blankenship, and Ray Irani salaries: Forbes.com, "CEO Compensation: Oil and Gas Operations," Forbes.com, Lists page (December 2006), www.forbes.com/lists/2006/12/Oil_Gas_Operations_Rank_1.html.

Page 73. Lee Raymond's parting gift from Exxon: ABC News, "Oil: Exxon Chairman's $400 Million Parachute," abcnew.go.com, *Good Morning America* page (April 14, 2006), www.abcnews.go.com/GMA/story?id=1841989.

Page 73. Friends of the Earth federal policies study: Friends of the Earth (FOE), "Big Oil, Bigger Giveaways," FOE (February 22, 2007), www.saveourenvironment.org/FriendsOfEarth_Report.pdf/, p. 1.

Pages 73–74. Earth Track report for the Organization for Economic Cooperation and Development: Doug Koplow, "Subsidies in the US Energy Sector: Magnitude, Causes, and Options for Reform," Earth Track library (November 2006), www.earthtrack.net/earthtrack/library/SubsidyReformOptions.pdf.

Page 74. U.S. federal energy subsidies in 2006 were $74 billion, in Koplow's estimate: Mark Clayton, "US House Takes on Big Oil," *Christian Science Monitor,* January 18, 2007.

Page 74. Environmental Law Institute on cost of fossil-fuel subsidies contrasted with support for renewable energy: Clifton Yin, "A Repeal of Fossil Fuel Subsidies Is Long Overdue," Americans for Energy Leadership Web site, July 23, 2010, http://leadenergy.org/2010/07/a-repeal-of-fossil-fuel-subsidies-is-long-overdue/.

Page 75. Spadaro quote: Interview with Clara Bingham, "Under Mined: When a Flood of Toxic Mining Sludge Wreaked Havoc in Appalachia, How Did the White House Respond? By Letting the Coal Company off the Hook and Firing the Whistleblower," *Washington Monthly,* January–February 2005, p. 5. See also www.wvgazette.com/static/series/buffalocreek/.

Page 75. Spadaro was asked to help lead an investigation: Ibid., p. 2.

Page 75. Coal executives gave $3.65 million in the 2000 election: Center for Responsive Politics: "Coal Mining: Long-Term Contribution Trends," opensecrets.org, Industries page (2002), www.opensecrets.org/industries/indus.asp?Ind=E1210.

Page 75. James H. "Buck" Harless: Spadaro interview with Bingham, p. 6.

Page 75. Harless quote: Tom Hamburger, "A Coal-Fired Crusade Helped Bring Crucial Victory to Candidate Bush," *Wall Street Journal,* June 13, 2001.

Page 76. Massey Energy fined $55,000 for one of the worst environmental disasters in the history of the southeastern U.S.: Phillip Babich, "Dirty Business: How Bush and His Coal Industry Cronies Are Covering Up One of the Worst Environmental Disasters in U.S. History," Salon.com (November 13, 2003), http://dir.salon.com/story/tech/feature/2003/11/13/slurry_coverup/index.html?source=search&aim=/tech/feature.

Page 77. Providing for Head Start and for medical care for uninsured U.S. kids: Head Start is a national program to help the advancement of low-income students. Read more at www.acf.hhs.gov/programs/hsb. The $2 billion figure for the cost of this program can be found on the National Institute for Early Education Research (NIEER) Web site at the Facts and

Figures page, http://nieer.org/resources/facts/index.php?FastFactID=12. The $6 billion figure for health-care costs for uninsured children can be found in an article by Pam Pohly, "Bush May Require 4 Million Uninsured Children to Suffer," Everyday Citizen's Web site (September 22, 2007), www.everydaycitizen.com/2007/09/bush_may_require_4_million_uni.html.

Page 77. Steve Kretzmann and *Rolling Stone:* Dan Baum, "Revolution 101: The Ruckus Society," *Rolling Stone,* July 5, 2001, p. 83.

Page 78. Midterm election results in 2006: Lindsay Renick Mayer, "Big Oil, Big Influence," PBS, *Now* page (November 23, 2007), www.pbs.org/now/shows/347/oil-politics.html.

Page 78. Congress acted in 2010 to require that extraction companies disclose how much they pay: Karin Lissakers, "Wall Street Reform Includes Big Steps on Oil and Mining Transparency," HuffingtonPost.com, July 15, 2010, www.huffingtonpost.com/Karin-lissakers/wall-street-reform-include_b_643399.html.

Page 78. Kretzmann quote: Telephone interview, October 10, 2007.

Page 79. Newman quote: Telephone interview, October 12, 2007.

Page 79. After some experimentation and exploration on MAPLight.org, the reader will be able to track what contributions were made—and when—for many bills in Congress. Here are the specific steps to take to get more information on the Pombo bill: Visit MAPLight.org, click "U.S. Congress," then "Bills," then enter "American-Made Energy and Good Jobs Act" into the search engine. Select the bill number: H.R. 5429. You'll come to a screen that lists the groups that did—and did not—want this bill to pass. To determine the role that the oil and gas industry played, take the following steps: Click "Customize" on the bottom, right-hand portion of your screen. Select "Energy/Nat resources," then "Oil and Gas," then click "support" next to "major (multinational) oil and gas producers" and "Oilfield service, equipment, and exploration" to see which oil and gas companies supported the bill. Then scroll down to the bottom of the screen and click "remove" next to all the other industries that may have supported the bill, including "trucking," the "Teamsters union," and so on. Once you've isolated just "major (multinational) oil and gas producers" and "oilfield service, equipment and exploration," click the "Votes" tab at the top of the page to find out how much each legislator who voted yes received from those sectors. Click on another tab at the top, "Timeline of Contributions" to learn more about when these donations were made.

Page 80. Newman quote: Telephone interview, October 12, 2007.

Page 80. Newman quote: Ibid.

Page 80. The House passed a bill: "House Rolls Back Oil Company Subsidies," *USA Today,* January 18, 2007, www.usatoday.com/news/washington/2007-01-18-house-oil_x.htm.

Page 80. Senate narrowly defeated a similar provision: Steven Mufson and Jonathan Weisman, "Senate to Rework Ambitious Energy Bill," *Washington Post,* December 8, 2007.

Page 80. Bush quote: President George W. Bush, State of the Union Address, January 31, 2006. View the full address at www.whitehouse.gov/stateoftheunion/2006.

Chapter 4: Follow the Money

Page 82. Mayer Anselm Rothschild epigraph: U.S. Senate document no. 23, 76th Congress, 1939.

Page 83. Bank of America press materials: Anne Finucane, "Bank of America Climate Change Position," Bank of America Web site, Environment page, www.bankofamerica.com/environment/index.cfm?template=env_clichangepos.

Page 83. Bank of America announces $20 billion commitment to climate change: Bank of America press release, "Bank of America Announces $20 Billion Environmental Initiative," Bank of America Web site, Newsroom page (Charlotte, NC, March 6, 2007), http://newsroom.bankofamerica.com/index.php?s=press_releases&item=7697.

Pages 83–84. Citi pledges $50 billion toward climate change: Dominic Rushe, "Green Ideals Inflate Bottom Line," *Australian Business,* May 15, 2007.

Page 84. AES Corporation seeks to build new coal-fired power plants in four states: Coal Moratorium Now! "State-by-State Descriptions of Proposed Coal-Fired Power Plants," Coal Moratorium Now! Web site, Proposed Coal Plants page (January 15, 2008), http://cmnow.org/Proposed%20Coal%20Plants.pdf.

Page 84. Dynergy planned to build up to eight or more new coal-fired power plants: Ibid.

Page 84. Peabody Energy poisoned the groundwater for Hopi and Navajo and planned to build new power plants: Information on the poisoning of groundwater can be found in a paper written by Kimberly Smith of Black Water Mesa Coalition, "Pollution of the Navajo Nation Lands," presented to the United Nations Department of Economic and Social Affairs at an International Expert Group Meeting on Indigenous Peoples and Protection of the Environment, Khabarovsk, Russian Federation, August 27–29, 2007. The full document can be accessed at the UN Department of Economic and Social Affairs Web site, www.un.org/esa/socdev/unpfii/documents/workshop_IPPE_smith.doc. Information about Peabody Energy's plans to build new coal-fired power plants can be found at Coal Moratorium Now! "State-by-State Descriptions of Proposed Coal-Fired Power Plants."

Page 84. American Electric Power: Coal Moratorium Now! "State-by-State Descriptions of Proposed Coal-Fired Power Plants."

Page 84. Florida Power and Light: Ibid.

Page 84. Southern Company: Environmental Integrity Project (EIP), "Dirty Kilowatts: America's Most Polluting Power Plants," dirtykilowatts.org, "Dirty Kilowatts" 2007 Database (July 2007), www.dirtykilowatts.org/Dirty_Kilowatts2007.pdf/, p. 10, table 2, "Top 50 Most Polluting Power Plants for CO_2 by Tons CO_2" (2006).

Page 84. TXU: Ibid.

Page 85. Some banks adopt policies that begin to limit financing for mountaintop removal: Bank Track, Rainforest Action Network, and Sierra Club, *Policy and Practice: Report Card on Banks and Mountaintop Removal*; see also *Grading the Banks: Mountaintop Removal Report Card*, ran.org/content/grading-banks-mountaintop-removal-report-card.

Page 85. Citi's largest shareholder was Abu Dhabi: Dan Wilchins and James Cordahi, "Citigroup to Sell $7.5 Billion Stake to Abu Dhabi," Reuters, November 27, 2007, www.reuters.com/

article/wtMostRead/idUSSP7190720071127. Another large shareholder: Eric Dash, "Citigroup to Sell $7.5 Billion Stake to Abu Dhabi," *New York Times,* November 27, 2007.

Page 85. Leslie Lowe quote: E-mail, November 14, 2007.

Page 85. One plant produces more carbon dioxide in three weeks than Citi will reduce in one year: From calculations by RAN campaigner Matt Leonard: Citi's operational emissions were 1,243,800 metric tons in 2005, according to Citi, "Citizenship Report, 2006," citigroup.com, Corporate Citizenship page, www.citigroup.com/citigroup/citizen/community/data/citizen06_en.pdf. On May 16, 2007, Citi announced it is "committing to reduce our carbon emissions by 10 percent from our 2005 level by 2011" ("The Environment," citigroup.com, Corporate Citizenship page, www.citigroup.com/citigroup/environment/climatechange.htm). If this goal is met, Citi would reduce its CO2 footprint by approximately 124,380 metric tons by 2011. In comparison, a single medium-sized coal-fired power plant will emit more than 3 million tons of CO2 annually.

Page 85. One large plant releases as much carbon as six hundred thousand cars and trucks: Union of Concerned Scientists (UCS), "The Costs of Coal," UCS Web site, Clean Energy page, www.ucsusa.org/clean_energy/fossil_fuels/costs_of_coal.html.

Page 86. Citi will spend an average of $3.1 billion on climate change per year: Citi, "The Environment," citigroup.com, Corporate Citizenship page (May 8, 2007), www.citigroup.com/citigroup/environment/climatechange.htm.

Page 86. Citi's corporate credit portfolio, $63 million dedicated to petroleum sectors: Citi Web site, Investor Relations, Financial Information, Annual Reports, and Proxy Information page, *Annual Report* (2006), www.citigroup.com/citigroup/fin/data/ar06c_en.pdf.

Page 86. Bank of America will spend $1.8 billion a year to help clients reduce gas emissions: Bank of America press release, "Bank of America Announces $20 Billion Environmental Initiative."

Page 86. Bank of America extended $35.6 billion in credit to oil and utilities: Bank of America Web site, Shareholders and Investors page, *Annual Report* (2006), http://phx.corporate-ir.net/phoenix.zhtml?c=71595&p=irol-reportsannual.

Page 86. Citigroup statistics: Cnnmoney.com, "Fortune 500, 2006: Our Annual Ranking of America's Largest Corporations; Citigroup," cnnmoney.com, Fortune 500 Data page, http://money.cnn.com/magazines/fortune/fortune500/snapshots/309.html.

Page 86. Bank of America statistics: Cnnmoney.com, "Fortune 500, 2006: Our Annual Ranking of America's Largest Corporations; Bank of America," Cnnmoney.com, Fortune 500 Data page, http://money.cnn.com/magazines/fortune/fortune500/snapshots/164.html.

Page 87. Time names Home Depot story as top environmental story of 1999: Published in the Canadian version of *Time,* December 20, 1999, p. 60.

Page 88. Citi's "Live Richly" campaign: In 2003 Citi launched the Live Richly campaign. From May to August 2003, Citi ran a series of ads. Copies of the ads can be viewed on Citi's Web site, Citigroup Advertising Showcase page, www.citi.com/citigroup/showcase/liverichly.htm.

Page 88. Joe Chemo campaign: Adbusters, "Joe Chemo," Adbusters Web site, Spoof Ads page, www.adbusters.org/spoofads/tobacco/jc2.

Page 88. Absolute on Ice ad: Adbusters, "Absolute on Ice," Adbusters Web site, Spoof Ads page, www.adbusters.org/spoofads/alcohol/absolutonice.

Page 88. Lowe's agrees to phase out wood products from endangered forests: Commitment made on October 13, 1999, in a letter to Rainforest Action Network.

Page 88. Kinko's adopts strongest environmental policy in the country: Kinko's adopted its Environmental Vision Statement, committing to not purchase paper or wood products from old-growth or endangered forests, and to increase the use of recycled and tree-free paper. Several years later, the policy was further strengthened: FedEx Kinko's press release, "Kinko's Forest-Based Products Policy Sets New Standard for Protecting the World's Forests," Corporate Social Responsibility Newswire, News Archive (March 11, 2003), www.csrwire.com/PressRelease.php?id=1650.

Page 89. Hogue quote: Telephone interview, October 11, 2007.

Page 89. Citi executive quote: In-person interview, 2004.

Page 89. Chan quote: Telephone interview, November 8, 2007.

Page 90. Firger quote: E-mail, November 14, 2007.

Pages 90–91. New York Times ad: RAN placed the advertisement on November 13, 2002.

Page 91. International Herald Tribune ad: RAN placed the advertisement on August 30, 2002.

Pages 91–92. Sandy Weill's speech at Cornell University in 2003: Linda Myers, "Weill Calls Economic Growth an Answer to Global Poverty and Conflict," *Cornell Chronicle,* April 10, 2003, *Chronicle* page on the Cornell Web site, www.news.cornell.edu/chronicle/03/4.10.03/Weill_cover.html.

Page 92. RAN Citibank ads: "Not with My Money" advertisements were placed on New York cable television, April 2003.

Page 92. Sixty-seven banks have adopted the principles: Web site of The Equator Principles, Official Adopters list, www.equator-principles.com/.

Page 92. Citi goes beyond the Equator Principles: Rainforest Action Network (RAN), "Citigroup New Environmental Initiatives," RAN Web site, Campaigns, Global Finance, Resources, Bank Policies page (January 2004), http://ran.org/fileadmin/materials/global_finance/Bank_Policies/CitiEnvPolicy.pdf.

Page 93. Hogue quote: Telephone interview, October 11, 2007.

Page 93. World Bank Group has provided more than $8 billion to the oil industry since 1992: Oil Change International, "Aiding Oil, Harming the Climate: A Database of Public Funds for Fossil Fuels" (December 2007), dev-zone.com, Knowledge Center page, www.endoilaid.org/wp-content/uploads/2008/01/aidingoilreport.pdf.

Page 93. U.S. Export-Import Bank and the Overseas Private Investment Corporation have given more than $21 billion: Judy Pasternak, "A Mixed Message on CO_2: Bush Seeks Overseas Curbs as U.S.-Backed Banks Help Emit More," *Los Angeles Times,* August 12, 2007.

Page 94. In the United Kingdom, it is the right-wing Conservative Party that is calling for an elimination of such "perverse subsidies": Quality of Life Policy Group, Conservative Party (U.K.), "Blueprint for a Green Economy," Conservatives.com, News page (September 13, 2007), www.conservatives.com/tile.do?def=news.story.page&obj_id=138484 (scroll down the page to download pdf file). The mention and description of "perverse subsidies" is found on p. 391.

Page 94. Cameron quote: ePolitix.com, "Conservative 'Quality of Life' Report," ePolitix.com Stakeholders comment on the Conservative Party's quality of life policy review, www. epolitix.com/EN/ForumBriefs/200709/e1a74739-521b-4ae9-86d2-ea4ceca94c2a.htm.

Page 94. World Bank approved a $3.75 billion loan to build coal-fired power plant in South Africa: Suzanne Goldenberg, "World Bank's $3.75bn coal plant loan defies environment criticism: US, Britain, the Netherlands, Italy and Norway abstain from vote in protest," *The Guardian,* April 9, 2010, www.guardian.co.uk/business/2010/apr/09/world-bank-criticised-over-power-station. For details on local opposition to the project, see Bruce Nilles and Mark Kresowik, "Stop Government Funding of Coal," Sierra Club Climate Crossroads blog, March 18, 2010, http://connect.sierraclub.org/post/ClimateCrossroads-Blog/stop_government_funding_of_coal.html.

Page 95. Joseph Stiglitz describes World Bank and IMF: "What I Learned at the World Economic Crisis," *The Insider,* April 17, 2000.

Page 95. World Bank Group: About Us section on the World Bank Group Web site, www.world-bank.org.

Page 95. World Bank Group committed $28 billion to fossil-fuel projects: Sustainable Energy and Economy Network (SEEN), "Key Facts on the G-8, World Bank, and Climate Change," SEEN Web site, Climate Change page (July 2005), www.seen.org/pages/keyfacts.shtml.

Page 96. Salim quote: E-mail, March 17, 2008.

Page 96. Kretzmann quote: Telephone interview, October 10, 2007.

Pages 96–97. Indigenous Peoples' Declaration on Extractive Industries: "Preamble to Indigenous Peoples' Declaration on Extractive Industries" (Oxford, England, April 15, 2003), Tebtebba Web page, www.tebtebba.org/tebtebba_files/susdev/mining/eir/eirdec.html.

Page 97. EIR official report: Extractive Industries Review, *Striking a Better Balance: Consultation on the Future Role of the World Bank Group in the Extractive Industries,* 6 vols. (December 2003), World Bank Web site, Extractive Industries Review page, http://web.worldbank.org/WBSITE/EXTERNAL/TOPICS/EXTOGMC/0,,contentMDK:20306686~menuPK:592071~pagePK:148956~piPK:216618~theSitePK:336930,00.html/, 1: xiii.

Page 97. Nobel Peace Prize letter: February 9, 2004, letter to World Bank president James Wolfensohn from Nobel peace laureates Jody Williams, Archbishop Desmond Tutu, Rigoberta Menchu Tum, Sir Joseph Rotblat, Betty Williams, and Mairead McGuire; reported by Bob Burton, "Nobel Laureates Ask World Bank to Curb Extractive Industries," Environmental New Service (February 13, 2004), www.ens-newswire.com/ens/feb2004/2004-02-13-01.asp.

Page 97. World Bank's response to EIR report: "Striking a Better Balance: The World Bank Group and Extractive Industries," final report of the Extractive Industries Review, World Bank Group Management Response, World Bank Web site, Resources page (September 17, 2004), http://siteresources.worldbank.org/INTOGMC/Resources/finaleirmanagementresponse.pdf/, p. iii.

Page 98. International Finance Corporation increased its loans: From statistics generated by Heike Mainhart-Gibbs, Bank Information Center. Quote from e-mail, December 13, 2007.

Page 98. Mainhart-Gibbs quote: Andrew Revkin, "Money for India's 'Ultra Mega' Coal Plants Approved," *New York Times,* Science, April 9, 2008. See also www.nytimes.com/2008/04/06/weekinreview/06revkin.html?scp=7&sq=april+6%2C+2008&st=nyt.

Page 98. Financing for Indian coal plant: Leslie Wroughton, "World Bank Approves Funds for Indian Coal-Fired Plant," Reuters, April 8, 2008, www.reuters.com/article/latestCrisis/idUSN08412737.

Page 98. Goodland quote: E-mail, November 17, 2007.

Pages 98–99. President Obama called on world leaders to phase out fossil-fuel subsidies: "Obama on G-20: No pancakes, but good groundwork," Top of the Ticket blog, *Los Angeles Times,* September 25, 2009, latimesblogs.latimes.com/washington/2009/09/obama-g-20-news-conference-text.html.

Page 99. Polar bears withdraw $27,000: This was part of a protest hosted by RAN on November 27, 2007. The activists were two folks dressed up in polar bear costumes to protest Bank of America's investments in coal-fired power plants and the effect that climate change is having on polar bear habitat. Frustrated with Bank of America's policies, these two people strolled into Bank of America, cameras in tow, to withdraw all their money as a statement to the bank. You can check out a video of this action on RAN's Web site, on the Understory (RAN's blog) page (posted November 27, 2007): http://understory.ran.org/2007/11/27/polar-bears-make-a-run-on-bank-of-america.

Page 99. Local residents at Kayford Mountain, West Virginia: You can see pictures of the banner and read about the National Day of Action against Coal: RAN, "Coal Finance Day of Action in West Virginia," RAN Web site, the Understory (RAN's blog) page (posted November 18, 2007), http://understory.ran.org/2007/11/18/coal-finance-day-of-action-in-west-virginia.

Page 99. Over a hundred demonstrations were held in November 2007: RAN press release, "Thousands Take to the Streets to Protest Citi and Bank of America Coal Investments," RAN Web site, Media Center page (November 16, 2007), http://ran.org/media_center/news_article/?uid=2443.

Page 99. Carbon Principles: Jeffrey Ball, "Wall Street Shows Skepticism over Coal," *Wall Street Journal,* February 4, 2008.

Pages 99–100. ShoreBank Pacific: Details of the EcoDeposits program can be found at the ShoreBank Pacific Web site, home page, www.eco-bank.com.

Page 100. Liu quote: Telephone interview, October 27, 2007.

Page 100. Barclay quote: In-person interview, January 7, 2007.

Page 102. Bank Track's report: See "A Challenging Climate: What International Banks Should Do to Combat Climate Change," Bank Track Web site, Documents page, www.banktrack. org/doc/File/banks,%20climate%20and%20energy/banktrack%20on%20climate%20 and%20energy/0_071212%20A%20challenging%20climate%20final.pdf.

Chapter 5: Redesigning Mobility

Page 103. New *shinkansen* trains decrease electricity use by 19 percent over earlier models: Alex Hutchinson, "World's Fastest Train You Can Ride Dumps Energy Like a Prius," *Popular Mechanics,* September 2007, www.popularmechanics.com/technology/transportation/4219935.html.

Page 103. Speed of trains exceeds 350 mph during test runs: Railway Technical Research Institute (RTRI), "Overview of Maglev R and D," RTRI Web site, Maglev page (February 20, 2004), www.rtri.or.jp/rd/maglev/html/english/maglev_frame_E.html.

Page 103. Nineteen-mile demonstration line at Pudong International Airport: Shanghai Municipal Tourism Administrative Commission, New Scenes of Shanghai page, http://lyw.sh.gov. cn/en/scenic_spot/maglev.html.

Pages 103–4. Japan has over twelve thousand miles of train tracks: Japan Railways Group, www. japanrail.com/JR_japanrailpass.html (scroll down a bit to the heading, "What Is the Japan Rail Pass?"). See the following note for the source of another statistic under this heading: that Japan's railways have twenty-six thousand runs daily.

Page 104. Eight hundred thousand daily riders: Japanese Guest Houses (JGH), "The Joy of Trains in Japan," JGH Web site, Travel Tips page, http://japaneseguesthouses.com/ about/travel/trains.htm.

Page 104. Amtrak daily ridership: Sam Abuelsamid, "Amtrak Could Set Ridership Record in 2010," AutoBlogGreen, April 9, 2010; the writer says, "2008 . . . turned out to be Amtrak's best ridership year in company history when America's passenger railroad carried 28.7 million passengers." http://green.autoblog.com/2010/04/09/amtrak-could-set-ridership-record-in-2010/.

Page 104. Shinkansen as safest form of transport in the world: Japan Railways Group, "Shinkansen (Bullet Train)": "In the almost 40 years since it opened, the Shinkansen network has carried over 6 billion passengers without a single major accident." See Japan Railways Web site, www.japanrail.com/JR_shinkansen.html. For Amtrak information, see the Amtrak Web site, National Fact Sheet page, www.amtrak.com/servlet/ ContentServer?pagename=Amtrak/am2Copy/Title_Image_Copy_Page&c=am2Copy&cid =1081442674300&ssid=542.

Page 104. China is coming up fast: Zachary Shahan, "Fastest High Speed Train Rolls off Production Line in China," *Earth & Industry*, June 3, 2010, http://earthandindustry. com/2010/06/fastest-high-speed-train-rolls-off-production-line-in-china/.

Page 104. China will have more high-speed train tracks: Keith B. Richburg, "China Is Pulling Ahead in Worldwide Race for High-Speed Rail Transportation," *Washington Post*, May 12, 2010, www.washingtonpost.com/wp-dyn/content/article/2010/05/11/AR2010051104950.html.

Page 104. Speed of boarding process: Boarding timed by author, August 4, 2006.

Page 105. More than 70 percent of the oil consumed in the United States: EIA, Independent Statistics & Analysis, "U.S. Primary Energy Consumption by Source and Sector, 2008," diagram in Annual Energy Review, www.eia.doe.gov/aer/pecss_diagram.html.

Page 106. High-speed train as catalyst for economic growth: Katsumasa Harada, "Technological Innovation and the Development of Transportation in Japan," *New Developments in Transportation (1955–1980)* (Tokyo: United Nations University Press, 1993), pp. 222–23.

Page 107. In 2003, Amtrak received two-thirds of what it received twenty years earlier: National Association of Railway Passengers (NARP), "Information on Amtrak Federal Funding," NARP Web site, www.narprail.org/cms/images/uploads/fund.pdf.

Page 107. Federal spending on highways and aviation has doubled in twenty years: Tim Gillespie, "Growth Capital: A Possible New Source," *Railway Age* (January 2004), www.bnet.com, Find Articles page, http://findarticles.com/p/articles/mi_m1215/is_1_205/ai_n6010943.

Page 107. More than $49 billion for the Federal Highway and Federal Aviation Administrations in 2007; and total budget outlays: NARP, "Information on Amtrak Federal Funding."

Page 107. Most of the stimulus money went to three major projects: Josh Voorhees of Greenwire, "High-Speed Rail Cash Lays Congressional Track for Billions More to Follow," *New York Times*, February 12, 2010, www.nytimes.com/gwire/2010/02/12/12greenwire-high-speed-rail-cash-lays-congressional-track-11511.html.

Page 107. Opponents say government shouldn't run railroads: John Sullivan, "New Jersey's Amtrak Blues," *New York Times,* June 30, 2002.

Page 108. China's investments in rail construction: Austin Ramzy, "Engines of Growth," *Time*, August 16, 2010, www.time.com/time/magazine/article/0,9171,2008791,00.html.

Page 108. Amtrak more energy efficient than domestic airlines and cars: NARP, "Oak Ridge Data on Fuel Efficiency," NARP Web site, www.narprail.org/cms/index.php/resources/more/oak_ridge_fuel. Data are contained in edition 26 of the *Transportation Energy Data Book*.

Page 109. One hundred twenty-seven million Americans lived in counties that violated Clean Air Act regulations: EPA, *Our Nation's Air—Status and Trends through 2008—Highlights*, www.epa.gov/airtrends/2010/report/highlights.pdf.

Page 109. Traffic congestion, productivity costs, and gas wasted: Texas Transportation Institute, *2009 Annual Urban Mobility Report*, http://mobility.tamu.edu/ums/; summarized in press release, http://mobility.tamu.edu/ums/media_information/press_release.stm.

Page 109. Mexico plans route from Guadalajara to Mexico City: Chris Hawley, "Mexico Reviving Travel by Train," *Arizona Republic,* January 6, 2006.

Pages 109–10. Lomax quote: TTI press release, "Annual Study Shows Traffic Congestion Worsening."

Page 110. Americans are far less likely to use public transportation: Kaid Benfield, "NatGeo Surveys Countries' Transit Use: Guess Who Comes in Last," Switchboard, Natural Resources Defense Council staff blog, National Geographic Society's 2009 Greendex report at http://switchboard.nrdc.org/blogs/kbenfield/natgeo_surveys_countries_trans.htm. See also

National Geographic Society's 2009 Greendex report, *Consumer Choice and the Environment, A Worldwide Tracking Survey,* at http://environment.nationalgeographic.com/environment/greendex/.

Page 110. Streetcar lines were removed: Paul Matus, "GM and the Streetcar—American Ground Transport—Street Railways: 'U.S. vs. National City Lines' Recalled," Third Rail Online (May 1999), http://thethirdrail.net/9905/agt1.htm.

Page 110. Commute distances for Americans increase every year: Richard J. Jackson, "Driving Ourselves Sick," *Western City Magazine,* August 2005.

Page 110. Suburban development as "greatest misallocation of resources in history": James Howard Kunstler, quoted in documentary film *The End of Suburbia: Oil Depletion and the Collapse of the American Dream* (2004). Check out the movie's Web site at www.endofsuburbia.com.

Page 110. Goal of the New Urbanist movement: Congress for the New Urbanism (CNU), "Charter of the New Urbanism," CNU Web site, www.cnu.org/charter.

Page 111. Neighborhoods with public transit also reduce transportation costs and make housing more affordable: Center for Neighborhood Technology, Housing + Transportation Affordability Index, http://htaindex.cnt.org/.

Page 111. The need for transit-friendly places to be walkable: Telephone interview with Sheila Poticha, president and CEO of Reconnecting America, June 27, 2007.

Page 111. Maryland adopts New Urbanism as core planning element: Delaware Valley Regional Planning Commission (DVRPC), "Smart Growth," DVRPC Web site, Regional Plans and Policy page, www.dvrpc.org/planning/regional/SmartGrowth.htm.

Page 111. Examples of New Urbanist design: CNU, "Chapters," CNU Web site, www.cnu.org/chapters.

Page 111. New Urbanist critics: See Alex Marshall, *How Cities Work: Suburbs, Sprawl, and the Roads Not Taken* (Austin: University of Texas Press, 2001). His critiques of New Urbanism can be found at his Web page: www.alexmarshall.org/am_categoryPagesFolder/newUrbanism.htm.

Page 111. Transit-oriented development (TOD) increases property values: Federal Transit Administration (FTA), "Transit-Oriented Development and Joint Development," FTA Web site, Planning and Environment page, www.fta.dot.gov/planning/planning_environment_6932.html.

Page 111. More than a hundred cities around the country have or are planning to install streetcar lines: Overhead Wire (blog), "The Rapid Streetcar" (July 2, 2007), http://theoverheadwire.blogspot.com/2007/07/rapid-streetcar.html.

Page 111. Poticha quote: Telephone interview with Sheila Poticha, June 27, 2007.

Page 111. Denver FasTraks ballot measure: See "FasTracks 2006 Team Factbook," Metro Denver Economic Development Corporation Web site, www.metrodenver.org/files/Documents/Transportation-Infrastructure/Mass-Transit/Trans_Mass_FasTracksFactBook.pdf/, p. 2.

Page 111. Hickenlooper quote: Global Public Media, transcript of interview at Association for the Study of Peak Oil and Gas (ASPO), Denver World Oil Conference, Denver, November 11, 2005.

Page 112. Poticha quote: Telephone interview, June 27, 2007.

Page 112. The $1 billion drained from our economy daily for oil used in transportation: Rebecca Lefton and Daniel J. Weiss, "Oil Dependence Is a Dangerous Habit," Center for American Progress (January, 2010), www.americanprogress.org/issues/2010/01/pdf/unstable_oil.pdf.

Page 113. New York City plans to have two hundred miles of bike trails by 2010: *The Villager,* "City Rolls Out Plan for 200 Miles of New Bike Lanes," www.thevillager.com (September 20–26, 2006), www.thevillager.com/villager_177/cityrollsout.html.

Page 113. Chicago is planning five hundred miles of bike trails by 2015: City of Chicago, "Bike 2015 Plan," www.bike2015plan.org/chapter1/chap1.html.

Page 113. Austin will spend $250 million: Daniel B. Wood, "Cities Build New Bike Paths: Will Cyclists Come?" *Christian Science Monitor,* June 19, 2007, www.csmonitor. com/2007/0619/p03s03-ussc.html.

Page 113. Robin Stallins, Texas Bicycle Coalition: Ibid.

Page 113. Steele quote: Telephone interview, June 18, 2007.

Page 113. Most people will walk to a bus or train if it is within a half-mile radius: Victoria Transport Policy Institute (VTPI), "Bike/Transit Integration," VTPI Web site (March 12, 2007), www.vtpi.org/tdm/tdm2.htm.

Page 114. Cost to construct a car parking space versus a bike rack: Ibid.

Page 114. Only a third of all buses in North America have bike racks: Victoria Transport Policy Institute (VTPI), "Bike/Transit Integration," VTPI Web site, *TDM Encyclopedia* (updated March 12, 2007), www.vtpi.org/tdm/tdm2.htm.

Page 114. Percentages for countries whose residents bike to work: Nancy Keates, "Building a Better Bike Lane," *Wall Street Journal,* May 4, 2007.

Page 114. Cities in Europe make bicycles available for free or at a very low cost: John Ward Anderson, "Paris Embraces Plan to Become City of Bikes," *Washington Post,* March 24, 2007.

Page 114. Paris and bikes: Ibid.

Page 114. Washington, D.C., initiated the first U.S. public bike-sharing program: Bernie Becker, "Bicycle-Sharing Program to Be First of Kind in U.S.," *New York Times*, April 27, 2008, www.nytimes.com/2008/04/27/us/27bikes.html. See also www.treehugger.com/ files/2010/05/washington-dc-bike-sharing-smartbike-getting-10x-bigger-expanding.php.

Pages 114–15. Shahum quote: Telephone interview, June 18, 2007.

Page 116. Hybrid buses: Jordan Schrader, "More Cities Get on Board with Hybrid Buses," *USA Today,* January 21, 2008.

Page 116. Hybrid and natural-gas-fueled buses made up nearly 30 percent of all transit buses: American Public Transportation Association press release, "Telling the Story of Public Transportation's Positive Environmental Impact," April 21, 2010, www.apta.com/media-center/pressreleases/2010/Pages/100421_EarthDay.aspx.

Page 116. U.S. public transportation saves 4.2 billion gallons of gasoline and reduces CO_2 emissions by 37 million metric tons each year: Ibid.

Pages 116–17. Griffith quote: Thomas Heath, "Zipcar and Flexcar Driven Together, *Washington Post,* October 31, 2007.

Page 117. Nonprofit car shares: Carsharing.net, "Where Can I Find Car Sharing?" www.carsharing.net/where.html.

Page 117. Zipcar helps people sell their cars: Zipcar.com, "Green Benefits," www.zipcar.com/carsharing-greenbenefits.

Page 117. Research by the company shows: Statistics from Zipcar, Green Benefits, www.zipcar.com/is-it/greenbenefits.

Page 117. Car-sharing statistics: Ibid.

Page 117. Zipcars are available in many cities: Zipcar.com, Find Cars page, www.zipcar.com/find-cars.

Chapter 6: Jump-Start Detroit

Page 120. Lynn Hinkle epigraph: Telephone interview, June 29, 2007. Used by permission of Lynn Hinkle.

Page 120. Woman's voice on voice mail: Call from Heather Bernikoff-Raboy to Jennifer Krill, January 2005.

Page 120. Dave Bernikoff-Raboy quote: Telephone interview, November 17, 2007.

Page 121. Heather Bernikoff-Raboy quote: Telephone interview, November 17, 2007.

Page 121. Auto industry opposes California mandate: For a detailed explanation of industry and government objections, check out the movie *Who Killed the Electric Car?* written and directed by Chris Paine (Sony Pictures, DVD released in 2006), www.whokilledtheelectriccar.com.

Page 122. Heather Bernikoff-Raboy quote: Telephone interview, November 17, 2007.

Page 122. Bernikoff-Raboys staged a round-the-clock vigil in their truck: Eric Bailey, "He Refuses to Put Down Electric-Powered Pickup: A Mariposa County Rancher Who Leases an Experimental Ford Ranger Wants to Keep It, but the Company Has Pulled the Plug on Such Vehicles, *Los Angeles Times,* January 18, 2005.

Page 122. Dave Raboy interview: Eric Bailey, "Ford Will Sell Its Electric Pickup Trucks to Lessees," *Los Angeles Times,* January 22, 2005.

Page 123. Golightly quote: Eric Bailey, "Ford Shifts Gears on Its Plan to Scrap Electric Pickup Trucks," *Los Angeles Times,* January 19, 2005.

Page 124. The Obama administration pushed things along: Peter Baker, "Obama Mandates Rules to Raise Fuel Standards," *New York Times,* May 20, 2010, www.nytimes.com/2010/05/21/business/energy-environment/21fuel.html.

Page 124. One out of every seven barrels of the world's oil is consumed on American highways: Thomas Friedman, "Let's Roll," *New York Times,* January 2, 2002.

Page 124. Seventy percent of oil consumed daily in the United States is used for transportation: EIA, Independent Statistics & Analysis, "U.S. Primary Energy Consumption by Source and Sector, 2008," diagram in Annual Energy Review, www.eia.doe.gov/aer/pecss_diagram.html.

Page 124. Big Three automakers emit more greenhouse gases than almost every country: Sierra Club Factsheet, "Driving Up the Heat: SUVs and Global Warming," Sierra Club Web site, Smart Energy Solutions page, www.sierraclub.org/globalwarming/suvreport/pollution.asp.

Page 124. Increase in number of vehicles, from 1950 to present: United Nations Environment Program (UNEP), "20 Issues to Keep You Awake at Night," UNEP Web site, GEO 2000 page, www.unep.org/GEO2000/pressrel/issues.htm.

Page 124. In 2008 there were about 668 million cars and trucks: U.S. Department of Energy (DOE), "Transportation Energy Data Book," DOE Center for Transportation Analysis Web site (July 2010), http://cta.ornl.gov/data/chapter3.shtml.

Page 124. Analysis by Union of Concerned Scientists and the Center for Auto Safety: Union of Concerned Scientists (UCS), "Drilling in Detroit: Tapping Automaker Ingenuity to Build Safe and Efficient Automobiles," UCS-USA Web site, Clean Vehicles page (June 2001), www.ucsusa.org/assets/documents/clean_vehicles/drill_detroit.pdf/, p. xiv.

Page 124. Hitting this average would save more oil each year: Sierra Club, "The Biggest Single Step," introduction, Sierra Club Web site, Global Warming and Energy page, www.sierraclub.org/globalwarming/biggest_single_step/intro.asp.

Page 125. Rebirth of electric vehicles might change the automotive industry: Rocky Mountain Institute (RMI), "What Is a Hypercar Vehicle?" RMI Web site, Transportation page, www.rmi.org/sitepages/pid191.php.

Page 125. Car companies plan to build plug-in hybrids: Information available on home page of Plug In America, www.pluginamerica.org.

Page 125. Golightly quote: Elizabeth Weise, "Think Drivers Strive to Save Their Cars from the Crusher," *USA Today,* September 2, 2004, www.usatoday.com/tech/news/2004-09-02-thinkcar_x.htm.

Page 126. Dorgan quote: Zachary Coile, "House to Vote on 'Historic' Deal to Raise Fuel Economy to 35 mpg," *San Francisco Chronicle,* December 5, 2007.

Page 126. The 2007 energy bill passed by Congress: John M. Broder and Micheline Maynard, "Lawmakers Set Deal on Raising Fuel Efficiency," *New York Times,* December 1, 2007.

Page 126. Auto companies lose money: Cnnmoney.com, "Fortune 500, 2007: Our Annual Ranking of America's Largest Corporations; General Motors," Cnnmoney.com, Fortune 500 Data page, http://money.cnn.com/magazines/fortune/fortune500/2007/snapshots/563.html. For Ford Motor Company: http://money.cnn.com/magazines/fortune/fortune500/2007/snapshots/529.html.

Page 126. GM loses about 150,000 workers: Thomas Friedman, "Et Tu, Toyota?" *New York Times,* October 3, 2007.

Pages 126–27. Hinkle quote: Telephone interview, June 29, 2007.

Page 127. Ford plant shuts down: Jeff Horwich et al., Minnesota Public Radio, "Ford Confirms Shutdown of St. Paul Plant," Minnesota Public Radio Web site, New and Features page (April 13, 2006), http://minnesota.publicradio.org/display/web/2006/04/13/fordclosure. Update on Ford plans to close plant in 2011: Leigh Phillips, "Obama Fuel Standards Lag behind EU Effort," EUobserver Web site (May 21, 2009), http://euobserver.com/885/28171.

Page 127. Increased fuel efficiency creates more jobs: Union of Concerned Scientists, "Jobs, Energy, and Fuel Economy, 2004," UCS-USA Web site, Clean Vehicles page (July 2004), www.ucsusa.org/clean_vehicles/fuel_economy/jobs-energy-fuel-economy.html.

Page 127. Lawmakers resist modernizing the vehicle industry: Thomas Friedman, "The Capital Energy Crises," *New York Times,* June 24, 2007.

Page 128. Frank quote: Telephone interview, June 22, 2007.

Page 128. Toyota is largest automaker: Jim Zarroli, National Public Radio, "Toyota Moves Past GM in First-Quarter Sales," NPR Web site, Business page (April 24, 2007), www.npr.org/templates/story/story.php?storyId=9803216.

Page 128. Toyota sold its millionth hybrid vehicle worldwide: David Welch, "Prius: Over 1 Million Sold," Bloomburg Business Week Web site (May 15, 2008), http://nybw.businessweek.com/autos/autobeat/archives/2008/05/prius_over_1_million_sold.html.

Page 128. U.S. Department of Energy study: "Tackling Climate Change in the U.S.," American Solar Energy Society (ASES) Web site (January 2007), www.ases.org/climatechange/climate_change.pdf/, p. 74.

Pages 128–29. Sexton quote: Chelsea Sexton interviewed in Google.org, "RechargeIT: Plug-In Hybrids," video, produced by Google.org, RechargeIt program (2007), available on YouTube, www.youtube.com/watch?v=oDjSbWTJbdo.

Page 129. Rick Wagoner quote: Gavin Green, "Interview: Rick Wagoner, General Motors Co.," *Motor Trend* (June 2006), www.motortrend.com/features/112_0606_rick_wagoner_general_motors/jobs_sales.html.

Page 129. Seventy-eight percent of commuters live within twenty miles of their employers: U.S. Department of Transportation, Bureau of Transportation Statistics, "Omnibus Household Survey," Department of Transportation Research and Innovative Technology Administration (October 2003), www.bts.gov/programs/omnibus_surveys/household_survey/2003/october/pdf/entire.pdf/, p. 1.

Page 129. Cost of plug-ins: John Fialka, "Coalition Turns On to Plug-In Hybrids," *Wall Street Journal,* January 25, 2006. Frank quote is from this article.

Page 129. Frank and his team modernize a Ford Explorer: Mark Clayton, "Hybrids? Some Opt to Go All-Electric," *Christian Science Monitor,* January 27, 2005.

Page 130. Woolsey quote: Telephone interview, June 28, 2007.

Page 130. Sexton quote: Google.org, "RechargeIT: Plug-In Hybrids."

Pages 130–31. Plug-In Partners coalition members: "Plug-In Partners National Campaign," Plug-In Partners Web site, Plug-In Partner List page (2010), www.pluginpartners.org/campaignOverview/partnerList.cfm.

Page 131. Wynn quote: "Plug-In Partners National Campaign," Plug-In Partners Web site, Information Packet page, http://pluginpartners.org/includes/pdfs/PluginPartnersPacket.pdf/, p. 19.

Page 131. CalCars manual: Electric Auto Association (EAA), "PriusPlus," EAA Web site, Plug-In Hybrid page, www.eaa-phev.org/wiki/PriusPlus. See chapter 8 on "greening the grid."

Page 131. Kramer quote: Telephone interview, June 22, 2007.

Page 131. Lithium ion battery conversion federal tax credit: Hybrid Center, "State and Federal Hybrid Incentives," Hybrid Center Web site, http://go.ucsusa.org/hybridcenter/incentives.cfm.

Page 131. A hybrid conversion takes two hours: Green Car Congress, "A123Systems to Market PHEV Conversion Packs in 2008," Green Car Congress Web site (May 1, 2007), www.greencarcongress.com/2007/05/a123systems_to_.html.

Page 132. Silicon Valley Leadership Group pledges to buy plug-ins: Matt Nauman, "Valley Executives Join Plug-In Hybrid Push" *San Jose Mercury News,* September 23, 2007.

Page 132. Tesla Roadster: Read about the Tesla Roadster at www.teslamotors.com.

Page 133. Tesla press statement: Tesla Motors, "Tesla Motors and Toyota Motor Corporation Formalize Agreement to Develop Electric Version of RAV4," news release (July 16, 2010), www.teslamotors.com/about/press/releases/tesla-motors-and-toyota-motor-corporation-formalize-agreement-develop-rav4.

Page 133. Straubel quote: Telephone interview, November 2, 2007.

Page 133. Musk quote: Telephone interview, November 5, 2007.

Page 133. Google.org's RechargeIT program: You can learn more about Google's RechargeIT program on its Web site, www.google.org/recharge.

Page 133. Frank quote: Telephone interview, June 22, 2007.

Page 133. Sodium-sulfur batteries: Both American Electric Power and Xcel Energy have announced purchases of sodium-sulfur batteries from NGK Insulators, of Japan, to store wind energy. For American Electric Power's purchase, see "Today in Business," *New York Times,* September 11, 2007; for Xcel Energy's, "Xcel Energy Launches Groundbreaking

Wind-to-Battery Project," Xcel Energy Web site, News Releases page (February 28, 2008), www.xcelenergy.com/XLWEB/CDA/0,3080,1-1-1_15531_46991-45134-0_0_0-0,00.html.

Page 133. Mechanical process to store electricity: Gene Berry, "Present and Future Electricity Storage for Intermittent Renewables," from workshop proceedings, "The 10-50 Solution: Technologies and Policies for a Low-Carbon Future," prepared by the Pew Center on Global Climate Change, March 2004.

Page 134. Frank quote: Telephone interview, June 22, 2007.

Page 134. Proudfoot quote: Alec Proudfoot, Google.org, "RechargeIT: Plug-In Hybrids."

Page 135. Brilliant quote: Google.org, "RechargeIT: Plug-In Hybrids."

Page 136. This tax credit could be paid for by eliminating subsidies to the oil industry: David Sandalow proposed recommendations for the federal government purchase order and tax credits for plug-in hybrid buyers in his book *Freedom from Oil: How the Next President Can End the United States' Oil Addiction* (New York: McGraw-Hill, 2007).

Page 136. "Feebate" legislation: At the time of this writing, California was considering such a move. For more information, see Margot Roosevelt, "Bill Offers Rebates, Exacts Fees Based on Car Emissions," *Los Angeles Times,* February 14, 2008.

Page 137. Some 11 million new cars and trucks sold in the U.S. annually: Matthew Keegan, "11 Million Auto Sales—The New Normal?" in EZine Articles, http://ezinearticles.com/?11-Million-Auto-Sales---The-New-Normal?&id=4790563.

Chapter 7: Growing Gas

Page 138. Joel K. Bourne, Jr., epigraph: "Green Dreams," *National Geographic,* October 2007.

Page 138. Galdikas quote: Telephone interview, October 24, 2007.

Page 138. Orangutans and their intelligence: Jonathan Leake and Roger Dobson, "Chimps Knocked Off the IQ Tree," *Sunday Times*, April 15, 2007.

Page 139. Indonesia and Malaysia produced 87 percent of the world's palm oil: U.S. Department of Agriculture (USDA), Foreign Agriculture Service, Commodity Intelligence Report, "Indonesia: Palm Oil Production Prospects Continue to Grow," USDA Web site, Global Crop Production Analysis page (December 31, 2007), www.pecad.fas.usda.gov/highlights/2007/12/Indonesia_palmoil.

Page 139. Borneo fires, 1997–98: M. J. Wooster and N. Strub, "Study of the 1997 Borneo Fires: Quantitative Analysis Using Global Area Coverage (GAC) Satellite Data," *Global Biogeochemical Cycles* 16, no. 1 (2002), American Geophysical Union (AGU) Web site, Publications page (February 12, 2002), www.agu.org/pubs/crossref/2002/2000GB001357.shtml. You will access an abstract of the article here; the full article is available to subscribers.

Page 139. Smits quote: Ian MacKinnon, "Palm Oil: The Biofuel of the Future Driving an Ecological Disaster Now," *The Guardian*, April 4, 2007.

Page 140. UNEP and Orangutans: United Nations Environment Programme, World Conservation Monitoring Centre (UNEP-WCMC), "The Last Stand of the Orangutan," UNEP-WCMC Web site, Information Resources page (February 2007), www.unep-wcmc. org/resources/publications/LastStand.htm.

Page 140. Biodiesel produces up to ten times the greenhouse gases: Wetlands International press release, "Biofuel Less Sustainable Than Realized," (August 12, 2006), www.wetlands. org/news.aspx?ID=804eddfb-4492-4749-85a9-5db67c2f1bb8.

Page 141. If all corn were devoted to ethanol, it would only replace 12 percent of gasoline: Jason Hill et al., "Environmental, Economic, and Energetic Costs and Benefits of Biodiesel and Ethanol Biofuels," Proceedings of the National Academy of Sciences (PNAS) Web site archives (June 2, 2006), www.pnas.org/cgi/reprint/0604600103v1/, p. 1.

Page 141. Global biodiesel and ethanol production: Crystal Davis, "March 2007 Monthly Update, Global Biofuel Trends," World Resources Institute (WRI), EarthTrends Environmental Information, Updates page (April 6, 2007), http://earthtrends.wri.org/updates/node/180.

Page 141. Ethanol production in the United States totaled 10.6 billion gallons in 2009: Renewable Fuels Association, Statistics, "Historic U.S. Fuel Ethanol Production," www. ethanolrfa.org/pages/statistics.

Page 143. Producing ethanol consumed 29 percent of U.S. corn crop in 2009, yet ethanol displaced less than 10 percent of the gasoline used: For corn production used to make ethanol, see www.nass.usda.gov/Statistics_by_Subject/result.php?553A7E5F-2FA4-3CCA-B77F-D8BF10FB1F0&sector=CROPS&group=FIELD%20CROPS&comm=CORN; for 10 percent of gas replaced by ethanol, see Renewable Fuels Association, Statistics, "Weekly U.S. Fuel Ethanol/Livestock Feed Production," www.ethanolrfa.org/pages/ statistics#weekly.

Page 143. Production of ethanol and biodiesel has tripled: William Coyle, "The Future of Biofuels: A Global Perspective," U.S. Department of Agriculture, Economic Research Service Web site, *Amber Waves* 5, no. 5 (November 2007): 1, www.ers.usda.gov/AmberWaves/ November07/PDF/Biofuels.pdf.

Page 143. Total production of ethanol and biodiesel reached 23.4 billion gallons in 2009: For ethanol, see Cindy Zimmerman, "Record Global Ethanol Production Forecast," Domestic Fuel Web site (March 29, 2010), http://domesticfuel.com/2010/03/29/record-global-ethanol-production-forecast/. According to Zimmerman, "Total ethanol production for 2009 was 73.9 billion litres (19.5 billion gallons) according to data assembled by F.O. Licht." For biodiesel, see Earth Policy Institute, *World Annual Biodiesel Production, 1991–2009* (world total for 2009 was 3,926 million gallons), www.earth-policy.org/datacenter/xls/ book_pb4_ch4-5_34.xls or www.earth-policy.org/index.php?/data_center/C23/.

Page 143. EU commits to use biofuels for transportation: Despite wide criticism, the EU confirmed its goal in early 2008. David Cronin, "Climate Change: EU Persists with Biofuels," Inter Press Service News Agency Web site (Brussels, January 23, 2008), http:// ww.ipsnews.net/news.asp?idnews=40890. For one percent statistic, see James Kanter, "Europe May Ban Imports of Some Biofuel Crops," *New York Times,* January 15, 2008.

Page 143. Iowa State University study: Simla Tokgoz et al., "Emerging Biofuels: Outlook of Effects on U.S. Grain, Oilseed, and Livestock Markets," Center for Agricultural and Rural Development (CARD), Iowa State University, CARD Web site, Publications page (July 2007), www.card.iastate.edu/publications/synopsis.aspx?id=1050.

Page 143. Advisories about rising food prices: Food and Agriculture Organization (FAO) press release, "FAO Forecasts Continued High Cereal Prices," FAO Web site (November 7, 2007), www.fao.org/newsroom/en/news/2007/1000697/index.html.

Page 143. Nearly 2.5 billion people live off less than $2 a day: World Bank, *World Development Report 2008: Agriculture for Development*, World Bank Web site, Data and Research page (October 2007), http://go.worldbank.org/ZJIAOSUFU0.

Page 143. Brown quote: Lester R. Brown, "Massive Diversion of U.S. Grain to Fuel Cars Is Raising World Food Prices," Earth Policy Institute Web site, Eco-Economy Updates page (March 21, 2007), www.earth-policy.org/Updates/2007/Update65.htm.

Page 144. More than 450 pounds of corn are needed to fill an SUV: C. Ford Runge and Benjamin Senauer, "How Biofuels Could Starve the Poor," *Foreign Affairs* (May–June 2007), Foreign Affairs Web site, www.foreignaffairs.org/20070501faessay86305/c-ford-runge-benjamin-senauer/how-biofuels-could-starve-the-poor.html.

Page 144. UN warns of food shortages: Javier Blas and Jenny Wiggins, "UN Warns It Cannot Feed the World," *Financial Times,* July 15, 2007.

Page 144. Jean Ziegler quote: Grant Ferrett, "Biofuels 'Crime Against Humanity,'" BBC News (October 27, 2007), http://news.bbc.co.uk/2/hi/americas/7065061.stm. Remarks were made at a press conference at the UN headquarters in New York.

Page 144. Eighteen thousand children die everyday: Associated Press, "18,000 Children Die Every Day of Hunger, U.N. Says," *USA Today,* February 17, 2007.

Page 144. ADM and Watergate: Tom Philpott, "Give Green, Go Yellow: How Cash and Corporate Pressure Pushed Ethanol to the Fore," *Grist: Environmental News and Commentary* (December 6, 2006), www.grist.org/news/maindish/2006/12/06/ADM.

Page 144. ADM leads United States in ethanol production: Antonio Regalado, "Sugar Rush: Ethanol Giants Struggle to Crack Brazil Market," *Wall Street Journal,* September 10, 2007.

Page 144. ADM receives billions of dollars in ethanol subsidies: Sasha Lilley, "Green Fuel's Dirty Secret," CorpWatch Web site, Energy page (June 1, 2006), www.corpwatch.org/article.php?id=13646.

Page 144. Cato Institute quote: James Bovard, "Archer Daniels Midland: A Case Study in Corporate Welfare,"*Cato Policy Analysis*, no. 241 (September 26, 1995), Cato Institute Web site, Publications page, www.cato.org/pubs/pas/pa-241.html.

Page 145. Toptiro quote: Institute for Agriculture and Trade Policy (IATP), "Biofuels and Development." Account from speech given by Mr. Toptiro to IATP staff, Minneapolis, November 2007.

Page 145. ADM's position regarding the antislavery pact: Based on meetings in which the author was involved and his personal knowledge of events.

Page 145. Cargill contributes to deforestation: Greenpeace, "How the Palm Oil Industry Is Cooking the Climate," Greenpeace Web site, Press Centre page (November 2007), www. greenpeace.org/international/press/reports/cooking-the-climate-full.

Page 145. ADM invests in Wilmar: A joint publication of Milieudefensie (Friends of the Earth Netherlands), Lembaga Gemawan, and KONTAK Rakyat Borneo: "Policy, Practice, Pride and Prejudice: Review of Legal, Environmental and Social Practices of Oil Palm Plantation Companies of the Wilmar Group in Sambas District, West Kalimantan Indonesia," Reda-pes.org, Orangutan Outreach blog archive (July 2007), http://redapes.org/news-updates/policy-practice-pride-and-prejudice-review-of-legal-environmental-and-social-prac-tices-of-oil-palm-plantation-companies-of-the-wilmar-group-in-sambas-district-west-kalimantan-indonesia.

Page 146. More displaced citizens in Colombia than in any other country except Sudan: Chris-tian Aid, "Human Tide: The Real Migration Process," Global Policy Forum Web site, Social and Economic Policy page (May 2007), www.globalpolicy.org/socecon/envronmt/climate/2007/0514humantide.pdf.

Page 146. Many palm plantations have been established illegally: Ibid., p. 28.

Page 146. Milvia Dias quote: Ibid., p. 31.

Page 146. "If you don't negotiate with us": Tony Allen-Mills, "Biofuel Gangs Kill for Profit," *Lon-don Sunday Times,* June 3, 2007.

Page 147. Up to 5 million indigenous people will be displaced: Justin Bergman, "Biofuels Dis-place Indigenous People," Associated Press, May 15, 2007, Mongabay.com, http://news.mongabay.com/2007/0516-indigenous.html.

Page 147. Indigenous people being pushed from their land: Biofuelwatch, Transnational Insti-tute et al., "Agrofuels: Towards a Reality in Nine Key Areas," Carbon Trade Watch Web site, Publications page (June 2007), www.carbontradewatch.org/pubs/Agrofuels.pdf.

Page 147. Villager in West Kalimantan loses farm: James Painter, "Losing Land to Palm Oil in Kalimantan," BBC News (August 3, 2007), http://news.bbc.co.uk/2/hi/asia-pacific/6927890.stm.

Page 147. Dead zone in Gulf of Mexico: Associated Press, "'Dead zone' in Gulf of Mexico among Top 3 Ever Mapped," Cnn.com (July 29, 2007), www.cnn.com/2007/TECH/science/07/29/dead.zone.ap/index.html.

Page 147. The Gulf's dead zone is expected to grow as large as eighty-five hundred square miles: Carolyn Lockhead, "Dead Zone in Gulf Linked to Ethanol Production," *San Francisco Chronicle,* July 6, 2010, www.sfgate.com/cgi-bin/article.cgi?f=/c/a/2010/07/05/MNF91E84SL.DTL.

Page 148. Report warned of a "considerable" increase in damage to the gulf if ethanol production rises: Ibid.

Page 148. Nitrates in drinking water cause health effects: EPA, "Consumer Fact Sheet on Nitrates/Nitrites," EPA Web site, Ground Water and Drinking Water page (November 28, 2006), www.epa.gov/OGWDW/contaminants/dw_contamfs/nitrates.html.

Page 148. Researchers believe that ethanol has a positive energy balance: Food and Water Watch and the Network for New Energy Choices, in collaboration with the Institute for Energy and the Environment at Vermont Law School, "The Rush to Ethanol: Not All Biofuels Are Created Equal," analysis and recommendations for U.S. biofuels projects, Network for New Energy Choices Web site, Uploads page (2007), www.newenergychoices.org/uploads/RushToEthanol-rep.pdf.

Pages 148–49. About 20 percent of greenhouse gas emissions come from land use changes: Intergovernmental Panel on Climate Change, "Summary for Policymakers: Land Use, Land Use Change, and Forestry," U.S. Environmental Protection Agency Web site, Yosemite page, http://yosemite.epa.gov/OAR/globalwarming.nsf/UniqueKeyLookup/SHSU5BVRTK/$File/sum_lulucf.pdf/, pp. 11–15.

Page 149. Science examined the life-cycle impacts of many agrofuel sources: Timothy Searchinger et al., "Use of U.S. Croplands for Biofuels Increases Greenhouse Gas Emissions from Land Use Change," *Science,* February 29, 2008, p. 1238; Joseph Fargione et al., "Land Clearing and the Biofuel Carbon Debt," *Science,* February 29, 2008, p. 1235.

Page 149. Wetlands International study: Wetlands International press release, "Bio-fuel Less Sustainable Than Realised," December 8, 2006.

Page 150. Wright quotes: Telephone interview, August 23, 2007.

Page 150. Biofuel provides less than 5 percent of all production: U.S. gasoline consumption totals 140 billion annually. Biofuel production is currently at less than 6 billion gallons. Comparatively, only approximately 100 million gallons of restaurant waste oil are generated each year. Steve Hargreaves, "Can Vegetable-Oil Cars Save the World?" Cnnmoney.com (July 24, 2006), http://money.cnn.com/2006/07/21/news/economy/vegetable_cars/index.htm.

Page 150. Pacific Biodiesel: For a list of places to buy Pacific Biodiesel, visit the Pacific Biodiesel Web site, www.biodiesel.com/index.php/fuel_sales/where_to_buy_biodiesel.

Page 151. Sustainable Biodiesel Alliance requirements: Read more about the Sustainable Biodiesel Alliance's requirements at its Web site, Mission page, www.sustainablebiodiesel-lalliance.com/principles.html.

Page 152. In 2007, federal subsidies for ethanol and other biofuels were more than eighteen times larger: EIA, "Federal Financial Interventions and Subsidies in Energy Markets 2007," table ES6, www.eia.doe.gov/oiaf/servicerpt/subsidy2/pdf/execsum.pdf. In 2007 ethanol/biofuels got $3,349,000,000 in federal subsidies compared to $184 million for solar.

Page 152. In 2009 ethanol subsidies were worth roughly $5 billion: Jeff Coombe, "Should Ethanol Subsidies Be Renewed?" Alt Energy Stocks Web site (June 16, 2010), www.altenergystocks.com/archives/2010/06/should_ethanol_subsidies_be_renewed.html.

Page 152. Quante quote: Telephone interview, July 6, 2007.

Page 153. Kholsa quote: Amanda Griscom Little, "Something Ventured, Something Gained," *Grist: Environmental News and Commentary* (December 8, 2006), www.grist.org/news/maindish/2006/12/08/little.

Chapter 8: Greening the Grid

Page 156. Tim Pawlenty epigraph: In a speech on May 25, 2007, when he signed the Next Generation Energy Act of 2007.

Pages 156–57. Harvey Wasserman calls industries King CONG: Harvey Wasserman, "Totally Boom/Doom Solartopian Green by 2030," Free Press, Columns page (June 26, 2007), http://freepress.org/columns.php?strFunc=display&strID=1557&strYear=2007&strAuthor=7.

Page 157. Coal generates about 47 percent of the electricity in the United States: EIA, *Electric Power Monthly,* August 2010 edition, Executive Summary, EIA Web site, www.eia.doe.gov/cneaf/electricity/epm/epm_sum.html.

Page 158. Analysts estimate that 20 percent of existing coal plants could be retired by 2015: Timothy Gardner, "Health Rules Could Cut Greenhouse Emissions," *New York Times,* July 25, 2010, www.nytimes.com/2010/07/26/business/global/26green.html.

Page 158. Wide range of research groups show how the U.S. economy can be carbon-free and nuclear-free: Several reports have been released in just the last year detailing the gains to be found in energy efficiency and renewables. They include McKinsey and Company, "Reducing Greenhouse Gas Emissions: How Much and at What Cost?" McKinsey and Company Website, Special Initiative: Climate Change page (December 2007), www.mckinsey.com/clientservice/ccsi/pdf/US_ghg_final_report.pdf/; Arjun Makhijani, "Carbon-Free and Nuclear-Free: A Roadmap for U.S. Energy Policy," Institute for Energy and Environmental Research (IEER), Joint Project of the Nuclear Policy Research Institute and the Institute for Energy and Environmental Research (July 2007), www.ieer.org/carbonfree/CarbonFreeNuclearFree.pdf/, p. 9; American Solar Energy Society (ASES), "Tackling Climate Change in the U.S.: Potential Carbon Emissions Reductions from Energy Efficiency and Renewable Energy," ASES Web site (January 2007), www.ases.org/climatechange/climate_change.pdf/, p. 5; Ken Zweibel, James Mason, and Vasilis Fthenakis, "A Solar Grand Plan," *Scientific American,* January 2008, p. 73.

Page 158. Through the first half of 2010, 4.6 percent of the United States' electricity was generated by renewables: EIA, *Electric Power Monthly,* August 2010 edition, Executive Summary, EIA Web site, www.eia.doe.gov/cneaf/electricity/epm/epm_sum.html.

Pages 158–59. Union of Concerned Scientists estimates on increasing renewable energy: Union of Concerned Scientists (UCS), "Cashing In on Clean Energy: A National Renewable Electricity Standard Will Benefit the Economy and the Environment," UCS-USA Web site, Clean Energy Policies page (2007), www.ucsusa.org/clean_energy/clean_energy_policies/cashing-in.html..

Page 159. Apollo Alliance 2004 report: Jointly produced by the Institute for America's Future and the Center on Wisconsin Strategy, "The Apollo Jobs Report: For Good Jobs and Energy Independence New Energy for America," Apollo Alliance Web site, Jobs page (January 2004), www.apolloalliance.org/jobs.php.

Page 159. A typical coal plant costs $1 billion to build: National Energy Technology Laboratory (NETL), "Tracking New Coal-Fired Power Plants," NETL Web site, Coal and Power Systems page (May 1, 2007), www.netl.doe.gov/coal/refshelf/ncp.pdf.

Page 159. University of California report: Daniel M. Kammen, Kamal Kapadia, and Matthias Fripp, "Report of the Renewable and Appropriate Energy Laboratory—Putting Renewables to Work: How Many Jobs Can the Clean Energy Industry Generate?" University of California, Berkeley (April 13, 2004; corrected January 31, 2006), United Nations Environment Programme Web site, Civil Society page, http://unep.org/civil_society/GCSF9/pdfs/karmen-energy-jobs.pdf. The paper analyzes thirteen independent reports and studies regarding the economic and employment impacts of renewable energy.

Page 159. Quote from report by the American Wind Energy Association et al.: BlueGreen Alliance, United Steelworkers, and American Wind Energy Association press release, "New Report Provides Blueprint for Building Domestic Wind Energy Supply Chain" (June 28, 2010), www.bluegreenalliance.org/press_room/press_releases?id=0094.

Page 160. The eventual Democratic candidate and forty-fourth president later said: Barack Obama, "Remarks by the President to the Nation on the BP Oil Spill" (June 15, 2010), White House Web site, www.whitehouse.gov/the-press-office/remarks-president-nation-bp-oil-spill.

Page 160. Jones quote: Telephone interview, December 8, 2007.

Page 160. McGeoy quotes: Telephone interview, December 8, 2007.

Page 161. The average American home uses 920 kilowatt-hours monthly, and breakdown: EIA, "Frequently Asked Questions—Electricity," EIA Web site, http://tonto.eia.doe.gov/ask/electricity_faqs.asp#home_consumption.

Page 161. Oil produces less than 2 percent of the nation's electricity: EIA, "Electric Power Overview," EIA Web site, Electricity page (October 22, 2007), www.eia.doe.gov/cneaf/electricity/epa/epa_sum.html.

Page 161. Coal remains the largest source of electricity, and other statistics on electricity sources: EIA, *Electric Power Monthly*, August 2010 edition, Executive Summary, EIA Web site, www.eia.doe.gov/cneaf/electricity/epm/epm_sum.html. "Year-to-date [as of mid-2010], coal-fired plants contributed 46.9 percent of the power generated in the United States. Natural gas-fired plants contributed 20.9 percent, and nuclear plants contributed 20.3 percent. Of the 0.9 percent contributed by petroleum-fired plants, petroleum liquids represented 0.5 percent, with the remainder from petroleum coke. Conventional hydroelectric sources provided 6.4 percent of the total, while other renewables (biomass, geothermal, solar, and wind) and other miscellaneous energy sources generated the remaining 4.6 percent of electric power."

Page 162. Renewable energy enjoyed a surge in 2009: American Wind Energy Association press release, "U.S. Wind Energy Industry Breaks All Records, Installs Nearly 10,000 MW in 2009" (January 26, 2010), www.awea.org/newsroom/releases/01-26-10_AWEA_Q4_and_Year-End_Report_Release.html.

Page 162. A typical coal-fired power plant is often described in terms of the maximum number of megawatts, etc.: American Wind Energy Association (AWEA), "Wind Power Today," AWEA Web site, Publications page, www.awea.org/pubs/factsheets/WindPowerToday_2007.pdf/; Clifford Krauss, "Move Over Oil, There's Money in Texas Wind," *New York Times,* February 23, 2008.

Page 162. The total generating capacity of U.S. coal plants is about 313,000 megawatts: EIA, "Summary Statistics for the United States, 2008," EIA Web site, www.eia.doe.gov/cneaf/electricity/epa/epates.html.

Page 162. There are just under six hundred power plants in this country using coal as a predominant fuel source: EIA, "Count of Electric Power Industry Power Plants, by Sector, by Predominant Energy Sources within Plant" (2008), EIA Web site, www.eia.doe.gov/cneaf/electricity/epa/epat5p1.html.

Page 163. Gyr quotes: In-person interview, June 2002, confirmed February 10, 2008.

Page 164. By 2010, solar PV installations worldwide reached 7,300 megawatts: James Russell (vitalsigns.worldwatch.org), "Record Growth in Photovoltaic Capacity and Momentum Builds for Concentrating Solar Power"(June 24, 2010), Global Energy Network Institute Web site, www.geni.org/globalenergy/library/technical-articles/generation/solar/vitalsigns-worldwatch.org/record-growth-in-photovoltaic-capacity/index.shtml.

Page 164. The solar industry has grown at a 35 percent annual rate globally since 1998: Greenpeace, "Solar Generation IV, 2007: Solar Electricity for over One Million People and Two Million Jobs by 2020," ed. Crispin Aubrey, Greenpeace Web site, International Reports page (September 3, 2007), www.greenpeace.org/raw/content/international/press/reports/solar-generation-iv.pdf/, p. 22.

Page 164. The solar industry growth rate akin to PC industry in heyday: Joel Makower, Ron Pernick, and Clint Wilder Clean, "Energy Trends, 2007," Clean Edge Web site, Reports page (March 2007), www.cleanedge.com/reports/Trends2007.pdf.

Page 164. Kennedy quote: In-person interview, August 7, 2007.

Page 164. Google builds largest solar array in the United States: Google, "Google Solar Panel Project," Google Web site, Corporate Information page (July 18, 2007), www.google.com/corporate/solarpanels/home.

Page 164. Wal-Mart sets goal to use 100 percent renewable power: Lee Scott (current president and chief executive officer of Wal-Mart Stores, Inc.), "Twenty-First Century Leadership," Wal-Mart Watch Web site (October 24, 2005), walmartwatch.com/img/documents/21st_Century_Leadership.pdf.

Page 164. Other firms have installed solar arrays on their stores across the country: Information on Staples and its environmental initiatives can be found on its About Staples page, www.staples.com/sbd/content/about/soul/energyclimate.html. For information on Whole Foods, its Company page, www.wholefoodsmarket.com/company/sustainablefuture.html; and on Walgreens, its Flex Your Power Web site, www.fypower.org/pdf/Walgreens_PV.pdf.

Page 164. Bradford quote: David Roberts, "The Revolution Will Be Solarized: An Interview with Travis Bradford, Author of *Solar Revolution*," *Grist: Environmental News and Commentary,* Grist Web site, Main Dish page (November 30, 2006), www.grist.org/news/maindish/2006/11/30/roberts/index.html; Makower, Pernick, and Wilder Clean, "Energy Trends, 2007."

Page 165. We had just over 400 megawatts of solar PV installed in 2009: Graham Jesmer, "US Solar Sees 38% Growth in PV Capacity in 2009," Renewable Energy World Web site (April

16, 2010), www.renewableenergyworld.com/rea/news/article/2010/04/us-solar-sees-38-growth-in-pv-capacity-in-2009.

Page 165. The solar industry grew over sevenfold globally in the five years from 2004 to 2009: Ron Pernick and Clint Wilder with Dexter Gauntlett and Trevor Winnie, *Clean Energy Trends 2010* (April 2010 update), www.cleanedge.com/reports/pdf/Trends2010.pdf, p.3.

Page 165. Results of California's SB1 legislation of 2007: California Public Utilities Commission (CPUC) staff progress report, "California Solar Initiative," CPUC Web site (January 2008), www.cpuc.ca.gov/puc/Energy/solar.

Page 165. Renewable portfolio standards enacted in twenty-nine states: EIA, "What Are Renewable Portfolio Standards (RPS) and How Do They Affect Generation of Electricity from Renewable Sources?" Energy in Brief, EIA Web site, http://tonto.eia.doe.gov/energy_in_brief/renewable_portfolio_standards.cfm.

Page 166. Every day, more solar energy falls on the planet in forty minutes: Ken Zweibel, James Mason, and Vasilis Fthenakis, "A Grand Solar Plan," *Scientific American,* January 2008, p. 64.

Page 166. Science magazine 1999 report: John A. Turner, "A Realizable Renewable Energy Future," *Science Magazine,* July 30, 1999.

Page 166. SEGS statistics: John Carey, with Adam Aston, "Solar's Day in the Sun," *Business Week,* October 15, 2007, www.businessweek.com/magazine/content/07_42/b4054053.htm.

Page 167. Solel Energy Systems signed contract in July 2007: Felicity Barringer and Matthew L. Wald, "California Utility Agrees to Buy Power Generated by Solar Array," *New York Times,* July 25, 2007.

Page 167. Ausra has agreement with PG&E: PG&E press release, "PG&E and Ausra Announce 177 Megawatt Solar Thermal Power Agreement," PG&E Web site, News and Alerts page (November 5, 2007), www.pge.com/about/news/mediarelations/newsreleases/q4_2007/071105.shtml.

Page 167. Darbee quote: John Carey with Adam Aston, "Solar's Day in the Sun," *Business Week,* October 15, 2007.

Page 167. Stirling Energy has signed contracts: Barringer and Wald, "California Utility Agrees to Buy Power Generated by Solar Array."

Page 167. The largest PV solar array in North America: Seamus O'Connor, "Solar Panels at Nellis Could Be Win-Win," Air Force Times Web site, Air Force News page (November 19, 2007), www.airforcetimes.com/news/2007/11/airforce_nellis_solar_071119w.

Page 167. Public Service of New Mexico seeks bid for solar array: Jesse Broehl, "New Mexico Solar Market Expected to Boom," Renewable Energy Access Web site, Magazine page (March 13, 2006), www.renewableenergyworld.com/rea/news/story?id=44328.

Page 167. PG&E announces that it will double amount of solar-power purchase: PG&E press release, "PG&E Commits to Double Its Solar Thermal Power Purchases During Clinton Global Initiative," PG&E Web site, News and Alerts page (September 27, 2007), www.pge.com/about/news/mediarelations/newsreleases/q3_2007/070927.shtml.

Page 167. Three new concentrating solar projects came online in 2009; three more likely by end of 2010: Power-Gen Worldwide, "Concentrating solar power projects showed growth in 2009, April 15, 2010, www.powergenworldwide.com/index/display/articledisplay/ 1802812473/articles/powergenworldwide/renewables/solar/2010/04/CSP-2009.html.

Page 168. Installed wind power exceeded 35,000 megawatts in 2009, and wind accounted for 39 percent of all new installed power plants: "U.S. Wind Energy Industry Breaks All Records, Installs Nearly 10,000 MW in 2009," press release (January 26, 2010), www.awea.org/ newsroom/releases/01-26-10_AWEA_Q4_and_Year-End_Report_Release.html.

Page 169. Wind farms compete with coal prices: Makower, Pernick, and Wilder Clean, "Energy Trends, 2006."

Page 169. Sixteen-mile-an-hour wind energy per hour can create 50 percent more wind energy: American Wind Energy Association, "The Economics of Wind Energy," AWEA Web site, Publications page (February 2005), www.awea.org/pubs/factsheets/EconomicsOfWind-Feb2005.pdf.

Page 169. A modern wind turbine can generate fifty-five times more energy: Ibid.

Page 169. A 51-megawatt wind project delivers electricity 40 percent more cheaply: Ibid.

Page 169. The amount of wind energy that is available in states: Makhijani, *Carbon-Free and Nuclear-Free,* p. 31.

Page 170. An average of two to five birds is killed per wind turbine per year: American Wind Energy Association, "Wind Energy and Wildlife: Frequently Asked Questions," AWEA Web site, Publications page, www.awea.org/pubs/factsheets/050629_Wind_Wildlife_ FAQ.pdf.

Page 170. Davies quote: Elinor Burkett, "A Mighty Wind," *New York Times Magazine,* June 15, 2003.

Page 170. The advantages of wind technology: American Wind Energy Association, "Wind Energy: The Fuel of the Future Is Ready Today," AWEA Web site, Publications page (2007), www.awea.org/pubs/factsheets/wetoday.pdf.

Page 171. Fortune Small Business says: Justin Martin, "Dan Juhl, Founder, Danmar and Associates, Woodstock, Minn.: As Investors Like Warren Buffett Recognize Wind Power's Potential, This Consultant Is Helping Farmers Cash In," Cnnmoney.com, Fortune Small Business page (June 1, 2003), http://money.cnn.com/magazines/fsb/ fsb_archive/2003/06/01/346435/index.htm.

Page 171. Juhl quote: Telephone interview, December 6, 2007.

Page 171. U.S. General Accounting Office study showed that local ownership of wind generates 2.3 times more jobs and 3.1 times economic impact: U.S. Government Accountability Office (USGAO), "Renewable Energy: Wind Power's Contribution to Electric Power Generation and Impact on Farms and Rural Communities," USGAO Web site (September 2004), www.gao.gov/new.items/d04756.pdf/, p. 84.

Page 171. Department of Energy study for Arizona, Colorado, and Michigan: S. Tegen, "Comparing Statewide Economic Impacts of New Generation from Wind, Coal, and Natural Gas in Arizona, Colorado, and Michigan," National Renewable Energy Laboratory Web site (May 2006), www.nrel.gov/docs/fy06osti/37720.pdf/, p. 2.

Page 172. Juhl quote: Telephone interview, December 6, 2007.

Page 172. Solar power in the dark: Marianne Lavelle, "Big Solar Project Planned for Arizona Desert," *U.S. News and World Report,* February 21, 2008.

Page 173. Germany is world's top consumer of solar energy: Rachel Oliver, "All About: Solar Energy," Cnn.com (November 13, 2007), www.cnn.com/2007/WORLD/asiapcf/10/01/solar.energy/index.html#cnnSTCText.

Page 173. Enrollment in Oregon's feed-in tariff program filled up: Lee van der Voo, "Solar Feed-in Tariff Rush Shakes Out for Oregon Businesses," Sustainable Business Oregon Web site (July 13, 2010), www.sustainablebusinessoregon.com/articles/2010/07/solar_feed-in_tariff_rush_shakes_out_for_oregon_businesses.html.

Page 173. California's $0.50 charge: For a description of California's Public Goods Charge and other energy efficiency programs, see "CPUC's Role in Energy Efficiency Programs," California Public Utilities Commission Web site, Energy Efficiency Program page, www.cpuc.ca.gov/PUC/energy/eep/cpucrole.htm.

Page 173. In Berkeley, California, a policy was approved enabling homeowners to install rooftop solar: Todd Woody, "Berkeley to Finance Solar Arrays for Homeowners," Green Wombat blog on Cnnmoney.com (October 31, 2007), http://blogs.business2.com/greenwombat/2007/10/berkeley-to-fin.html.

Page 174. Campus Climate Challenge: "The Campus Climate Challenge is a project of more than thirty leading youth organizations throughout the U.S. and Canada. The Challenge leverages the power of young people to organize on college campuses and high schools across Canada and the U.S. to win 100% Clean Energy policies at their schools. The Challenge is growing a generation-wide movement to stop global warming, by reducing the pollution from our high schools and colleges down to zero, and leading our society to a clean energy future." To find out more about the Campus Climate Challenge, visit http://climatechallenge.org/about.

Page 174. Sierra Club Cool Cities: Read more about Sierra's Club Cool Cities program on its Web site, http://coolcities.us/about.php. You can also find more information about specific cities' action plans at seattle.gov: www.seattle.gov/climate/govResources.htm.

Page 175. Lack of public awareness as obstacle: Zweibel, Mason, and Fthenakis, "A Grand Solar Plan," p. 64.

Page 175. Investment of $10 billion per year from 2011 to 2050: Ibid., p. 73.

Page 176. California Energy Commission evaluated the cost of generating new capacity: Study by Energy and Environmental Economics, "CPUC CGH Modeling," www.ethree.com/cpuc_ghg_model.html. At this site, select "GHG Calculator v2b"; download this spreadsheet and select the "Gen Cost" tab at the bottom. Look for "All-in Levelized Busbar Cost California." To convert to kilowatt-hour prices, move the decimal point one space to the left.

Page 176. Coal prices rising: Shai Oster and Anne Davis, "China Spurs Coal-Price Surge," *Wall Street Journal,* February 12, 2008, http://online.wsj.com/article/SB120275985736359763. html?mod=hpp_us_pageone. See also the EIA, "Average Weekly Coal Commodity Spot Prices," www.eia.doe.gov/cneaf/coal/page/coalnews/coalmar.html. Cost to build new power plants increase: Bernie Woodall, "US Power Plant Costs Up 130 Pct since 2000," Reuters, February 14, 2008, www.reuters.com/article/idUSN1339129420080214.

Page 176. Cost of building U.S. coal-fired power plants has increased 130 percent: Ibid.

Page 176. Vinod Khosla quote: Vinod Khosla, "Solar Flare, Sustainable or Not?" slide no. 35 (Solar Power 2006, San Jose, CA, October 16 2006). Khosla's presentation can be accessed at www.khoslaventures.com/resources.html.

Chapter 9: Less Is More

Page 178. Amory Lovins epigraph: David Stipp, "Can This Man Solve America's Energy Crisis? Amory Lovins Thinks Business and Nature Can Work in Concert to Cut U.S. Reliance on OPEC," *Fortune,* May 12, 2002.

Page 178. Corbett quote: Bill Browning and Kim Hamilton, "Village Homes: A Model Solar Community Proves Its Worth," *In Context* (Spring 1993), Context Institute Web site, www.context.org/ICLIB/IC35/Browning.htm.

Page 179. Lovins quote: Amory Lovins, "More Profit with Less Carbon," *Scientific American,* September 2005.

Page 179. McKinsey and Company estimates: McKinsey and Company, "Reducing Greenhouse Gas Emissions: How Much and at What Cost?" McKinsey and Company Web site, Special Initiative, Climate Change page (December 2007), www.mckinsey.com/clientservice/ ccsi/pdf/US_ghg_final_report.pdf/, p. xv.

Page 180. Energy efficiency on a date: Patty Limerick and Howard Geller, "What Every Westerner Should Know about Energy Efficiency and Conservation," Center of the American West Web site, Publications page (2007), www.centerwest.org/publications/pdf/ energycons.pdf.

Pages 180–81. Efficient systems are cheaper: For cost saving for efficiency, see McKinsey and Company, "Reducing Greenhouse Gas Emissions," p. xii. For reference regarding energy efficiency, see the University of California, Berkeley, report by Daniel M. Kammen, Kamal Kapadia and Matthias Fripp, "Report of the Renewable and Appropriate Energy Laboratory: Putting Renewables to Work: How Many Jobs Can the Clean Energy Industry Generate?" (April 13, 2004; corrected January 31, 2006), p. 19, http://rael.berkeley.edu/ old-site/renewables.jobs.2006.pdf.

Page 182. Rosenfeld autobiography: Arthur H. Rosenfeld, "The Art of Energy Efficiency: Protecting the Environment with Better Technology" (1999), California Energy Commission Web site, Commission Info Page, www.energy.ca.gov/commission/commissioners/rosen-feld_docs/2000-10_ROSENFELD_AUTOBIO.PDF/, p. 37.

Page 182. Oil statistics from 1977 to 1985: Mark Clayton, "To Boost US Security, an Energy Diet," *Christian Science Monitor,* September 23, 2004. Persian Gulf statistic from Amory Lovins and L. Hunter Lovins, "Fools Gold in Alaska," *Foreign Affairs,* July–August 2001.

Pages 182–83. California produces savings: California Public Utilities Commission (CPUC) and California Energy Commission (CEC), "Lowering Energy Costs, Protecting Economic Growth, and Protecting the Environment," California Public Utilities Commission Web site, Energy Efficiency Program page (August 2006), ftp://ftp.cpuc.ca.gov/Egy_Efficiency/CalCleanEng-English-Aug2006.pdf/, p. 2.

Page 183. Good news for everyone involved: Ibid., pp. 2, 3.

Page 183. California New Energy Action Plan: Ibid., p. 5.

Page 183. California invests in efficiency projects: CPUC press release, "PUC Launches Ground-breaking Energy Efficiency Effort," CPUC Web site, Press Release page (September 22, 2005), http://docs.cpuc.ca.gov/Published/News_release/49757.htm.

Page 183. Kennedy quote: Ibid.

Page 184. Efficiency program will produce net ratepayer savings: Ibid.

Page 184. California's per capita electricity consumption remains constant: California Energy Commission, "The Loading Order: How Are We Doing?" Independent Energy Producers Annual Meeting, CEC Web site, Publications page (October 10, 2006), www.energy.ca.gov/2006publications/CEC-999-2006-020/CEC-999-2006-020.PDF.

Page 185. Arnold quote: In-person interview, June 27, 2007.

Page 185. Cost of saving energy is half what it costs to produce it: CPUC and CEC, "Lowering Energy Costs, Protecting Economic Growth, and Protecting the Environment," p. 4.

Page 185. Efficiency Vermont: Learn more about Efficiency Vermont on its Web site, the About Us page, www.efficiencyvermont.com/pages/Common/AboutUs.

Page 186. California, Vermont, and Connecticut tied for first: American Council for an Energy-Efficient Economy (ACEEE), summary of "The State Energy Efficient Scorecard," American Council for an Energy-Efficient Economy, Publications page (June 2007), www.lcv.org/scorecard.

Page 186. Statistics on Bayer, DuPont, and Johnson and Johnson. All these statistics can be found on the Climate Group's Web site, http://theclimategroup.org. To read about the specific case studies mentioned in this text once on the Web site, go to the Low Carbon Solutions page, and then click on Case Studies.

Page 186. "Negawatt revolution": Amory Lovins, "The Negawatt Revolution," *Across the Board: The Conference Board Magazine* 27, no. 9 (September 1990), Rocky Mountain Institute Web site, www.rmi.org/images/PDFs/Energy/E90-20_NegawattRevolution.pdf.

Page 186. Investments in energy efficiency will pay off: McKinsey and Company, "Reducing U.S. Greenhouse Gas Emissions: How Much at What Cost?" U.S. Greenhouse Gas Abatement Mapping Initiative Executive Report, McKinsey and Company Web site, Special Initiative: Climate Change page (December 2007), www.mckinsey.com/clientservice/ccsi/pdf/US_ghg_final_report.pdf/, p. xvi.

Pages 187–88. Cavanagh quote: Telephone interview, August 21, 2007.

Page 188. Rogers quote: American Public Media, "Getting More Power Out of Using Less," *Marketplace* (October 23, 2007). Listen to the full story at http://marketplace.publicradio.org/display/web/2007/10/23/power_conservation.

Page 188. Eight states had enacted decoupling legislation for gas: Natural Resources Defense Council (NRDC), "Gas and Electric Decoupling in the U.S." (August 2009), http://www.raponline.org/docs/NRDC_Decoupling%20Maps%20US_2009_08.pdf.

Page 188. Average lightbulb is only 3 percent efficient: Lovins, "More Profit with Less Carbon."

Page 189. Australia bans incandescent lightbulbs: BBC News, "Australia Pulls Plug on Old Bulbs" (February 20, 2007), http://news.bbc.co.uk/2/hi/asia-pacific/6378161.stm.

Page 189. Turnbull quote: Ibid.

Page 189. Nevada bill saves money and power: Southwest Energy Efficient Project (SWEEP), "2007 Nevada Legislative Activities," SWEEP Web site (January 28, 2008), www.swenergy.org/legislative/2007/nevada/index.html.

Page 189. U.S. lightbulb legislation: Paul Davidson, "It's Lights Out for Traditional Light Bulbs," *USA Today,* December 17, 2007.

Pages 189–90. Steele quote: Telephone interview, November 23, 2007.

Page 190. Ann Arbor, Michigan, converts to LED technology: Tom Gantert, "City to Be First in LED Lights," *Ann Arbor News,* October 17, 2007.

Page 190. Wal-Mart announces it will install LED lighting: Business Wire, "Wal-Mart Uses GE LED Refrigerated Display Lighting to Save Green" (November 16, 2006), www.businesswire.com/portal/site/ge/?ndmViewId=news_view&newsId=20061116005286&newsLang=en.

Page 190. Steele quote: Telephone interview, November 23, 2007.

Page 190. Harman's bill: Congresswoman Jane Harman, 36th Congressional District, "Harman Introduces Bill to Phase Out Low-Efficiency Light Bulbs," Jane Harman's Web site, News Archive page (March 15, 2007), www.house.gov/harman/press/archive.shtml.

Page 190. Vampire appliances: Julie Carr Smyth, "Another Kind of 'Vampire' Invades Home This Halloween: Energy Sucking 'Standby Mode,'" Associated Press (October 31, 2007), www.investmentmoats.com/investment-ideas/vampire-electronics-drain-homes-of-energy. Twenty-four coal plants: Lovins, "More Profit, Less Carbon."

Page 191. As of 2009, 76 percent of all coal-fired electricity was consumed by residential, commercial, and industrial buildings: Architecture2030, "Problem: The Building Sector, Architecture 2030 Will Change the Way You Look at Buildings," http://architecture2030.org/the_problem/buildings_problem_why.

Page 191. Mazria quote: Tim Folger, "Blueprint for Disaster?" *OnEarth Magazine* (Summer 2005), National Resources Defense Council (NRDC) Web site, OnEarth page, www.nrdc.org/OnEarth/05sum/livgreen.asp.

Page 192. Architecture 2030: Read more about Architecture 2030 at www.architecture2030.org.

Page 192. Mayors sign Architecture 2030 pledge: American Institute of Architects (AIA), "Mayors Adopt AIA Position on Sustainability," *The Angle* 4, no. 15 (June 15, 2006), AIA Web site, Sustainability Articles from *The Angle* page, www.aia.org/nwsltr_angle. cfm?pagename=angle_nwsltr_20060615&archive=1&#Mayors.

Page 192. Churchill quote: The International Centre for Facilities Web site says that "Churchill used this statement twice, first in 1924 at the English Architectural Association, then in 1943 upon the occasion of requesting that the bombed-out Parliament be rebuilt exactly as before. The first time he said it a little differently: 'There is no doubt whatever about the influence of architecture and structure upon human character and action. We make our buildings and afterwards they make us. They regulate the course of our lives.'" International Centre for Facilities Web site, Quotes page, www.icf-cebe.com/quotes/quotes.html.

Page 192. The Home Star Act of 2010: Efficiency First, "Home Star Coalition Fact Sheet" (2010), http://homestarcoalition.org/documents/HOME_STAR_Fact_Sheet.pdf.

Chapter 10: Power Shift

Page 198. Philip Morris report: Arthur D. Little International, "Public Finance Balance of Smoking in the Czech Republic," p. 2 of executive summary. An excerpt: "Public finance saved between 943 mil. CZK and 1,193 mil. CZK (realistic estimate: 1,193 mil. CZK) from reduced health-care costs, savings on pensions and housing costs for the elderly—all related to the early mortality of smokers." Campaign for Tobacco-Free Kids Web site, Reports page (November 28, 2000), http://tobaccofreekids.org/reports/philipmorris/pmczechstudy.pdf.

Page 198. BP rebrands itself: Susan Bryce, "Global Manipulators Move beyond Petroleum," *New Dawn Magazine,* no. 63 (November–December 2000), www.newdawnmagazine.com/articles/Beyond_Petroleum.html.

Page 198: BP ads: Visit Ogilvy Public Relations Web site to learn about the launching of BP's advertising campaign in 2001: "Case Studies: BP; Launching 'Beyond Petroleum' Worldwide," Ogilvy Web site, Case Studies page, www.ogilvypr.com/case-studies/bp.cfm.

Page 198. BP invests more in oil than renewables: Steven Mufson and Juliet Eilperin, "For BP, a Pair of Repairs," *Washington Post,* August 9, 2006.

Page 198. Chevron urges visitors to "join the discussion": Read the full manifesto at Chevron's willyoujoinus.com Web site, www.willyoujoinus.com/register.

Page 199. Chevron ads: See the Media Gallery page, www.willyoujoinus.com.

Page 199. Walbridge quote: E-mail, March 2, 2008.

Page 200. Global Climate Science Communications Team: Global Climate Science Communications Team, "Action Plan" (April 3, 1998), p. 3. Document can be found at the Environmental Defense Fund Web site, www.environmentaldefense.org/documents/3860_GlobalClimateSciencePlanMemo.pdf.

Page 200. Victory would be achieved: Ibid., p. 3.

Page 201. Media continue to express doubt about climate change: Maxwell Boykoff and Jules M. Boykoff, "Balance as Bias: Global Warming and the U.S. Prestige Press," *Global Environmental Change* 14, no. 2 (September 2004), North Arizona University Web site, College of Engineering and Natural Sciences, Environmental Sciences and Education page, www.envsci.nau.edu/sisk/courses/env555/Readings/BoykoffBias.pdf.

Page 201. Mother Jones article: Chris Mooney, "Some Like It Hot," *Mother Jones,* May–June 2005.

Page 201. Exxon donates to think tanks who say climate change is false: "Put a Tiger in Your Think Tank," *Mother Jones* special report, May–June 2005.

Page 201. Exxon donates to American Enterprise Institute: Ibid.

Page 201. Friends of Science: Excerpt from Friends of Science Web page, the About Us page, www.friendsofscience.org/index.php?id=1.

Page 201. Friends of Science gets its funding from oil companies: Charles Montgomery, "Meet Mr. Cool: Nurturing Doubt about Climate Change Is Big Business," *Globe and Mail* (Toronto), August 12, 2006.

Pages 201–2. Frank Luntz quote: From the Luntz Research Companies, "Straight Talk" (July 2002), photocopy of memo at the Environmental Working Group (EWG) Web site, www.ewg.org/files/LuntzResearch_environment.pdf. More information from EWG is available at www.ewg.org/node/8684.

Page 204. Eighty percent of population in cities will be able to reject the automobile: David Whitehouse, "Half of Humanity Set to Go Urban," BBC News (May 19, 2005), http://news.bbc.co.uk/1/hi/sci/tech/4561183.stm.

Pages 205–6. Foust quote: Clifford Krauss, "Move Over Oil, There's Money in Texas Wind," *New York Times,* February 23, 2008.

Page 206. Chavez quote: "What the Future Holds for Farm Workers and Hispanics," address given to the Commonwealth Club, San Francisco, November 9, 1984, Mindfully.org Web site, www.mindfully.org/Reform/Cesar-Chavez9nov84.htm.

Page 206. Gibbs's book: Lois Marie Gibbs, *Love Canal: My Story* (Albany: State University of New York Press, 1982).

Page 207. America spends $4 billion a week on the war in Iraq: David Leonhardt, "What $1.2 Trillion Can Buy," *New York Times,* January 17, 2007.

Page 207. 1. The president requested an additional $20 million for the Afghanistan war for fiscal year 2011: Karen DeYoung, "Afghan War Spending Faces New Scrutiny," *Washington Post,* July 30, 2010, www.washingtonpost.com/wp-dyn/content/article/2010/07/29/AR2010072905729.html.

Page 208. Hawken quote: The official Web site for *The 11th Hour* (Warner Independent Pictures, 2007) is http://wip.warnerbros.com/11thhour.

Afterword: Beyond the Gulf Oil Disaster

Page 209. Largest U.S. oil spill in history: Justin Gillis, "Estimates of Oil Flow Jump Higher," *New York Times,* June 15, 2010, www.nytimes.com/2010/06/16/us/16spill.html?_r=1&partner=rss&emc=rss.

Page 210. Brown pelican status: U.S. Department of the Interior press release, "Brown Pelican Populations Recovered, Removed from Endangered Species List," November 11, 2009, www.doi.gov/archive/news/09_News_Releases/111109.html.

Page 210. Number of rigs in the Gulf: NOAA Ocean Explorer website (updated June 8, 2010), http://oceanexplorer.noaa.gov/explorations/06mexico/background/oil/media/platform_600.html.

Page 210. Sally Bingham quote: Bruce Nolan, "BP's Gulf Oil Spill Is a Sin, Visiting Clergy Say After Touring the Coast," *Times-Picayune,* July 7, 2010.

Page 211. Quantity of dispersants in the Gulf: Kate Sheppard, "Is the EPA Playing Dumb on Dispersants?" *Mother Jones,* July 20, 2010, http://motherjones.com/environment/2010/07/epa-whistleblower-bp-dispersants.

Page 211. Obama expands offshore oil activities: Department of the Interior press release, "Secretary Salazar Announces Comprehensive Strategy for Offshore Oil and Gas Development and Exploration" (March 31, 2010), www.doi.gov/news/pressreleases/2010_03_31_release.cfm.

Page 211. Obama change of heart: Department of the Interior press release, "Salazar Calls for New Safety Measures for Offshore Oil and Gas Operations; Orders Six Month Moratorium on Deepwater Drilling" (May 27, 2010), www.doi.gov/news/pressreleases/Salazar-Calls-for-New-Safety-Measures-for-Offshore-Oil-and-Gas-Operations-Orders-Six-Month-Moratorium-on-Deepwater-Drilling.cfm.

Page 211. EPA improves fuel-efficiency standards again: Peter Baker, "Obama Mandates Rules to Raise Fuel Standards," *New York Times,* May 20, 2010, www.nytimes.com/2010/05/21/business/energy-environment/21fuel.html.

Page 212. Obama oil spill address: White House press release, "Remarks by the President to the Nation on the BP Oil Spill" (June 15, 2010), www.whitehouse.gov/the-press-office/remarks-president-nation-bp-oil-spill.

Page 213. Lindsey Graham quote: WVOC, June 24, 2010, www.youtube.com/watch?v=eEPH7k_R_4c.

Page 213. Oil industry lobbying expenditures in 2009: Center for Responsive Politics, OpenSecrets.org, "Oil & Gas Summary," www.opensecrets.org/industries/indus.php?ind=E01.

Page 213. Markey quote: Bradley Blackburn and Andrew Miller, "BP Oil: Government Ups Flow Estimate as Congress Targets Flawed Spill Response Plans," *ABC World News,* June 15, 2010, http://abcnews.go.com/WN/oil-executives-face-congressional-criticism-disaster-response-plans/story?id=10919846.

Page 213. Blowout in Timor Sea: "Montara Oil Spill," Wikipedia, http://wikipedia.org/wiki/Montara_oil_spill.

Page 213. China spill: Lily Kuo, "China Says Ocean Cleared of Oil 10 Days After Spill," *Los Angeles Times*, July 26, 2010, www.latimes.com/news/nationworld/world/la-fg-china-oil-spill-20100727,0,3917306.story.

Page 213. Toll taken by oil development in Gulf: MSNBC, "Potential for Big Spill after Oil Rig Sinks" (April 22, 2010), www.msnbc.msn.com/id/36683314/ns/us_news-life/.

Page 214. "BP to Donate Net Revenue from MC252 Well Leak to Protect and Rehabilitate Wildlife in Gulf States," BP website (June 8, 2010), www.bp.com/genericarticle.do?categoryId=2012968&contentId=7062799.

Page 214. On oil residue at Prince William Sound: Riki Ott, "Lessons from the Exxon Valdez Spill," Environmental Forum, Reuters (May 1, 2010), http://blogs.reuters.com/environment/2010/05/02/lessons-from-the-exxon-valdez-spill/.

Page 217. *Nation* quotation on coal campaign: Christine MacDonald, "The Spill's Silver Lining," *The Nation*, July 15, 2010, www.thenation.com/article/37526/spills-silver-lining.

Page 218. Jon Powers quote: "Tens of Thousands Join Hands Across the Sand," Scrapbook, Sierra Club, June 28, 2010, http://sierraclub.typepad.com/scrapbook/.

Page 219. Oil consumption statistics: U.S. Energy Information Administration, "Oil: Crude and Petroleum Products Explained," 2008 data for petroleum, www.eia.doe.gov/energyexplained/index.cfm?page=oil_home#tab2.

Page 219. BP profits: "First Quarter 2010 Results," BP website, (April 27, 2010), www.bp.com/extendedgenericarticle.do?categoryId=2012968&contentId=7061409.

Page 219. Sima J. Gandhi quote: David Kocieniewski, "As Oil Industry Fights a Tax, It Reaps Subsidies," *New York Times*, July 3, 2010, www.nytimes.com/2010/07/04/business/04bptax.html.

Index

change, 74, 82, 84–87, 93–99, 196–97;
greening of corporate practices, 20, 83–84,
85–86; public-pressure campaigns against,
86–93, 99; taking action against fossil-fuel
financing, 101–2; Wall Street Reform and
Consumer Protection Act, 78
Barclays, 92
battery technology, 124, 131–32, 133–35, 203
Bayer, 186
Bechtel, 93
Bernikoff-Raboy family, 120–23, 130
Beyond Coal campaign, 21, 46, 59, 85, 158, 217
Beyond Oil campaign, 21, 217, 218
bicycling, 110–11, 112–15, 117, 119
Big Branch mine collapse, 18, 69
biodiesel: buses fueled by, 115, 116; crops
used to produce, 140, 141, 142, 150; global
production, 143; from recycled cooking
oil, 150; Sustainable Biodiesel Alliance,
151, 154
biofuels: agrofuels, defined, 141; vs. food
production, 22, 138, 140–41, 142–44, 149;
need for global standards, 151–52; net
energy balance, 148–49; from palm oil,
138–40, 141, 145–47, 149, 155; prioritization
of, with other solutions, 152–54; types of,
explained, 140, 141–42. See also biodiesel;
ethanol
Birol, Fatih, 31–32
bitumen, 36
black lung disease, 50
Blagojevich, Rod, 58, 59
Blankenship, Don, 73
BMW, 123
Bolivia, 141, 144
Bouler, Olivia, 216–17
Bowen Power Plant, 61
Boxer, Barbara, 69
BP (formerly British Petroleum):
accountability of, 214, 220; greenwashing
of corporate brand, 43, 198; Tony Hayward
(ex-CEO), 34; negligence of, 198, 214;
political donations and lobbying expenses,
67, 72, 80; profits, 19, 211, 214, 219. See also
Gulf oil spill
Brazil, 141, 144–45, 146, 149
Brockovich, Erin, 40

Brown, Jerry, 168, 182
building efficiency standards, 191–92, 205
Bunge, 144–45
Burma, 42
buses, 113–14, 115–16, 119
Bush, George H. W., 34
Bush, George W.: campaign contributions, 68,
69, 75–76; climate-change policies, 16–17,
60, 71; and coal plants, 58; and energy bill
of 2007, 189; lifting of offshore drilling
moratorium, 35

California: energy crisis, 68; energy
purchasing collectives, 204; energy-
efficiency programs, 181–84, 185, 186,
188; greenhouse gas restrictions, 16–17,
121–22, 137; high-speed rail, 107; legislators
receiving oil money, 79–80; Los Angeles
energy plans, 62; renewable energy
mandate, 165; Santa Barbara oil spill, 34,
213; solar energy, 160–61, 164, 166–67, 173;
Unocal lawsuit, 40; wind energy, 168
Cameron, David, 94
Campbell, Colin, 30
Canada: bicycling initiatives, 114; carbon
sequestration project, 53; climate skeptics
in, 201; incandescent bulb ban, 189; tar
sands oil production, 26, 35–39, 44, 201,
208
cancer: and fertilizer runoff, 148; and fossil
fuels, 35–36, 38, 39–40, 56, 195
Cape Wind project, 170, 211
car shares, 116–18
carbon dioxide emissions: carbon offsets, 83;
and "clean coal," 49, 50, 52–55; dirtiest U.S.
coal plants, 61–62; from homes, 192; from
palm-oil production, 149; pounds per gas
tank, 42; reductions of, from CFLs, 15, 189;
reductions of, from wind energy, 170. See
also greenhouse gas emissions
Carbon Principles, 99
carbon sequestration, 49, 52–55, 60
Cargill, 144–45
cash-for-clunkers program, 135
Cerrado, 144–45
Chan, Michelle, 88
Chao, Elaine, 69

Cheney, Dick, 58, 68, 201
Chevron: bank financing of, 85; denial of
climate change, 200; greenwashing of
corporate brand, 43, 198–99; political
donations and lobbying expenses, 67, 80
China: bicycling rates, 114; coal prices, 176;
fuel-efficiency standards, 66, 126; oil
consumption, 29, 32; oil spill, 213; plug-in
hybrid production, 130; railways, 103, 104,
108, 109; renewable energy, 171, 206
Chrysler, 22, 126
Chukchi Sea drill project, 34
Citi (Citigroup): and Carbon Principles,
99; and Equator Principles, 92–93; as
financing climate change, 82, 84–87;
greening of corporate practices, 20, 83–84,
85–86; public-pressure campaigns against,
86–93, 99
Citizens Against Ruining the Environment, 58
Clean Air Act, 23, 39, 57, 67, 109, 117
Clean Energy Jobs and Oil Company
Accountability Act of 2010, 192
Clean Water Act, 23, 54, 67
Clear the Air coalition, 57
climate change: bank financing of, 74, 82,
84–87, 93–99, 196–97; and "clean coal,"
49, 50–51; denial of, 69, 70, 197, 200–202;
holding oil industry accountable for,
77; media coverage of, 14, 70–71, 200;
scientific consensus on, 70; socioeconomic
consequences of, 65; and weather, 14–15,
17, 21, 50, 59–60, 158; wedge theory, 182
climate data controversy, 14, 201
Clinton, Bill, 34–35
coal: "clean coal" myth, 48–55, 62; historic
role of, 18; U.S. consumption, 58; U.S.
production, 50
coal-fired power plants: and asthma, 18,
56–58; cost comparisons to wind power,
169, 171, 176; generating capacity of, 162,
165, 168; greenhouse gas emissions from,
16, 18, 50–51, 58, 60–62, 84, 85, 195; IGCC
("clean coal") plants, 52–55; as leading
source of U.S. electricity, 16, 24, 50, 157,
161; moratorium on new construction,
60, 63, 157, 217; number of, in U.S., 50, 58;
outdated technology of, 60–62, 157–58;

and plug-in hybrids, 128; solid waste from,
51, 54, 195
coal industry: American attitudes toward,
14, 15; bank financing of, 84–85, 94, 98, 99;
denial of climate change, 69, 197; flouting
of health and safety standards, 51, 54, 67,
69, 70; opposition to renewable energy,
156–57; political donations and lobbying
expenses, 66, 69, 75; profits, 73; promotion
and expansion efforts, 50–51, 58–60, 62,
84; subsidies to, 49, 51, 72–74, 98–99;
taking action against, 63–64
coal mining: deaths, 18, 47, 69, 75; health and
safety concerns, 18, 50, 51, 54–55, 67, 69;
waste-impoundment spills, 74–76. See also
mountaintop-removal mining
Coal River Mountain Watch, 64
Colombia, 42, 141, 146
Colorado, 111, 114, 171
Communities for a Better Environment, 44
community-based energy development,
171–72, 202, 205
commuting, 109, 110, 113, 131
Competitive Enterprise Institute, 71
Congress: and donations from fossil-fuel
industry, 66, 67, 68–69, 76–78, 78–80;
and Gulf oil spill, 220; increases in
fuel standards, 66, 123, 126; and Kyoto
Protocol, 200–201; and offshore drilling
moratorium, 34, 68; and oil-industry
subsidies, 17, 67, 72–74, 80; transportation
spending, 107, 112, 116. See also politics and
politicians and specific legislation
Connecticut, 16, 185–86, 188
ConocoPhillips, 27, 44
conservation vs. energy efficiency, 179
consumer protection act (2010), 78
Cool Cities program, 174
Cooney, Phil, 70–71
Copenhagen climate talks, 94
coral reef destruction, 17
Corbett, Michael, 178
corn, for ethanol: and Archer Daniels
Midland, 144; vs. cellulosic ethanol, 153;
and fertilizer runoff, 140, 147–48; net
energy balance, 148–49; U.S. production,
141, 142–43, 145

Fisk Generating Station, 57, 62
flexible-fuel vehicles, 142, 154
Florida, 107, 111, 214
Florida Power and Light, 84
Ford Motor Company, 16, 66, 120–23, 125–27, 128
Four Corners Power Plant, 61
Fox News, 200
France, 108, 109, 114
Frank, Andrew, 127–30, 133–34
Friedman, Lisa, 162
Friedman, Thomas, 14, 127
Friends of the Earth, 73, 89, 91
Frontiers of Freedom, 200
fuel efficiency: in airline industry, 43, 108, 208; automakers' resistance to improving, 16, 23, 66, 123–27; federal increases in standards, 66, 123, 124, 211; and jobs, 127; for plug-in hybrids, 124–25, 129, 137; standards outside U.S., 66, 126

G-20 Summit (2009, Pittsburgh), 98–99
Galdikas, Birute, 138–40, 155
gas taxes, 136
gasoline, amount saved by public transportation, 116; use in hybrid vehicle engines, 128–29; replaced by biofuels, 140–41. *See also* oil and gas; oil and gas industry
General Electric, 15–16, 52
General Motors: bankruptcy and bailout, 22, 126, 129; electric vehicles, 121, 123, 125; vs. Toyota, 128; truck factory closures, 15
Georgia, 59, 61
geothermal energy, 172
Gerard, Jack, 72
Germany, 108, 109, 141, 173
Ghana, 141
Gibbs, Lois, 206–8
Gibson, Larry, 45
glacier melt, 21, 59, 60
Global Community Monitor, 40, 44
global warming. *See* climate change
Goldman Environmental Prize, 48
Goldman Sachs, 20, 93
Gollin, James, 88
Goodland, Robert, 98

Google, 132, 133–35, 164
Gore, Al, 26
Gotschall, Ben, 39
government, federal: agribusiness subsidies, 144, 152, 154; and auto industry, 126, 129, 135–36, 207; aviation spending, 107; defense spending, 207; fossil-fuel subsidies, 17, 49, 51, 67, 72–74, 76–78, 80, 98–99, 175, 197, 214; fossil-fuel tax credits, 72, 73–74, 173, 219; and Gulf oil spill, 19, 214, 215, 220; and high-efficiency vehicles, 131–32, 135–36, 152, 203; increases in fuel standards, 66, 123, 124, 211; and solar energy, 152, 175. *See also* Congress *and specific presidents*
government, state. *See specific states*
Graham, Lindsey, 212–13
Great Bear Rainforest, 38, 87, 199–200
greenhouse gas emissions: automakers' resistance to reducing, 16–17, 22, 43, 121–22; and biofuels, 140, 142, 148–49; from buildings, 191–92, 205; and Campus Climate Challenge, 174; carbon offsets, 83; by Chevron, 43; and "clean coal," 49, 50, 52–55; from coal plants, 16, 18, 50–51, 58, 60–62, 84, 85, 195; corporate reductions of, 84, 186; Obama's auto-emission standards, 17, 124; oil industry's resistance to reducing, 70, 71; reductions of, from energy efficiency, 183, 184; reductions of, from plug-in hybrids, 128; statistics on U.S. increase, 65; from tar sands oil production, 36. *See also* carbon dioxide emissions
Greenpeace, 78, 145, 217
greenwashing, 43, 197–99
Gulf of Mexico, 29, 35, 147–48, 211, 213
Gulf oil spill: and BP's greenwashing, 43, 198; and BP's negligence, 198, 214; and dead zone, 147–48; devastation of, 19, 209–10, 214–15; as impetus for change, 215–18; inadequate response to, 19, 210–11, 218; and lax government oversight, 19, 214, 215, 220; and offshore drilling moratorium, 34, 211–12, 218; oil industry's response to, 213, 218. *See also* BP (formerly British Petroleum)
Gunnoe, Maria, 45

Physicians for Social Responsibility, 59
Plug In America, 130
plug-in hybrid vehicles: conversions
    to, 131–32, 133, 137; development of,
    127–30; fuel efficiency of, 124–25, 129, 137;
    government support of, 131–32, 135–36,
    152, 203; "tribrids," 154; vehicle-to-grid
    power, 133–35, 203
Plug-In Partners, 130–31
politics and politicians: and agribusiness,
    144; and auto industry, 66; and coal lobby,
    51, 62; cronyism and corruption, 67–70,
    75–76; denial of climate change, 201–2;
    failure to enact meaningful legislation, 17,
    65–67, 196, 199, 215; failure to enforce laws,
    29, 67, 69, 76; oil lobbyists in government
    positions, 70–72, 75; rejection of new coal
    plants, 60, 157; taking action to clean up,
    81. *See also* Congress; government, federal
Pombo, Richard, 79–80
Poticha, Shelley, 111, 112
poverty and the poor: and air pollution, 40–41,
    56–57; and food security, 22, 143–44, 149;
    and green-collar jobs, 160–61; in oil-rich
    nations, 41–42; and World Bank, 95
Prairie State coal plant, 59
Pro-Regenwald, 27
Public Citizen, 78

Quinn, Pat, 59

Racimos de Ungurahui, 91
railways: Amtrak, 104, 106, 107–9, 119;
    Japanese *shinkansen*, 103–5, 106–7, 108;
    streetcars and light rail, 110, 111, 113–14
Rainforest Action Network: and Archer
    Daniels Midland, 145; Citi campaigns,
    85, 86–93; and electric vehicles, 120, 122;
    Randy Hayes (founder), 27, 91–92; Home
    Depot campaign, 20, 87, 90; "oil-free
    Congress" campaign, 78
rainforests: Amazon, 17, 27–29, 31, 42,
    145; biodiversity of, 17, 27, 139; carbon
    absorption of, 149; Great Bear, 38, 87,
    199–200; palm oil production in, 138–40
Raymond, Lee, 73
Reagan, Ronald, 163

Reconnecting America, 111
Rell, Jodi, 16
renewable energy: American attitudes
    toward, 15; arguments against, 156–57,
    172; benefits of, summarized, 206–8;
    jobs created by, 22, 158–61, 171, 192, 196,
    205–6; net metering of, 174–75; storage of,
    134, 172; taking action to support, 176–77;
    transitioning to, 152, 157–58, 172–76,
    202–6, 218–20. *See also* solar energy; wind
    energy
Rhode Island, 204
Rodgers, Michael, 31
Rolfes, Anne, 41
Rosenfeld, Art, 178, 181–82
Royal Dutch Shell, 34, 37, 77, 80
Rubin, Robert, 91
Ruckus Society, 78, 91
rural economies, 171–72, 205–6

Salim, Emil, 96
San Diego Gas and Electric, 167, 183
Santa Barbara oil spill, 34, 213
Sarayaku (Ecuador), 27, 29, 31, 42
Saro-Wiwa, Ken, 77
Saudi Arabia, 19, 30–31, 32, 85
Schwarzenegger, Arnold, 16
sea levels, rising, 17, 158
Senegal, 141
Service Employees International Union, 91
Sexton, Chelsea, 128–29, 130
Shell Oil (Royal Dutch Shell), 34, 37, 77, 80
Sherburne County Generating Plant, 62
ShoreBank Pacific, 99–100, 101
Sierra Club: Beyond Coal campaign, 21, 46,
    59, 85, 158, 217; Beyond Oil campaign, 21,
    217, 218; Cool Cities program, 174; "oil-free
    Congress" campaign, 78; organizational
    reach of, 20–21, 217
Silicon Valley Leadership Group, 132
Simmons, Matthew, 30
Socolow, Robert, 182
solar energy: commercial use of, 133, 164;
    cost comparisons to coal, 176; federal
    investments in, 152, 175; and Four Corners
    Power Plant, 61; generating capacity, long-
    term, 175; generating capacity, typical, 162;

global production, 164; industrial facilities, 166–68, 172; jobs created by, 159–61, 206; residential financing, 100, 173, 176, 220; residential use of, 162–65; storage of, 134, 172. *See also* renewable energy
Solar Energy Generating Systems, 166–67
Solel Energy Systems, 167
South Africa, 94
Southern California Edison, 167, 183
Southern Company, 61, 84, 200
Spadaro, Jack, 74–76
Staples, 164
Steele, Kristen, 113
Stiglitz, Joseph, 95
stimulus bill (2009), 107, 108, 131–32, 135
Stirling Energy Systems, 167
streetcars and light rail, 110, 111, 113–14
suburban sprawl, 110
Sudan, 42
sugarcane, for ethanol, 140, 141, 148, 149
sulfur dioxide, from fossil fuels, 39, 56, 57, 61, 170
Sungevity, 164, 220
Sunoco, 73
Surfrider Foundation, 217
Syncrude, 36

tar sands oil production, 26, 35–39, 44, 201, 208
tax credits: for ethanol, 152; to fossil-fuel industry, 72, 73–74, 173, 219; for high-efficiency vehicles, 131–32, 136
terrorism, 207, 208
Tesla Motor Company, 132–33
Texas: bicycling initiatives, 113; carbon sequestration, 54; coal plants, 61; New Urbanism, 111; oil and gas industry, 40, 198; plug-in hybrid promotion, 130; wind energy, 169, 205–6
Thompson, Tim, 70, 75–76
Toptiro, Hiparidi, 145
Towns, Edolphus, 72
Toyota: electric vehicles, 121, 122, 123; plug-in hybrids, 125, 129–30; Prius hybrids, 128, 131; and Tesla, 132–33
trade deficits, 19, 21, 42, 208
transesterification, and biodiesel, 142

transit-oriented development, 109–12
transportation, public: air travel, 108, 208; Americans' use of, 105–6, 110, 204; bicycling, 110–11, 112–15, 117, 119; buses, 113–14, 115–16, 119; and car shares, 117; railways, 103–5, 106–9, 119; streetcars and light rail, 110, 111, 113–14; taking action to support, 118–19; as underinvested, 43, 107–9, 112
"tribrid" vehicles, 154
Trillium Asset Management, 91, 101
Twist, Bill, 27
TXU Energy, 61, 84

Uganda, 141, 145, 146
Union Oil spill, 34
United Airlines, 208
United Kingdom, 94, 99, 201
Unocal lawsuit, 40
U.S. Export-Import Bank, 93
Uzbekistan, 42

vehicle-to-grid power, 133–35, 203
Venezuela, 141
Vermont, 185, 186, 188
Villasenor, Sam, 57
Virginia, 46, 84
Volkswagen, 123

Wagoner, Rick, 129
Walgreens, 164
Walid bin Talal, Prince, 85
walking, 110–11, 117, 118, 204
Wall Street reform act (2010), 78
Wal-Mart, 164, 190
wars, for oil, 17, 32, 77
Washington, D.C.. *See* District of Columbia
Washington (state), 114, 128, 170
Wasserman, Harvey, 157
water pollution: from coal mining and processing, 46, 47, 48, 50, 84, 195, 204; from fertilizer runoff, 140, 147–48; from tar sands oil production, 35–36, 38
water shortages, 17
water usage, industrial, 37, 50
Waterkeeper Alliance, 72, 85
Waxman, Henry, 68

About the Author

Michael Brune, executive director of the Sierra Club, has seen firsthand the devastation caused by the BP oil disaster in the Gulf of Mexico. He served for seven years as executive director of Rainforest Action Network, providing strategic direction for its programs, and previously worked with Greenpeace and the Coastal Rainforest Coalition (since renamed ForestEthics). Brune wrote the original edition of *Coming Clean: Breaking America's Addiction to Oil and Coal* in 2008, and he blogs regularly for the *Huffington Post, SolveClimate,* and *Daily Kos.* Brune holds bachelor of science degrees in economics and finance from West Chester University. He lives with his wife and their two young children in Alameda, California.